Creating Memory and Cultural Identity in African American Trauma Fiction

Critical Approaches to Ethnic American Literature

General Editors

Jesús Benito Sánchez (*Universidad de Valladolid*)
Ana María Manzanas (*Universidad de Salamanca*)

Editorial Board

Babs Boter (*Vrije Universiteit Amsterdam*)
Isabel Caldeira (*University of Coimbra*)
Nathalie Cochoy (*Université Toulouse*)
Astrid Fellner (*Universität des Saarlandes*)
Cristina Garrigós (*National University of Distance Education*)
Markus Heide (*Uppsala University*)
Paul Lauter (*Trinity College, Hartford, Connecticut*)
Shirley Lim (*University of California, Santa Barbara*)
Angel Mateos (*University of Castilla-La Mancha*)
Silvia Schultermandl (*University of Graz*)

Assistant Editors

Amanda Gerke
Paula Barba

VOLUME 6

The titles published in this series are listed at *brill.com/aeal*

Creating Memory and Cultural Identity in African American Trauma Fiction

By

Patricia San José Rico

BRILL

RODOPI

LEIDEN | BOSTON

Cover illustration: "Circumpolar 1", photograph by Alberto Rico Vélez, from ARV Estudio. Reproduced with kind permission of the photographer.

The Library of Congress Cataloging-in-Publication Data is available online at http://catalog.loc.gov
LC record available at http://lccn.loc.gov/2019933611

Typeface for the Latin, Greek, and Cyrillic scripts: "Brill". See and download: brill.com/brill-typeface.

ISSN 1871-6067
ISBN 978-90-04-36409-7 (hardback)
ISBN 978-90-04-36410-3 (e-book)

Copyright 2019 by Koninklijke Brill NV, Leiden, The Netherlands.
Koninklijke Brill NV incorporates the imprints Brill, Brill Hes & De Graaf, Brill Nijhoff, Brill Rodopi, Brill Sense, Hotei Publishing, mentis Verlag, Verlag Ferdinand Schöningh and Wilhelm Fink Verlag.
All rights reserved. No part of this publication may be reproduced, translated, stored in a retrieval system, or transmitted in any form or by any means, electronic, mechanical, photocopying, recording or otherwise, without prior written permission from the publisher.
Authorization to photocopy items for internal or personal use is granted by Koninklijke Brill NV provided that the appropriate fees are paid directly to The Copyright Clearance Center, 222 Rosewood Drive, Suite 910, Danvers, NV 01923, USA. Fees are subject to change.

This book is printed on acid-free paper and produced in a sustainable manner.

A quienes me dieron la vida y me enseñaron a vivirla

Contents

Acknowledgments XI

Introduction 1

1 **Cultural, Collective, and Literary Trauma: Foundations for Analysis** 9
　1　Trauma: What It Is, How it Feels, What It Does 11
　2　Collective Trauma 19
　3　A "Story to Pass on"? Trauma and Its Transmission 24
　4　Trauma, Memory and Space: Sites of Memory/Sites of Trauma 28
　5　Trauma Writing/Writing Trauma 34
　6　Trauma Fiction 48

2 **History, Roots and Myth: Toni Morrison's *Paradise* and Gloria Naylor's *Mama* Day** 56
　1　History and Traumatic Memory 56
　2　*Paradise*: The Perils of Sublimated History 62
　　2.1　*History Revisited* 62
　　2.2　*This, You Must Learn: the Elders' Exaltation of History* 63
　　2.3　Not *the Truth, After All: Archival Work and the Unearthing of the Secret* 71
　　2.4　*"An Endless Cycle of Repetition": Inverted Racism and Violence* 75
　　2.5　*Wind of Change: When the Out There Reaches Paradise* 84
　　2.6　*Breaking the Cycle of Repetition: Sharing Trauma* 86
　3　Know thy Roots: *Mama Day* and the Significance of the Past 89
　　3.1　*Dynamic Memory vs. Stagnant History* 90
　　3.2　*The Day Family: a Trauma within the Folds of Memory* 97
　　3.3　*The Need for Roots: George and Cocoa* 101

3 **The Dangers of Repression/Suppression: Toni Morrison's *Beloved*** 107
　1　Trauma and Hidden Memory 107
　2　*Beloved*: The F/Hateful Power of Repressed Trauma 114
　　2.1　*"The Unspeakable": Repressive Signs in* Beloved's *Characters* 115
　　2.2　*A Ghost (Hi)story: Beloved as the Return of the Repressed* 125

    2.3   *Voicing It out: the Attempt and Failure of the Talking Cure* 134
    2.4   *The Light at the End of the Tunnel: Denver and Recovery from Trauma* 137

4 The Recovery of History: Toni Morrison's *Song of Solomon* and David Bradley's *The Chaneysville Incident* 142

1. A Quest for One's Past: Individuals, Collectivities, and Recovered Memory 144
2. The Truth Shall Make You Fly: Unearthing the Past in *Song of Solomon* 148
   - 2.1 *Trauma in* Song of Solomon 148
   - 2.2 *That's Not My Thing: Milkman's Initial Disinterest in the Past* 152
   - 2.3 *Of Roots and Ancestors: the Recovery of History as a Treasure Hunt* 153
   - 2.4 *It Is All in There: Myth, Tales and Folk Culture as a Repository of Memory* 156
   - 2.5 Lieux de Mémoire: *Places of History and the History in Places* 160
   - 2.6 *Hallowed Be Thy Name: Naming and the Power of Designation* 163
   - 2.7 *Learning (in Order) to Fly: the Acquisition of Historical Knowledge as a Liberating Process* 172
   - 2.8 *Turning the Tables: Reversal of Stigmas and Our Debt to the Future* 175
3. Digging up History: *the Chaneysville Incident* and the Ethnic Historian 178
   - 3.1 *Historians vs. Archeologists: Study or Action?* 179
   - 3.2 *Scholarly Knowledge vs. Ancestral Wisdom* 183
   - 3.3 *The Contesting and Therapeutic Value of Recovering the Past* 189
   - 3.4 *The Coalescence of Fact and Fiction: Bridging Genres and Cultures* 194

Epilogue: Is Closure Possible? the Use of Trauma in Art as a Vehicle for Political Struggle 198

1. "National Amnesia": Searching for Its Cure 198
2. Fighting Our Own Battles: the Use of Trauma in Political Struggle 200

3   Trauma as Art or the Art of Trauma?   202
4   Is Closure Possible?   203

Works Cited   207
Index   217

Acknowledgments

When I embarked on my academic journey in the summer of 2009, still a master's student in search of a research field, I would never have thought that, almost ten years later, it would blossom into the publication of this volume. Many are the people that have contributed to this result and, although a few will be acknowledged here, many others will not. Rest assured that is not the case in my heart.

First and foremost, my gratitude goes to Dr. Jesús Benito and Dr. Ana Manzanas for their unrelenting support before, during and beyond my doctoral years. Without their assistance, advice—both personal and professional—and countless hours of work and revision, neither this volume nor my own growth as a researcher would have been possible. It is through their expertise and guidance that this and other professional successes have been achieved.

During these years I have spent time and shared ideas with many colleagues, some of whom I am honored to now call friends. Thank you Enrique Cámara, Laura Filardo, Marta Gutiérrez, Rosalía Martínez, Sara Medina, Toñy Mezquita, Sonja Mujcinovic and Tamara Pérez for all the coffee breaks, help and the occasional shoulder to lean on. Part of this book is also yours. I am also indebted to the rest of the people at the English Department at the University of Valladolid. I never thought that those that I admired as teachers would become such great colleagues and excellent friends. Thank you as well to Susana Gómez, Ana Muñoz, Mª Carmen Alario and Ana Díez for their encouragement and aid in the course of the many challenges that recent years have thrown my way. You showed me great warmth and welcome when our paths crossed, without you I would have found adjusting to these, at times, adverse circumstances markedly more difficult.

I must also express my gratitude to those scholars and reputed professionals that have devoted part of their precious time and insight to help me further this project: Dr. Isabel Caldeira and Dr. Maria Jose Canelo from the University of Coimbra, Teresa Cid from the University of Lisboa, Dr. Stephen Thomson from the University of Reading, Dr. Cristina Alsina from the University of Barcelona and Dr. Viorica Patea from the University of Salamanca. Their help at various stages of this venture and their continued generosity has manifested in other interesting projects across countries and universities that have no doubt benefitted this one as well.

Heartfelt thanks to my family and friends for putting up with me during the worst moments of the last few years. Many a crisis would not have been solved without your encouragement and affection. If our past influences our present,

I have been extremely lucky for your presence in my mine, and your help in my becoming who I am today. I look forward to continuing to evolve in the future with the best group of people anyone could wish for. As for my love and the most recent addition to this circle, may we continue to form a myriad of happy memories together!

I would like to acknowledge the assistance (and patience!) of Masja Horn, from Brill, during the editing process of this book, as well as the bibliographical sources and travelling expenses financed by the Ministerio de Ciencia e Innovación (MICINN) for the research projects "Critical History of Ethnic American Literature" (references FFI2009-07450, FFI2012-31250 and FFI2015-64137-P), and the Junta de Castilla y León through the projects "Borders and Identities in American and Spanish Cultural Studies" (reference SA007A10-1) and "The Frontiers of Hospitality in the Cultural Studies of The United States and Europe" (reference SA342U14).

Introduction

> If every age has its symptoms, ours appears to be the age of trauma.
> MILLER AND TOUGAW, *Extremities: Trauma, Testimony, and Community*

∴

More than a fashionable or catchy phrase, 'the age of trauma,' is a relevant concept that accurately summarizes the core of this work. Recent events like the attacks on the World Trade Center and the Pentagon on September 11th, 2001, Hurricane Katrina in 2005, the 2011 Japan earthquake, or the more recent attacks on Paris, Brussels, Istanbul, Berlin and London, are just a few examples of the pervasive presence of traumatic events in our day. Even though natural disasters and terrorist attacks cannot be equated, they do have one thing in common: they all create victims[1] that will have to face the psychological consequences of their experiences. The attention that the media, the academic world and the literary and cinematic spheres have given to these victims and events has helped create a generalized feeling of helplessness together with an increased compassion for the victims mingled with discomfort (what LaCapra has called "empathic unsettlement" (2001)) in a society that has learned to live with, and face, trauma and its consequences. This is not to say that our age is more 'trauma prone,' but rather more 'trauma aware.' That is, whereas traumatic events have occurred throughout the history of humanity, our society has developed a greater awareness of the long-lasting consequences that dramatic losses and other painful events can have for the minds and lives of their victims.

What used to be completely overlooked as a mental pathology or shunned as mere hysteria during the better part of the nineteenth and twentieth

---

1 The author is aware of the fact that the tern 'survivor' is often preferred when referring to people suffering from trauma, given its more positive connotations. However, in what follows, both terms will be used strictly in the sense of a person that has undergone a traumatic experience or set of experiences. Except when specifically referring to the actual process of coming out alive, in which 'survivor' will be employed, both terms, 'victim' and 'survivor,' are to be understood in their most neutral meanings.

centuries, has now erupted into the public's vocabulary and awareness. Psychiatrists, psychologists and scholars of all nationalities are striving to reach a better understanding of the pathology; theories and counter theories about its origin, consequences and modes of treatment are continually published. And yet, despite the overwhelming presence of modern discourses of trauma, trauma is still not a 'present' thing. Not only is its existence not restricted to the present time, trauma itself is inherently historical, insomuch as, given the peculiar ways in which its experience is encoded in the victim's psyche, there is always a temporal gap between its occurrence and the experience of it (see Caruth 1995 and 1996). Trauma, therefore, is always experienced after a period of latency. It is precisely because of this belatedness of trauma, this capacity of trauma to survive and be felt long after the occurrence of the traumatic event, that we can talk about people suffering from the consequences of an event that happened years, or even centuries, ago. In some cases, both the—belated—experience of trauma and its aftereffects become central to processes of identity formation in which both individuals and communities project new meanings onto the traumatic events of the past. These links between trauma, history and the development of identity both individual and collective have not escaped numerous sociologists, historiographers and literary theorists that have devoted their work to this emerging field called 'trauma studies.' Accordingly, the works of Cathy Caruth, Dominick LaCapra, Roger Luckhurst, Judith Herman, Ruth Leys, Shoshana Felman, Dori Laub, Kalí Tal or E. Ann Kaplan, among many others, are now considered canonical in this field and tackle the issue from various perspectives, ranging from clinical to cultural and representative.

As it is still an emerging field (trauma studies surfaced in the early to mid 1990s), the traumatic events that served as catalysts for its appearance and expansion are of fairly recent occurrence, namely the two World Wars, the Holocaust and the Vietnam War. There is a recent tendency to claim that those traumatic events—particularly the Holocaust—have received most of trauma theorists' attention and often occlude other histories of trauma and oppression. Consequently, the field of trauma studies is now expanding to the analysis of postcolonial traumas still lingering in the present. This is the case in the histories of slavery, racism and oppression in America, which are now being recovered in academic, political and literary fields.

The present volume places itself within this area of study to focus particularly on the issue of collective African American historical trauma and, more specifically, on its representation in contemporary literature. It therefore draws on the work of significant trauma scholars such as those already mentioned, as well as other critics focused on highlighting the relation between history, memory and the formation of collective identity, such as Paul Ricoeur or Nicola King, together with postcolonial trauma theorists such as Stef Craps, Michael Rothberg and J. Brooks Bouson in order to approach the recreation of history, the conflict between memory and history, the recovery of the past and its uses for identity formation as reflected by three contemporary African American authors: Toni Morrison, Gloria Naylor and David Bradley. I contend that a shared knowledge of a community's past, and most importantly, the particular ways in which that past is represented, recreated and remembered, are crucially important to determining how the members of a community regard themselves and their fellow individuals within that collective. Such historical knowledge, and the representation thereof, can operate in various modes of identity formation, joining individuals together in clusters while at the same time setting them apart from other communities. It is the appropriation of the past, its actualization in the present and its representation as a source of collective resilience and identity that works to enhance the internal cohesion of communities. Modern African American literature plays a central role in what we could call, following Sethe's words in Toni Morrison's *Beloved*, the process of "beating back the past" (2005: 87).

However, as Sethe herself would surely claim, not every community's historical foundations are joyful and easily transformed into sources of communal action and resilience. The history of the African American community, for instance, is demarcated by a series of painful and traumatic events that can be traced to the Middle Passage, the very moment of the slaves' forced dislocation from Africa, dating back to the seventeenth century. Even though the original members of what is now the African American community came from diverse backgrounds, nationalities, religions and languages, over the years they have tended to cluster together, taking as their unifying force their shared traumatic past and former status as Africans brought by force to a foreign country and compelled to work as slaves as well as their ongoing experience of racism and oppression in the US. It is that common historical layer that was later used as what LaCapra called "founding trauma" (2001: 23); a shared traumatic past event or situation around which a community's identity and cohesion evolves. Gayatri Chakravorty Spivak once referred to this kind of process as 'strategic essentialism,'[2] meaning that oppressed communities or minority groups can find political use in the adoption of one specific common trait—or in this case, traumatic past event—in order to construct their collective identity and

---

[2] An idea that she herself later "thoroughly repudiate[d]" (Spivak 2008: 260).

organize their resistance and their fight for political rights around it. And yet, a strictly essentialist, immobile and unchanging view of past traumas may result in further retraumatization and repetition of trauma, as I show in my analysis of Toni Morrison's *Paradise*. A dynamic and non-essentialist, yet still strategic revisiting and actualization of the times and sites of memory—or rather the times and sites of trauma—may be more significant in the process of giving voice to past traumas while at the same time making them bear into the present.

This use of the recovery of the past for socio-political, bonding and reconciliatory purposes is fairly recent for African Americans. For centuries, the community's history of trauma and oppression was not only not remembered, but actively silenced by both the dominant white community and by African Americans themselves. It was not until relatively recent times[3] that those unspeakable things were, to use Morrison's words, "spoken at last" (1989: 22). The recovery and representation of a traumatic history previously confined to silence was instrumental in raising awareness about the injustices of the past, promoting a collective sense of community and shared history, and achieving political agency. Novels like those analyzed here illustrate this process of giving voice to what trauma theorist Dominick LaCapra calls "the ghosts of the past" (2001: 215). These novels have been chosen for analysis because of their special emphasis on history and memory, as well as on the perils of forgetting the past, and the benefits that can be extracted from its recovery. Even though several other themes are touched upon in the analysis of each novel, I focus my study on each novel's particular approach to memory and trauma. Consequently, the analysis of Gloria Naylor's *Mama Day* and Toni Morrison's *Paradise* centers on their characters' obsession with history, and on their different approaches to it, from the history never being "breathed out" (Naylor 1988: 4) to being brought up "[o]ver and over and with the least provocation" (Morrison 1999a: 161). *Beloved*, on the other hand, shows a marked attention to the issue of traumatic repression/suppression, the constant and determined effort of "beating back the past," and the repercussions that it can have on the minds of victims. Finally, David Bradley's *The Chaneysville Incident* and Morrison's *Song of Solomon* both focus on a willful recovery of the past, finding "where they hid the bodies" (Bradley 1990: 186) through a return to the actual sites of memory and

---

3   Although African American artists have been acknowledging their traumatic past in their works for some time now (Frederick Douglass's speech "What to the Slave is the 4th of July" in 1841 comes to mind) it is only in recent decades that the retracing of the African American silenced history has attracted the most academic interest and that most African American fiction writers have chosen to tackle such events in their novels.

reconnection with the traditional and mythical elements embedded in them. Apart from this, they also center on the benefits that such a recovery of the past can bring about for the individuals and communities of the present.

Of the five novels analyzed here, three of them are by Nobel Prize Winner Toni Morrison. In my view, Morrison is one of the African American authors most evidently preoccupied with the necessity of recovering the past in literature as means of repaying a debt to those who lived through it, as she has expressed in several interviews: "That's all history means to me. It's a very *personal* thing—if their blood is in my veins, maybe I can do this little part right here" (Wilson 1994: 132). Morrison recognizes the former silence cast upon her community's history and the value and significance of its retrieval, and, because she is a prolific and internationally acclaimed author, her works are among the most accessible—to the public and critics alike, a fact that increases their potential to give voice to the African American trauma and makes them still more valuable.

The other two novels—Gloria Naylor's *Mama Day* and David Bradley's *The Chaneysville Incident*—present thematically similar topics to the two Morrison works with which they are respectively coupled—*Paradise* and *Song of Solomon*—while going one step further. Thus, *Mama Day* offers a warning against the repetitive patterns of unresolved traumas similar to that of *Paradise*, yet from a significantly different perspective: whereas the community's past in *Paradise* has been endlessly repeated to the point of harmful sublimation, the community in *Mama Day* has forgotten about the founding event at the heart of their collective identity with equally destructive consequences. We learn in *Paradise* that sublimation is not advisable, and *Mama Day* confirms the teaching and adds its own warning against forgetting. Likewise, *Song of Solomon* and *The Chaneysville Incident* are similar in their approach to reconnection with the past through myth and folklore, but whereas Morrison stays within the realm of folklore with her reinterpretation of the myth of the Africans who could fly, Bradley bases his narrative on the results of historical research carried out by his mother, a historian herself. We can sense the historical truth of the African American experience behind Morrison's text, but Bradley's novel goes one step further by showing the actual bodies left behind by the course of history. *Beloved* serves as a hinge between these four novels, showing how willful or unconscious forgetting is always in play when talking about history and memory, and the reasons that this should not be so.

Although the main focus of this work is the fictional recreation of collective trauma, some attention is paid to individual trauma, its manifestations and consequences and the literary representations thereof. Surely, even though I approach these novels from the point of view of the collectively shared memory of the African American traumatic past—and present—line of racial discrimination, and the novels themselves portray the stories of their characters against that backdrop, they also represent and deal with the specific problems of specific characters, some of which can be said to exhibit traumatic symptoms. It is important to separate the collective sense of a culturally and politically negotiated foundational trauma from the particular experience of individuals that have been influenced by it in a perhaps more direct, less politically mediated way. Whereas the former would revolve around the recreation of a particular historical situation used to join together the members of a community with the aim of gaining visibility and political agency, the latter would refer to the psychological consequences that may affect certain individuals in the present. Moreover, the notion of a collectively shared memory of a past trauma *clinically* affecting the individual members of a community is a highly contested theory and should be considered with extreme caution. The purpose of this volume is to analyze how contemporary African American writers represent the ways in which certain individuals and communities engage in different types of relationships with traumatic histories and memories, from repression/suppression to a desire to appropriate a historical trauma out of empathy or identification with the original victims or, most often, in accordance with a particular political position or in solidarity with a given group of people.

Having said that, it is true that during the analysis of the novels, I mainly focus on individual characters and the trauma symptoms and coping techniques they illustrate and not—or not normally—on the collective. The reason for this is that, even if the issue of the African American collectively shared memory of continuous trauma and racial oppression is in the background of every novel and at the core of this volume's main theoretical stance, the narratives primarily portray characters suffering from their private, personal traumas, although these are clearly linked to the collective traumas experienced by the community as a whole. For instance, even though *Beloved*'s Sethe is clearly a victim of the institution of slavery, the novel portrays the ways in which the institution was particularly traumatizing to *her*, and, only by extension, traumatizing to the community. When Sethe appears "loaded with the past and hungry for more" (Morrison 2005: 83), her trip back to the traumatizing spaces of southern slavery makes her face her own personal sites of memory. Similarly, even the novels that concern themselves with the issues of history and historical recovery deal with the particular family histories of specific individuals, although the experiences illustrated by each can be extrapolated to the community in general. It is the possible uses and intentions behind these novels, I argue, that are indeed related to the collective, to its shared memories of traumatic past events, and to its present recreation of that past for socio-political purposes, not the personal traumas of the individual characters that appear in them.

Since the representation of individual and collective trauma in African American fiction is treated here from the perspective of memory and the recovery and literary recreation thereof, the analytical body of the present work is divided into three interrelated parts, preceded by one more general chapter dealing with some basic theoretical concepts, theories and critical movements that are central for the subsequent analysis. Chapter One, "Cultural, Collective, and Literary Trauma: Foundations for Analysis," touches upon some of the basic concepts of individual clinical trauma as they have been represented in several literary works; later these will enable us to trace each of the characteristic traits of trauma in the literary descriptions of the characters portrayed in the novels to be analyzed in the subsequent three chapters. The chapter then addresses and problematizes notions of collective trauma, founding trauma and historical trauma, with special attention to the transmission of traumatic memories within collectives across generations and its impact on the formation of collective identity. Several possibilities for the transmission of traumatic memories are offered and analyzed, including the special relationship that exists between space, trauma and memory as addressed by Pierre Nora in his concept of *lieux de mémoire* and the potential use of places as reminders of a shared traumatic history in the process of collective identity formation. In its final sections, the chapter approaches the primary focus of this volume in its attention to the intersection between trauma and writing—fictional or otherwise—and explores the narrative techniques most often employed in the portrayal of both communal and individual trauma in fictional narratives.

Reconnecting with the issue of collective and historical trauma explored earlier, the second chapter, "History, Roots and Myth: Toni Morrison's *Paradise* and Gloria Naylor's *Mama Day*," begins with a discussion of the differences between memory and history and the diverse approaches to the past that they entail. I then move on to an analysis of Toni Morrison's *Paradise*, followed by Gloria Naylor's *Mama Day*. Although both novels deal with the issue of the crucial role that historical events play in the formation of communities and their identities, they approach the matter from opposite perspectives. Whereas *Paradise* portrays—and warns against—the imposition of a controlled, rigid version of history established as the central motif for the formation of the community's collective identity, *Mama Day* focuses on the ways in which time can continually shape the memory of a past event while at the same time preserving it as the community's foundation.

However, when the past is filled with harmful and traumatic reminiscences, the first response—both by individuals and communities—is not always to appropriate those traumatic events as the backbone of collective and individual identity formation, but rather to forget it, or—if forgetting is not wholly possible—to suppress it and block it from conscious and collective recall. The third chapter, "The Dangers of Repression/Suppression: Toni Morrison's *Beloved*," focuses on the issue of repression/suppression as one of the most frequent—and most dangerous—reactions to the impact of trauma. The first part analyzes the different ways in which traumatic memories can be encoded, remembered or re-enacted in the survivor's mind, and the often ambivalent and blurry relationship between willful forgetting and unconscious repression. The second section tackles the analysis of *Beloved* from the point of view of the "unspeakable," that is, the willful suppression of trauma that most of the characters in the novel exercise, proposing that the character of Beloved is the embodiment of that suppressed trauma, returned in physical form to haunt and prevent Sethe from working through it.

Because of the harmful potential of both repression and suppression, and the socio-political benefits that can be extracted from the recovery and remembrance of the past, the fourth chapter of this book, "The Recovery of History: Toni Morrison's *Song of Solomon* and David Bradley's *The Chaneysville Incident*," comes back full circle and focuses on the willful unearthing of the past. The chapter traces the evolution of the two protagonists, Milkman in *Song of Solomon* and John Washington in *The Chaneysville Incident*, from ignorance and indifference to their heritage, to the discovery of past truths and the liberation extracted therefrom. In both cases, places or sites of memory become the repository of ancient wisdom and folk tradition and figure as key catalysts for the retrieval of the past and the discovery—literally so in *The Chaneysville Incident*—of "where they hid the bodies" (Bradley 1990: 186).

Moving from the significance of the past for identity formation to the perilous practice of repression, and to the therapeutic or future-building value that "beating back the past" (Morrison 2005: 87) can have for individuals and collectives marked by traumatic experiences, this volume illustrates and explores the use of fictional works as valuable instruments for the disclosure, giving voice to and public recognition of the African American collective and historical trauma in order to leave yesterday's troubles behind and find "some kind of tomorrow" (Morrison 2005: 322).

CHAPTER 1

Cultural, Collective, and Literary Trauma: Foundations for Analysis

> Nescire autem quid ante quam natus sis acciderit, id est semper esse puerum. Quid enim est aetas hominis, nisi ea memoria rerum veterum cum superiorum aetate contexitur?
> CICERO, *Orator* XXXIV[1]

∴

History, roots and ancestors. Trauma, psychology and psychoanalysis. Apparently these two sets of concepts have little to do with each other, and certainly Cicero could have had no knowledge whatsoever of the latter when he talked about the former. So why are his words appropriate for the epigraph of a work that claims to deal with trauma? The key to understanding their relationship lies in the concept that another man, a much more recent one, had of history. When Walter Benjamin talked about history as "one single catastrophe" (2003: 392), he was not merely being pessimistic; he was—perhaps unknowingly—linking the concepts of trauma and history. If we accept that the past is but one single catastrophic event that spreads itself throughout the centuries, then 'history' automatically links with 'trauma.' Consequently, in order to keep ourselves from remaining children forever, we must delve into the folds of that past trauma in the hopes of understanding and overcoming it, thus approaching history in a comprehensive yet critical way.

Moreover, if the past is inherently traumatic, trauma itself can be understood as inherently past (yet often influencing the present) if we take Caruth's view of trauma as always experienced belatedly (Caruth 1995, 1996). Insomuch as, following Caruth, a traumatic event may only be experienced after a period of latency, and the psychological consequences that it triggers refer back to the event itself—an event always lurking in the past—trauma and history seem to be irrevocably coupled, and the study of one is always aided by the study

---

[1] To be ignorant of what occurred before you were born is to remain always a child. For what is the worth of human life, unless it is woven into the life of our ancestors by the records of history?

© KONINKLIJKE BRILL NV, LEIDEN, 2019 | DOI:10.1163/9789004364103_003

of the other. Just as Kalí Tal pointed out, "history is a compendium of past, and therefore inaccessible events—events not fully perceived as they occur—given meaning later in a process of narrative construction" (Tal 2003: n.p.). If we take Caruth's claim of the inaccessibility of trauma as valid, then the analysis of history from the point of trauma studies can be taken not only as justifiable, but as a valuable tool for "the ongoing process of generating narrative meaning out of an irretrievable past" (Tal 2003: n.p.).

This study of history from the point of view of clinical trauma and psychoanalytic theory was at the core of the emergence of the field of trauma studies in the early to mid-1990s. Drawing on Freud and Lacan, most of the early trauma theorists focused on the trauma of the Holocaust, its aftermath and the effect it has had both on its direct survivors and on the Jewish community as a whole.[2] This focalization on the Holocaust has turned it into the great trauma of the twentieth century; a process that was aided by the proliferation of books, films and museums, among other sites of remembrance, that commemorate and/or condemn the episode. However, as the more recent trend of postcolonial trauma studies often argues, this focus on the Holocaust seems to have obscured—even prevented—scholarly attention to other collective traumas equally dramatic and sometimes occupying a broader time-span, as is the case for the African American history of slavery and discrimination. However, we should not view this, as LaCapra argues, as a tendency to cover more recent problems "related to the heritage of slavery [...] [with] a focus on the Holocaust" (2001: 171), for there are clearly many factors behind this apparent disregard. In order to discern those reasons, we must not focus so much on why the Holocaust was apparently given special visibility, but on why the African American trauma was not. The answer to the latter question revolves around the silencing processes to which the African American history of trauma has been subjected. According to James Baldwin, "[f]or the horrors of the American Negro's life there has been almost no language" (1985e: 362), which has turned the narrative of the African American historical trauma into

---

2   See for example: Lawrence Langer, *The Holocaust and the Literary Imagination* (1975); James E. Young, *Writing and Rewriting the Holocaust: Narrative and the Consequences of Interpretation* (1988); Lawrence Langer, *Holocaust Testimonies: The Ruins of Memory* (1991); Shoshana Felman and Dori Laub, *Testimony: Crises of Witnessing in Literature, Psychoanalysis, and History* (1992); James E. Young, *The Texture of Memory: Holocaust Memorials and Meaning* (1993); Dominick LaCapra, *Representing the Holocaust: History, Theory, Trauma* (1994); Edward T. Linenthal, *Preserving Memory: The Struggle to Create America's Holocaust Museum* (1995); Geoffrey Hartman, *The Longest Shadow: In the Aftermath of the Holocaust* (1996); Raul Hilberg, *The Politics of Memory: The Journey of a Holocaust Historian* (1996); or Dominick LaCapra, *History and Memory after Auschwitz* (1998).

"a dangerous and reverberating silence" (1985c: 65). Therefore, I argue, the fact that the Holocaust has received a greater degree of attention from the point of view of trauma studies should not lead us to affirm that its study has obscured that of the African American trauma, but rather that it contributed to this phenomenon only secondarily since the processes that silenced the atrocities of slavery were in place long before the Holocaust occurred.

The reasons for this historical silencing of the African American traumatic experience are manifold and revolve around issues of guilt, shame and fear, as will be later analyzed. However, the apparent lack of focus on its reverberations—that is, the collective trauma thereof—could also be due to a simple question of chronology. The study of trauma in clinical terms is a fairly recent phenomenon. Even though its origins can be traced as far back as the 1860s, it was not until after the Vietnam War that the term *trauma* gained prominence. It was at that point that the attention devoted to the Holocaust experience began to heighten, that is, when there *were* direct survivors. We should not forget that the term trauma was initially applied to those individuals who had personally undergone a trying experience and that, therefore, the study of its psychological repercussions and the attempt to cure them was strictly reserved to its survivors. The leap from personal to collective trauma and thence to transgenerational and historical trauma was taken within the study of the broadest collective of direct trauma survivors that existed at the time, which justifies the fact that most of the early literature on trauma focused on the Holocaust and the fact that those works that center on the trauma of other collectives must inevitably draw on this early literature.

When, as time passed, scholars began to posit that those who had not directly experienced the Holocaust, but were descendants of those who had, could also somehow show signals of distress, the idea of a collective historical trauma began to develop. Alongside this, the emphasis shifted to other communities affected by traumas further back in history; like the African American. Thus, like the ring of a bell, whose sound reverberates through time even though the strike that originated it is long past and its noise silenced, the previously muted ripples of the African American trauma of slavery and oppression began to be heard in scholarly, social, political and—most importantly for the present volume—literary circles.

1   Trauma: What It Is, How it Feels, What It Does

It was in the seventeenth century that the word *trauma* was taken from the Greek *traumatizo* and first used to refer to "a bodily injury caused by an external agent" (Luckhurst 2008: 2), a meaning which is still applied in medical terms. A century later, several physicians and neurologists realized that this meaning could also be applied to certain mental illnesses. In fact, this definition does not differ greatly from what we understand nowadays as psychological trauma. Only, in this case, the injury would not be inflicted upon the body but upon "the tissues of the mind" (Erikson 1995: 183). Freud called traumatic those "external excitations [...] strong enough to break through the barrier against stimuli" (1922: 34) and reach the mind. Should this happen, he continues, it "will undoubtedly provoke a very extensive disturbance in the workings of the energy of the organism, and will set in motion every kind of protective measure" (Freud 1922: 34). When the term PTSD was introduced in 1980, the traumatic event causing it was defined as "generally outside the range of usual human experience" and as being able to "evoke significant symptoms of distress in almost everyone" (Leys 2000: 232). Subsequent definitions have classified trauma as an event that *"overwhelms existing defences against anxiety in a form which also provides confirmation of those deepest universal anxieties"* (Garland 2002: 11. Italics in the original) or, in Cathy Caruth's words, as "the response to an unexpected or overwhelming violent event or events that are not fully grasped as they occur, but return in repeated flash-backs, nightmares, and other repetitive phenomena" (1996: 91). Regardless of the different ways of defining it, it is clear that trauma is a) unexpected, b) sometimes repressed and/or suppressed and thus felt belatedly, c) unsettling, and d) the cause of numerous symptoms that may include nightmares, compulsions, numbness, dissociation and others.

Traumatic symptoms are multifaceted and extremely varied. They can range from different types of amnesia (from unconscious repression to wishful forgetting) to several compulsions, passing through flashbacks and compulsive repetition, dissociation of self and language, and numbing, among others. Some of these symptoms, if present in an isolated and attenuated variant, may be rather innocuous and the consequence of the natural defensive barriers of the psyche. However, the majority, if left untreated, can potentially be highly dangerous to the individual's mental stability. One of the most prevalent examples of this is the case of repression, since, in a way, other symptoms can be said to emerge from it. Repressed and/or suppressed memories, as will be seen in chapter three, tend to resurface somehow, and may reappear in the form of nightmares, compulsions, hallucinations and repetitive flashbacks in which the past is relived almost as an exact replica of the initial event. This kind of intrusive phenomena was defined in the DSM-IIIR (1987) in terms similar to these:

> The flashback takes the form of recurrent, intrusive images or sensation associated with the traumatic event, or of a sudden feeling that the traumatic event is literally happening all over again. The victim feels as if he has returned to the perceptual reality of the traumatic situation, and it has become orthodox to interpret such flashback experiences as the literal return of dissociated memories of the event. The term flashback implies the cinematic possibility of literally reproducing or cutting back to a scene from the past and hence expresses the idea that the trauma victim's experiences are exact 'returns' or 'replays' of the traumatic incident. (Leys 2000: 241)

Since a flashback is seen as "the cinematic possibility of literally reproducing or cutting back to a scene from the past," it has been widely used in literature to provide the reader with glimpses of a character's life at specific moments. Consequently, literature about trauma has made use of this narrative device not only to enlighten the reader about a character's past, but also to portray this specific characteristic of trauma as a psychological symptom. For instance, in Lan Cao's *Monkey Bridge*, we find the character of Mai, a young Vietnamese girl living in the US and marked psychologically by the experience of having survived an explosion while working as a nurse at a hospital in Saigon. Her flashback is triggered when entering a safe hospital in the States, and past and present are immediately intermingled:

> The smell of blood, warm and wet, rose from the floor and settled into the solemn stillness of the hospital air. [...]
> A scattering of gunshots tore through the plaster walls. Everything was unfurling, everything, and I knew I was back there again, as if the tears were always pooled in beneath my eyes. It was all coming back, a fury of whiteness rushing against my head with violent percussive rage. The automatic glass doors closed behind me with a sharp sucking sound.
> Arlington Hospital was not a Saigon military hospital. [...] I knew I was not in Saigon. I was not a hospital volunteer. It was not 1968 but 1978. Yet I also knew, as I passed a wall of smoked-glass windows, that I would see the quick movement of green camouflage fatigues, and I knew, I knew what I would see next. (Cao 1998: 1–2)

Similarly, in Toni Morrison's *Home*, a novel in which trauma has a central role, one of the protagonists suffers from recurrent memories of his experience and the death of his closest friends in the Korean War. Even though he tries to block those intrusive memories with drinking, still "[e]verything reminded him of something loaded with pain" (Morrison 2013: 8), which accounts for his frequent flashbacks:

> So, as was often the case when he was alone and sober, whatever the surroundings, he saw a boy pushing his entrails back in, holding them in his palms like a fortune-teller's globe shattering with bad news; or he heard a boy with only the bottom half of his face intact, the lips calling mama. And he was stepping over them, around them, to stay alive, to keep his own face from dissolving, his own colorful guts under that oh-so-thin sheet of flesh. [...] They never went away, those pictures. (Morrison 2013: 20)

This type of reliving of traumatic events may make victims feel literally "possessed," as Caruth says (1995b: 5), by the event in question, as if it was a ghost that were constantly coming back to haunt them. In Freud's words, "a thing which has not been understood inevitably reappears; like an unlaid ghost, it cannot rest until the mystery has been solved and the spell broken" (qtd. in Garland 2002: 180). As Kathleen Brogan points out, contemporary literature of all ethnicities and nationalities has widely used this ghost metaphor to refer to traumatic unresolved issues:

> Maxine Hong Kingston mined the ghost metaphor in the mid-seventies in *The Woman Warrior*; it appears in Native American literature as well, most recently in novels by Louise Erdrich (*Tracks*, 1988; *The Bingo Palace*, 1994) and Leslie Marmon Silko (*Almanac of the Dead*, 1991). William Kennedy's *Ironweed* (1983) is haunted by the ghosts of Irish Albany, New York. In 'The Management of Grief' (1989), Bharati Mukherjee invokes ghosts to dramatize the divided loyalties and ultimate transformation of immigrants to North America. The ghost of the folkloric La Llorona [...] weeps through the pages of much contemporary Mexican-American literature, including Rudolfo Anaya's *Bless me, Ultima* (1972) and Sandra Cisneros's *Woman Hollering Creek* (1991). In *World's End* (1987), T. Coreghessan [sic] Boyle moves his narrative back and forth between seventeenth-century New York, populated by Native Americans, Dutch, and English, and a twentieth century haunted by the ghosts of these earlier inhabitants. Robert Olen Butler's *A Good Scent from a Strange Mountain* (1992), a collection of stories documenting the lives of Louisiana Vietnamese, often stages the painful loss of old ways and the difficult cultural transition made by war refugees through confrontations between the living and ghosts of the Old Country. There are ghosts of old Ukraine in Askold Melnyczuk's 1994 *What is Told*, ghosts of the Sioux past in Susan Power's 1994 *The Grass*

Dancer, Cuban ghosts in Cristina Garcia's 1992 *Dreaming in Cuban*, and a ghostly cantor in Ira Levin's 1988 play *Cantorial*. (1995: 150–151)

Even more interestingly for the present volume, African American literature is also riddled with unwanted ghosts, ghosts that refuse to leave the living in peace and that keep bringing traumatic memories back to them. The novels of Toni Morrison are good examples of this. In *Tar Baby*, for example, the protagonist is confronted by the vision of several women (many of them already dead) that stare at her holding their breasts in their hands in an attempt to make her remember the cultural inheritance that she so strongly wants to leave behind. More clearly, in *Beloved*—perhaps Morrison's most renowned novel—the presence of the ghost is clear from the very words with which the novel opens: "124 was spiteful. Full of a baby's venom" (Morrison 2005: 3). The ghost in question here is that of Beloved, Sethe's one-year-old baby daughter that she murdered with her own hands to prevent her from being sent back to slavery. Once this act was committed, it was never spoken of in the house. This silence, this suppression of a traumatic memory, is what triggers the presence of the ghost in the house, until, after being expelled by Paul D, a family friend, it comes back in the body of Beloved, the young woman that the murdered infant might have grown to be had she lived. This coming back is explained, as I argue in chapter three of this book, by the fact that Paul D's exorcism was not accompanied by a proper working through of the trauma; the ghost was expelled, yes, but the trauma survived and therefore was bound to reappear.

Apart from the aforementioned cases of intrusive reappearance of the past, present events might be viewed in the victim's traumatized mind as repetitions of a past event:

> It is not simply that traumatic events in the present unearth events from the past, as of course they often do. It is more that in the survivor's mind the current event takes on some of the emotional resonance of past fears and phantasies, and may eventually be perceived as having some structural resemblance as well. To the extent that this link becomes entrenched, the trauma is felt to confirm existing unconscious phantasies about certain deeply troubling kinds of object relations, and this in turn contributes forcefully to the difficulty of 'getting over' the event in the present. (Garland 2002: 108)

This is what happens to Florens, the heroine in Toni Morrison's *A Mercy*. The story of this woman starts as a child on a plantation in Virginia ruled by a merciless Portuguese slaveholder that runs into debt with Jacob Vaark, a Dutch trader. As partial payment, he asks Jacob to take one of his slaves. Horrified though he initially is by the idea, he finally accepts and takes Florens with him after her mother begged him to. This, although ultimately done for her benefit, is felt by Florens as a rejection, and added to the trauma of separation from her mother is Florens's feeling of dejection, as she feels her mother prefers her little brother over her. A few years later, she meets a free black man who comes to work at the Vaark's plantation. She immediately falls madly in love with him, but even though they engage in a relationship while he is working at the plantation, when he finishes his job he suddenly leaves without even saying goodbye. This new rejection is seen by Florens as a repetition of her mother's. When, after being sent to fetch him, she finds him with a small boy, the parallelism is made even clearer. At this point, her already excited mind reenacts the imagined trauma of her mother preferring her over her little brother. When this happens, Florens sees her trauma repeated before her eyes:

> This happens twice before. The first time it is me peering around my mother's dress hoping for her hand that is only for her little boy. The second time it is a pointing screaming little girl hiding behind her mother and clinging to her skirts. Both times are full of danger and I am expel [sic]. Now I am seeing a little boy come in holding a corn-husk doll. He is younger than everybody I know. You reach out your forefinger toward him and he takes hold of it. [...]
> [...] I worry as the boy steps closer to you. How you offer and he owns your forefinger. As if he is your future. Not me. (133–134)

The repetitive characteristic of the trauma and the association done by Florens's mind regain here their full potential and she sees her past coming unexpectedly upon her. Insomuch as Florens's trauma has never been expressed or rationally remembered, she has not yet started to come to terms with it. It is for that reason that it still retains its full grasp upon her; a hold that is accentuated by yet another abandonment. Florens's trauma of rejection keeps repeating itself until she has no sense of time or reality. Past and present are intermingled and haunt Florens at night: "When I wake a minha mãe[3] is standing by your cot and this time her baby boy is Malaik. He is holding her hand. She is moving her lips at me but she is holding Malaik's hand in her own" (136). Florens identifies Malaik, the little boy she finds at the blacksmith's house and whom she is

---

3 "my mother" in Portuguese. This is how Florens always refers to her mother in the novel, since she grew up in a plantation owned by a Portuguese-speaking master.

commissioned to look after, with her little brother and transfers to him all the hatred she feels towards her sibling.

The fact that the repetition of a past trauma in any of the aforementioned forms may present itself as an exact replica of the past event in the present time entails a subsequent blurring of tenses between the past and the present, and even the future, that have to be cleared up in order to work through the trauma. As LaCapra explains it, when the past is uncontrollably relived by the patient, he/she is inadvertently brought back to the scene of the traumatic past as if he/she were really there, and the distinctions between past and present "collapse" (2001: 21). The future is likewise affected for it becomes "blocked or fatalistically caught up in a melancholic feedback loop" (2001: 21). Therefore, the realization that the repetition is just a repetition and not the event itself is crucial not only for working through the trauma, but also for the survival of the individual.

When this realization does not occur, when working through does not take place, the victim may undergo a process of decentering and dissociation. For Dominick LaCapra, a traumatic experience is by definition "disruptive," as it "disarticulates the self and creates holes in existence" and has normally "belated effects" (2001: 41). Some of these belated effects may be felt in the subject's feelings and his/her control over them. A victim of trauma may experience an event without emotion, a given emotion without an external cause for it, or can become hyper-vigilant and hyper-irritable without a conscious reason. Traumatized people behave, in sum, "as though their nervous systems have been disconnected from the present" (Herman 2001: 34–35). This, as mentioned before, is a result of the fact that traumatic emotions, insomuch as they are potentially harmful to the mental well being of the patient, become "severed from representations" and "hidden away deep in the unconscious" (Ferenczi 1995: 203). This can be seen as a mode of psychical defense against trauma (Leys 2000: 147), but it may be, in some cases, of such strength as to develop into a split personality. Nicholas T. Rand defines it as an "internal psychic splitting; as a result two distinct 'people' live side by side, one behaving as if s/he were part of the world and the other as if s/he had no contact with it whatsoever" (1994b: 100). Psychologist Pierre Janet explains how this peculiar behavior of the psyche could result from the impact of trauma in the following terms:

> [A] particular shocking moment or event might produce a defensive response of a narrowing of the field of consciousness. This would become an *idée fixe*, held outside the recall of memory of the conscious mind. It would accrue its own memory chain and associations, becoming a 'new system, a personality independent of the first.' (qtd. in Luckhurst 2008: 42)

This, to go back to African American literature, is once again represented in several of Toni Morrison's novels. In *The Bluest Eye*, for example, we find the case of Pecola, a young black girl whose only wish is to have blue eyes in order to be pretty like Shirley Temple. This desire hides a lifetime of being used and abused by the whole town, including her own father—who rapes her—and her mother—who beats her when she finds out. Towards the end of the novel, Pecola develops a pathology in which she sees herself as finally having blue eyes. In addition to this, her personality is split and she begins talking—even arguing—with an imaginary friend (Morrison 1999b: 152–162). Similarly, when Ayo, an African woman in Phyllis Alesia Perry's *Stigmata*, leaves the slave boat, she feels the necessity of mirroring the traumatic tearing apart from her roots with a personality split, in which she becomes two different persons, one Ayo from "Afraca" and the other Bessie, a slave. Her own daughter comments on this: "She never los that strange voice of hers from Afraca, but when she talk about her childhood and the bad times it seem like she really was Ayo and not Bessie after all. She once told me that Ayo got lost when she crossed the water. Bessie kinda took over. She had to think like her not like Ayo from Afraca" (Perry 1999: 50).

Again, in Morrison's *A Mercy*—which can be seen almost as a treatise on traumatic syndromes, so many of them are represented in its characters—we find Sorrow, a demented girl who carries a history of severe trauma. She spent her early years on board a ship with her father, the captain. After the ship is looted and everybody else is murdered or taken, she is found lying on the shore unable—or perhaps unwilling—to remember or speak about her whole past up to that moment: "Not then, not ever, had she spoken of how she got there or where she had been" (Morrison 2008: 49). Once again, we find ourselves looking at a case in which the victim has repressed the painful memories of her past either by means of unconscious repression or conscious denial. As a consequence, those memories have neither been remembered nor properly expressed and therefore pose an impediment to the correct working through of the trauma. Due to this circumstance, Sorrow suffers from several neuroses, the most radical of which is a severe fragmentation of the self, in which she is always accompanied by an exact replica of herself whom she calls Twin, and that seems to have a better knowledge of Sorrow's past identity than that of others in the 'exterior' world:

> She did not mind when they called her Sorrow so long as Twin kept using her real name. […] Having two names was convenient since Twin couldn't be seen by anybody else. So if she were scrubbing clothes or herding geese and heard the name Captain used, she knew it was Twin.

But if any voice called 'Sorrow,' she knew what to expect. Preferable, of course, was when Twin called from the mill door or whispered up close into her ear. Then she would quit any chore and follow her identical self. (114)

There are numerous other symptoms of trauma—see the fourth edition of the *Diagnostic and Statistical Manual of Mental Disorders* for an attempt at a classification—but the ones described above are among the most frequent and the ones that most recurrently appear in trauma narratives such as those analyzed here. We will pay special attention to the representation of these symptoms in the five novels to be analyzed in subsequent chapters, but in order to understand how the authors utilize the representation of individual trauma in their characters in order to generate narrative meaning about issues of collective, historical and cultural traumas, we must understand how the latter are understood and articulated in trauma theory.

2   Collective Trauma[4]

When Judith points out to John Washington—the protagonist of David Bradley's *The Chaneysville Incident*—the irony behind him being a "hot-stuff historian" that can "make a bonfire by rubbing two dry facts together" even though when he deals with his own personal history "it all goes out the window" (1990: 391), she is attempting to make him aware of the fact that, to know others, you must first know yourself. As I will show later in the analysis of the novel, John's problem as a historian is that he can dissect any historical event as long as it does not touch him personally, for when it does, he fails to make sense of it. Throughout the novel, he does not realize that the reason for his inability to understand the connection between the events in his predecessors' lives is not, as he claims, that he lacks the facts, but rather that he is trying to understand others while refusing to explore within himself. Lacking the necessary knowledge of himself and the extent to which his community's historical

---

4   Some scholars use the term 'collective trauma' to denote the type of trauma that, on befalling a collectivity, would disrupt the pre-established connections between the members of that collectivity, thus tearing them apart; as opposed to *cultural* trauma, in which a shared traumatic event or set of events can provoke the different individuals to cluster together. However, for the purposes of the present volume, collective trauma will henceforth be used to refer to any trauma that affects a collectivity, regardless of its effect within it.

trauma[5] has shaped his life prevents him from making sense of the lives of others. After all, understanding big concepts usually comes from understanding their smaller parts. That is, from the inside to the outside. Arguably, this technique is not useful in every case, but it is certainly applicable to collective traumas and works in a bi-directional motion. Not only is it of great help in understanding the workings of individual trauma in order to delve into the mysteries of traumatized collectivities, but also in getting to know how—and why—a traumatic event of the past affects a given community may be useful in making sense of the repercussions that it has for the lives of its individuals. Following this reasoning, I will now focus on the issue of collective trauma and the ways in which African American fiction writers have portrayed individuals suffering from personal traumas against the background of their community's historical sufferings.

In the same way that individuals suffer from trauma, collectives can also be subjected to an event or series of dramatic events that may radically change the manner in which they view themselves and their future. According to Jeffrey Alexander, communities that have experienced a "horrendous event" may feel that they have been marked by it in their collective consciousness and, as a result, find their memories and future identities changed in "fundamental and irrevocable ways" (2004a: 1). The horrendous event—or series of events—can take diverse forms, such as wars, natural disasters like Hurricane Katrina or a tsunami, a terrorist attack as in the events of September 11th, mass genocides like the Holocaust, or violent systems of oppression such as southern slavery, if we talk about the African American community. In those cases, not only are the individuals within a community left with psychological scars from their particular traumas (the loss of a loved one, situations of personal violence and/or the threat to one's life), but also with a shared sense of grief and disruption that may persist over years or even

---

5 Although sometimes used interchangeably, the terms 'historical trauma' and 'collective trauma' are not exact synonyms. As Carol Kidron describes it, historical trauma becomes embedded in the community's politics of memory and identity formation in its role as a "key national or ethnic founding event" (2004: 537). According to this definition, historical trauma contemplates the same characteristics of identity and memory formation as collective or cultural trauma. The main difference is that, in historical trauma, the emergent or founding event occurred in a distant past, and has been preserved through generations as a symbol and marker of collective identity. The term collective trauma has much less distant connotations and it can be applied to a community sharing a traumatic experience from the very moment that the event in question is acknowledged as such. In other words, although every historical trauma is collective, not every collective trauma is historical.

centuries within the collectivity. This is felt as a "tear in the social fabric" (Eyerman 2001: 2) and its consequences can be similar to those of individual trauma.[6]

And yet, collective trauma does differ from individual trauma in that it can be "mediated through various forms of representation and linked to the reformation of collective identity and the reworking of collective memory" (Eyerman 2001: 1). This differentiation is highly significant, for whenever a trauma—such as the Holocaust or the African American experience of slavery—is imbued with this particular characteristic of collective memory and identity formation, it becomes what we term 'cultural trauma.' In it, a particular traumatic event or set of traumatic events may become of such relevance to the community affected by it that they become the central elements around which the national or cultural identity is created, which is what Roger Luckhurst means when he refers to traumatic memory as being "at the root of many national collective memories" (2008: 2). Indeed, cultural or collective trauma is intrinsically related to the notion of collective memory and to the different ways in which communities remember past events, which need not be the same ways in which individuals build up memories. In fact, in my understanding of collective trauma, not every individual within a community needs to have been personally affected by the traumatic events in question and, consequently, not everyone needs to be able to maintain a mental imprint of their experience of the actual facts. They do need, however, a shared—and therefore unavoidably mediated—memory of the past in order for those traumatic events to become crucial in their collective identity formation process; a testimony of the events and—perhaps most especially—the forces that put those events in motion that can then be transmitted across generations through various and continuous retellings and recreations. Memory, like trauma, can indeed be shared in the sense that, according to

---

6 This view of collective trauma as a clinical issue is rather doubtful, and some theorists disagree. There is, in fact, a 'reasonable doubt' in this, insomuch as not every victim of a collective trauma suffers from clearly marked trauma-related symptoms and, in the cases in which this does happen, it may be as a consequence of a somehow artificial appropriation of those symptoms to serve a community's identity formation process. And yet, sometimes the use of psychoanalytic concepts in reference to collective trauma may be useful because "they undercut the standard opposition between the individual and the collectivity, may help us to rethink that opposition, and are to variable degrees applicable in individual or collective ways depending on contexts and situations" (LaCapra 2004: 73–74). Paul Ricoeur supports this last position when he states that it is because of the "bipolar constitution of personal and community identity" that Freudian concepts like that of mourning can be extended from individuals to collectives when dealing with trauma (2004: 78).

Halbwachs, it is "supra-individual" (Eyerman 2001: 6) and normally conceived in relation to a group whose identity is formed around several communally shared remembrances and sets of ideas.

That collective memory would serve as a model out of which individual memories are shaped suggests that identities may work in a similar manner and that individual identity can be a derivative of that of the group. In the cases in which a cultural trauma is not only accepted into the community's cultural background as a significant part of it but as the crucial element in the formation of the group's identity, we would be talking about a 'founding trauma,' which LaCapra defines as "traumas that paradoxically become the valorized or intensely cathected basis of identity for an individual or a group rather than events that pose the problematic question of identity" (LaCapra 2001: 23). It could even become what Kalí Tal calls a 'national myth,' which, like collective memory, "belongs to no one individual, though individuals borrow from it and buy into it in varying degrees" (1996: 115). Kai Erikson also refers to this process of adoption of the traumatic experience as a marker of collective identity by equating it to the sense of communality that sharing a common language or a common background creates (1995: 186). In sum, even though a traumatic event within a community may be a shattering experience, it often works counter intuitively, becoming the "basis of identity" of a group, even within groups that had not previously considered themselves as such (Garland 2002: 184). It differentiates the people that underwent a particular traumatic experience from those who did not; it helps define 'us' as different from 'them.' In the words of Michael Kreyling, "[s]hared, collective, cultural memory marks groups *as groups*, confers upon the individual members the identity of the collective and distinguishes them among the throng of groups threatened with dissolution in the acceleration of history" (2007: 111. Italics in the original). This is the reason that trauma has such a strong binding and community-making power. Once a collectivity has been touched by trauma, the individuals within it feel different and distanced from the rest of the people unaffected by the event in question, and thus they tend to cluster together in order to feel more comfortable in their uniqueness. Conjointly, feeling special can sometimes be a comforting feeling that you choose over, perhaps, a much more painful feeling related to trauma. Communities may choose—either voluntarily or unconsciously—to cluster together in order to feel comforted rather than oppressed by the experience of trauma; to gain something out of it. According to Judith Herman, the group as an environment may help its various individuals work through trauma precisely because it stands opposite from the trauma experience itself—solidarity versus isolation, affirmation and bearing witness versus stigmatization—which is why trauma is often treated in group therapy (2001: 214). Kai Erikson points to something similar when he recognizes the power that trauma has in making people cluster together. Still, he emphasizes, this is not due to "feelings of affection," but to a "shared set of perspectives and rhythms and moods that derive from the sense of being apart" (1995: 194).

The African American collective can be said to be one in which this process is more clearly visible. As I argue in this volume, their shared history of traumatic experiences has been fundamental in the formation of the community and, even now, there are numerous examples in which African American individuals can easily bond together and call each other 'brother' due to the recognition of a common background—though one perhaps not shared by everyone. This can also be clearly linked to the construction of ethnicity and race as a marker of identity. Insomuch as most of the African Americans' traumatic history is the result of the perpetuation of certain oppressive and segregationist systems based on racial difference, it follows that what we can call 'the African American trauma' can be understood simply as a trauma of racism and oppression across centuries. This way, since racial difference for African Americans has traditionally entailed being subjected to racial oppression and therefore to a collective sharing of individual traumas of racist origin, members of that community have tended to identify themselves as much in terms of race and ethnicity as in terms of the traumatic past derived from the system of racial discrimination that former and present members of the community have endured in the US.

Apart from this sense of shared memories, experiences of racism, and identity derived thereof, collective identity also serves as a link within groups since it is within the group that it is more easily possible for individuals to convert the trauma into a somehow positive experience rather than become absorbed and consumed by it. In fact, according to LaCapra, there exists a current tendency "to convert trauma into the occasion for sublimity, to transvalue it into a test of the self or the group and an entry into the extraordinary" (2001: 23). Members of a collectivity sharing a common traumatic past sometimes strive to extract a positive aspect from the experience that they and their community endured. A clear example of this positivistic frame of mind is the numerous cases in which a past trauma has been used to give political agency to the community affected by it. Museums, memorials, monuments and written and oral testimonies alike are proof of this tendency to turn the memory of a past trauma into a political manifestation of denunciation and reclamation of formerly denied collective rights.

3   A "Story to Pass on"? Trauma and Its Transmission

> Shit, we're all consequences of something. Stained with another's past as well as our own. Their past in my blood.
> GAYL JONES, *Corregidora*

For a collective trauma to be considered historical, it must be transmitted through generations from direct survivors of the original traumatic event to their descendants and the descendants of these, even when the latter did not experience the founding trauma. This process of transmission can be explained by the central role that empathy plays in the formation of collective—and therefore historical—traumas. According to Roger Luckhurst, trauma can be "worryingly transmissible" between victims and their listeners—doctors or mere bystanders—due to its capacity to provoke sympathy in the viewers (2008: 3). This capacity to be moved, this empathy on the part of the listener can in some cases reach such high levels of identification with the victim that it can lead to what has been called "secondary victimhood" (Luckhurst 2008: 3) or "vicarious victimhood" (LaCapra 2001: 47), even across centuries. In other words, secondary witnesses do not merely sympathize with the direct survivor; they acquire the trauma and become identified by it in such a way that they regard themselves as victims. This is not by any means to say that a person affected by vicarious victimhood may exhibit symptoms of a clinical trauma in the same way as a direct survivor would, but rather that the person in question may identify with direct victims and their suffering, or else—in the case of collective and historical traumas such as the ones affecting the African American community—recognize the structures that put the first traumatic experience (slavery, for instance) in motion as also affecting him/her in the present (racial discrimination). In other words: contemporary African Americans do not necessarily identify themselves as victims of slavery, but rather as victims of a perpetuation of the racist system that lay behind slavery itself, which makes the marking of the succession of traumatic experiences due to racism across time a self-defining feature among the community. When a traumatic event is as valorized as this for the formation of collective identity, special emphasis is made on its empathic aspect, and on its capacity of creating vicarious victimhood even through time. Historical traumas are thus created by a "continuous line of witnessing (telling and listening) from past to present" (Kreyling 2007: 112). According to LaCapra, empathy "is bound up with a transferential relation to the past," (2004: 135) and this is how the traumatic past can be passed on through generations. For Cathy Caruth, this capacity of the victim to "contaminate others" is what allows the "truth of the past" to live on to the present and be transmitted to others (qtd. in Leys 2000: 254).

In some occasions, especially those in which the traumatic past is conceived of as an injustice committed against the community, the necessity that that 'truth of the past' be remembered and transmitted to later generations is felt almost as an obligation. An example of this is the inscription at the Hall of Remembrance in the US Holocaust Memorial Museum in Washington DC which reads: "Only guard yourself and guard your soul carefully, lest you forget the things your eyes saw, and lest these things depart your heart all the days of your life. And you shall make them known to your children and to your children's children." This self-imposed obligation to maintain the memory of the past serves obvious socio-political purposes and the hope to rectify past wrongs, even if it takes several generations to do so. This survival of memory can be enacted through monuments and memorials such as the aforementioned, but also through public demonstrations, literature, or even tales and songs. According to Ron Eyerman, this is what spirituals, or—using Du Bois's term—'sorrow songs,' actually did in the time of slavery, thus becoming the vehicles for memory and hope of liberation to be passed along through generations and across territories (2001: 13–14).

The passing on of trauma and memory, however, is not always a conscious thing. Dominick LaCapra highlights this double route when he refers to the process of inheritance as "repetition or reproduction," and characterizes it as a combination of "conscious processes" like education and some unconscious or "less controlled processes" like identification and mimeticism (2004: 107). Therefore, when dealing with the trauma of a non-survivor (in this case, a descendant from someone who did experience the traumatic event or series of events directly) we cannot strictly speak of memory, but of 'postmemory,' which could be defined as "the acquired memory of those not directly experiencing an event such as the Holocaust or slavery" (LaCapra 2004: 108). This of course does not mean that the experience and memory of a trauma or a traumatic history is genetically transferred from parent to child, since memories are not genetically encoded, but I argue that such transference does take place by means of empathic, socio-political and identitary processes that perpetuate the memory of the past, such as narrative reconstructions like the novels analyzed here.

This type of transmission could even be enhanced by what I call 'concatenation of traumas.' It may happen that one generation experiences a particular type of trauma and passes it on to the next through the aforementioned processes while the latter generation suffers a trauma of their own. Admitting that non-survivors can experience the collective trauma of their parents—or at least carry the recollection of it—while at the same time being themselves confronted by a new traumatic situation inflicted upon their community, they are theoretically liable to transmit the memory of their collective trauma attached to and modified—even magnified—by the previous one to their descendants.

It would seem that in the case of the African American community there indeed exists such a concatenation of traumas, starting with the original trauma of the estrangement from the motherland, leading to the trauma of slavery, followed by the repression and segregation imposed by the Jim Crow laws, the situation of effective segregation in the big ghettos in the north, up to the racism still visible in modern-day America. Since, as aforementioned, the origin of all those traumatic experiences is one and the same (the perpetuation of racist structures and ideologies in the US), they are in fact all interrelated and it therefore seems plausible that present-day members of the African American community may still identify the original founding trauma with current traumatic experiences and tend to amalgamate them all into what we could term 'the African American trauma' or, rather, 'the African American traumatic experience of racism in the US'. This is what lies at the core of the Black Lives Matter movement, which is predicated on the argument that the perpetuation of a systematic oppression of people due to racial difference indeed exists in the US, and that the excessive police violence demonstrated in the deaths of Trayvon Martin in 2012 and Michael Brown or Eric Garner, both in 2014, among many others, are indicative of the continuation of the line of succession described above. Insomuch as all these traumas—up to and including the present situation of racial discrimination in the US—have continuously and repeatedly affected the African American community, they all need to be recognized as stemming from the same root cause and remembered from generation to generation until that root has effectively been eliminated. Gayl Jones's *Corregidora* is a very good literary representation of this self-imposed imperative, as it portrays the constant necessity of four generations to learn about the previous generation's traumatic story, add it to their own, and pass it on to the next:

> My great-grandmama told my grandmama the part she lived through that my grandmama didn't live through and my grandmama told my mama what they both lived through and my mama told me what they all lived through and we were suppose to pass it down like that from generation to generation so we'd never forget. (1975: 9)

Following this idea, I propose that, especially in cases of traumatic experiences lived across generations as a consequence of the perpetuation of violent or oppressive systems such as the racial discrimination exerted against African Americans, the transmission of trauma is not so much a passive act—something simply passed on to you by your parents—but rather an active and willful act; something that one is willing to do. An individual may voluntarily choose to identify himself with his ancestors' traumatic history out of love and solidarity, as the only subject position that seems ethical or even responsible, or following a political or activist schedule in the same vein as Spivak's concept of strategic essentialism. Since a founding trauma can function as a marker of collective identity, it may happen that a person that has not lived through a given set of events, but that has perhaps lived through others that he/she identifies as stemming from the same source, may choose to use them—and the trauma that they entail—to identify him/herself with the people who did suffer them in order to claim a common source and construct the self's own personal identity as equal to that of the rest of individuals within the community.

To go a step further, it may also happen that at a particular point in time, that community may see itself in need of gaining a degree of political agency that they otherwise lack. The trauma of its forefathers—that collective trauma that marks the community as special and that works as the perfect way of maintaining internal unity within its individuals—becomes then a more than valid vindicatory tool in order to make themselves heard and pitied. This is especially true when the strategies that put the original trauma in motion are felt to be still in force. Justice should be made *now* in honor of those who did not have it *then* and in order to work towards a better future. Stef Craps, one of today's most reputed postcolonial trauma scholars, reads this injunction to remember past traumas and reconstruct them into the future in her interpretation of Derrida's *Specters of Marx* in which, she argues, Derrida posits "an obligation to live not solely in the present but 'beyond all living present,' aware of and attentive to those already dead or not yet born" (Craps 2010: 467). For Derrida, she continues, some degree of responsibility towards the future can only be met by acknowledging the ghosts of the past, by which we can understand the gaps in narrative history left by silenced stories of injustice and oppression like that of African Americans. Those specters must be recognized and passed on to our descendants in order to work for a better future. And since they are often gaps, absences left by the silencing of atrocities put in motion by those that committed them, they must be recorded in order to leave evidence, in order to leave a trace of them for the future. Again, an example of this self-imposed imperative can be found in Gayl Jones's *Corregidora*:

> *When I'm telling you something you don't ever ask if I'm lying. Because they didn't want to leave no evidence of what they done—so it couldn't he held*

against them. And I'm leaving evidence. And you got to leave evidence too. And your children got to leave evidence. And when it come time to hold up the evidence, we got to have evidence to hold up. (1975: 14. Italics in the original)

4   Trauma, Memory and Space: Sites of Memory/Sites of Trauma

In addition to the aforementioned sociological and political reasons that a trauma can be passed on, it could also be claimed that trauma 'sticks' not only to the victims, but also to the place where such trauma occurred. Many scholars, such as Gaston Bachelard, have analyzed the ways in which a particular place can be, throughout time, imbued with memories and experiences, becoming inscribed by them and changing the way its inhabitants feel, act, and relate to that place. Indeed, "it is not by chance," Paul Ricoeur points out, "that we say of what has occurred that it took place" (2006: 41). Moreover, he continues, these "memory places" can offer an aid for failing memory, against forgetting and "the silent plea of dead memory" (Ricoeur 2006: 41). In this way, the space can stand almost as a document in which the memories of each of the events that happened there become inscribed as on a palimpsest. Those memories, naturally, can be both happy and tragic, which poses a great difference in the way that people refer and relate to the aforementioned places and allows us to speak of "memory sites" as opposed to "trauma sites" (LaCapra 1998: 10) or even "mourning sites" (LaCapra 1998: 44).

In the same way that people often nostalgically remember the places where they were cheerful, feelings of anger and pain are often reawakened and magnified when watching or going through the places in which a traumatic loss has occurred. The place becomes somehow impregnated with the tragedy that happened there and becomes a constant reminder of it. In other cases, artificially constructed sites of memory like museums or memorials can be erected in order to build up and transmit a collectively shared notion of trauma. By visiting those monuments to memory, a non-survivor can partake and share in the memories of the past trauma refered to and commemorated in such constructions and engage in a communal identification with the victims directly affected by that trauma or traumatic history. This practice, based on empathy and political and ideological identification, can be used to build up a sense of collectiveness among members of a community that has established a shared past trauma as the center of their identity formation process and for which the site of memory in question serves as a physical reminder of the founding trauma.

All of these enclaves—from the place in which a specific event occurred, to the place in which a reminder of it was erected—have been broadly called *lieux de mémoire*—even though Pierre Nora, who coined the term, used it to refer more specifically to the latter. For him, the appearance of *lieux de mémoire*— that is, spaces in which the memories of past events were transferred—is due to the disappearance of the 'true' memories of those past events accountable to the rapidity of modern life and the pre-eminence of history over memory itself. Thus, history would be the artificially constructed substitute of memory, which in turn would consist of the remembrance of events and ways of life carried by individuals through the generations. This endangered memory, Nora says, needs to be consecrated to museums, monuments, or other physical memorials that would function as reminders of the effacing "*milieux de mémoire*, real environments of memory" (1989: 7).

Nothing could be more appropriate in the case of the African American community. Insomuch as their original *milieux de mémoire* have been not only lost to the "acceleration of history" (Nora 1989: 7), but also forcibly erased, there exists no other choice but to resort to *lieux de mémoire*. Nevertheless, there are not many examples of monuments or memorials to the trauma of slavery—whereas there are several for the Holocaust. Consequently, I posit, other—perhaps non-spatial—*lieux de mémoire* must be invented, and literature is once again a more than acceptable substitute. A book can perform the function of a site of memory in Nora's sense just like a museum, since it can serve as a reminder of a past event—a traumatic event in this case. Trauma writing attempts to recreate the scenes of a lost, hidden, repressed, denied or silenced past and can provide an artificial—yet truthful—account of history when the original memories of that history cannot.

However, not only artificial places or artifacts can function as *lieux de mémoire*. As mentioned above, sometimes the actual enclave in which a trauma occurred becomes so imbued with traumatic memories as to become a constant reminder of that traumatic event and, thus, a site of memory. In fact, Nora's term has been broadly accepted by various authors in order to allude to those geographical spaces in which trauma took place as well as to the substitutes for memory to which Nora referred. In this sense, for the African American community, the *lieux de mémoire* are varied, and range from the original spaces of the lost motherland to the ghettoes within the cities of the north to the southern spaces of slavery and subsequent segregation, each standing as a memento of a different trauma within the African American experience. All those spaces have subsequently been prevalent in the formation of the African American identity and have therefore been the object of study in numerous works of fiction. Authors like Toni Morrison, James Baldwin, Alice

Walker, David Bradley, Ralph Ellison and Richard Wright set their works in one or several of these spaces in order to reconstruct the traumatic events, hopes of freedom or feelings of estrangement that have marked the African American collective identity.

Similarly, African American literature itself is plagued with instances in which a specific location is marked for its inhabitants with the reminiscences of a traumatic past. Those enclaves, located within the communal *lieux de mémoire*, become individual sites of memory for those characters related to them, and their very sight or mention may trigger a series of painful reminiscences that might be interwoven with—or even overpowered by—more pleasant memories. Such is the case of Sethe in *Beloved*, who remembers "[b]oys hanging from the most beautiful sycamores in the world" (Morrison 2005: 7) and is shamed by the fact that, in her mind, the beauty of the trees always trumps the tragedy of the lynched boys. Similarly, Vere—one of Paule Marshall's characters in *The Chosen Place, the Timeless People*—is overwhelmed, upon his return to his native island, by a mixture of good and bad memories awakened at the mere sight of the island from a plane window:

> Straining forward, Vere could just make out the old hill with the two craggy peaks rising like steeples from its crest. Hidden below to the left, where Westminster's long northern spur flattened out to almost level ground, was Cane Vale sugar factory, he knew. Cane Vale! where [sic] every morning as a boy he had taken his great-aunt Leesy's husband his eleven o'clock breakfast of rice and saltfish, before the latter had fallen into the deep pit which housed the rollers used to extract the juice from the canes, and been crushed to death. Out of sight also, between the broad foot of the hills and the sea, lay the small village which its inhabitants insisted on calling a town: Spinetown. It was there he had been born and his mother had died giving birth to him ... (1969: 14)

Because of its complexity and the effect it creates in the characters, the setting in this novel merits closer examination. The embeddedness of trauma in this island is so marked, that even those that have no previous personal relationship to it, and for whom none of their private history has taken place there, feel it. The island, and most specifically, the obvious division existing in it between Bournehills (one of its corners) and the rest, seems to be screaming out its pain; "*it* [Bournehills] gives the impression [...] that it has all the problems there are" (Marshall 1969: 23. Italics in the original). This secluded part of the island serves as a catalyst for other people's traumas, as we can extract from Harriet's reaction at the sight of it:

> Because of the shadows Bournehills scarcely seemed a physical place to her, but some mysterious and obscured region of the mind which ordinary consciousness did not dare admit to light. Suddenly, for a single unnerving moment, she had the sensation of being borne backward in time rather than forward in space. The plane by some perverse plan might have been taking her away from the present, which included Saul and her new life she was about to begin with him, back to the past which she had always sought to avoid. (Marshall 1969: 21)

Similarly, for Saul, her husband, this same place almost immediately becomes the epitome of all the other troubled and abused places, resonant with their specific traumas. Just as in the case of Harriet, although he has never set foot in that place before, he feels immediately—and troublingly—connected to it to the point that it seems "strangely familiar" (Marshall 1969: 99). The place itself, although new to Saul and thus strange and unfamiliar, is reminiscent of other, more recognizable spaces both external and internal to him, hence the oxymoronic expression. In an instant, Saul is reminded of all the spaces of trauma he has previously visited as well as those located within himself:

> He had gotten out of the car along with Harriet and Allen, leaving Merle behind, and was standing gazing around him on the sharply inclined shoulder of the road—and thinking that he had surely been there before. He was certain he had. Perhaps, he quickly told himself, it was because the place somehow, for some reason, brought to mind other areas up and down the hemisphere where he had worked. It resembled them all, not in physical detail so much, but in something he sensed about it as his eyes, half-closed against the glare, roamed slowly over the patchwork hills to the sea and back again. Bournehills, this place he had never seen before, was suddenly the wind-scoured Peruvian Andes. The highlands of Guatemala. Chile. Bolivia, where he had once worked briefly among the tin miners. Honduras, which had proved so fatal. Southern Mexico. And the spent cotton lands of the Southern United States through which he had traveled many times as a young graduate student on his way to do field work among the Indians in Chiapas. It was suddenly, to his mind, every place that had been wantonly used, its substance stripped away, and then abandoned. He was shaken and angered by the abandonment he sensed here, the abuse. [...] Moreover, the place, these ragged hills crowded out of sight behind the high ridge, with the night hiding in their folds, even seemed, suddenly, to hold some personal meaning for him, his thoughts becoming complex, circular, wheels within a wheel as he stood there.

Bournehills could have been a troubled region within himself to which he had unwittingly returned. (Marshall 1969: 99–100)

In some cases, especially when the aforementioned sites of memory become representative of the whole community's past—traumatic or otherwise—such sites can be almost mystified, and converted into places of cult that need to be protected in order to preserve the memories for which they stand. When, for instance, the younger generations of Ruby, in Toni Morrison's *Paradise*, deface the public oven that the city's founding fathers transported from their former location and rebuilt piece by piece as a reminder of their honored past, the whole town is set amiss in a confrontation with terrible consequences. On the other hand, even in cases in which the actual places—houses, barracks, ovens, etc.—no longer exist, the space in which they stood becomes reminiscent of them, and the recollections of the events that took place in them must be preserved as part of the community's collective memory and identity. Sometimes, the urge to protect these spaces against any external evil may move individuals to unprecedented actions, as in the case of the characters in Ernest Gaines's *A Gathering of Old Men*, where a group of elderly, long-abused men decide to finally face their oppressors not only in order to stand up for themselves, but also to protect the place in which the last remainders of their past survive:

> [Johnny Paul] wasn't looking at Mapes, he was looking toward the tractor and the trailer of cane out there on the road. But I could tell he wasn't seeing any of that. I couldn't tell what he was thinking until I saw his eyes shifting up the quarters where his mama and papa used to stay. But the old house wasn't there now. It had gone like all the others had gone. Now weeds covered the place where the house used to be. 'Y'all look,' he said. 'Look now. Y'all see anything? What y'all see?'
> [...]
> 'Y'all remember how it used to be?' [...] 'When they wasn't no weeds—remember? Remember how they used to sit out there on the garry—Mama, Papa, Aunt Clara, Aunt Sarah, Unc Moon, Aunt Spoodle, Aunt Thread. Remember? Everybody had flowers in the yard. [...]'
> 'That's something you can't see, Sheriff, 'cause you never could see it,' he said. 'you can't see the church with the people, and you can't hear the singing and the praying, you had to be here then to be able to don't see it and don't hear it now. But I was here then, and I don't see it now, and that's why I did it. I did it for them back there under them trees. I did it 'cause that tractor is getting closer and closer to that graveyard, and I was

scared if I didn't do it, one day that tractor was go'n come in there and plow them graves, getting rid of all proof that black people ever farmed this land with plows and mules—like if they had nothing from the starten but motor machines. Sure, one day they will get rid of the proof that we ever was, but they ain't go'n do it while I'm still here. Mama and Papa worked too hard in these fields. They mama and they papa worked too hard in these same fields. They mama and they papa people worked too hard, too hard to have that tractor just come in that graveyard and destroy all proof that they ever was. I'm the last one left. I had to see that the graves stayed for a little while longer. But I just didn't do it for my own people. I did it for every last one back there under them trees. And I did it for every four-o'clock, every rosebush, every palm-of-Christian ever growed on this place.' (1983: 88–92)

And yet, as mentioned above, in some instances the memories imbued in some places are so painful that the place itself becomes a source of pain and is avoided by the victims of the trauma present in it. This, as will be seen later, is the case of 'the other place' in Gloria Naylor's *Mama Day*; a house that was abandoned after a certain trauma, which was kept silent throughout the narrative to be gradually disclosed toward its end, occurred there. Even though the readers do not learn what horrific event took place in this house until late in the book, the secrecy surrounding the house—a secrecy manifested in the form of whispers and in the strong refusal of one of the characters, Abigail, to set foot there, she avoids the place "like the plague" (Naylor 1988: 279)—makes it clear from the beginning of the narrative that we are facing yet another *lieu de mémoire*. This kind of haunting is very much reminiscent of the one present in Morrison's *Beloved*. Similarly, in one of the most recent African American novels to retrace the trauma of slavery, Colson Whitehead's *The Underground Railroad*, one of the characters, Valentine, speaks of a specific location as permeated by the traumas of the past that occurred there, and as, probably, a place to be avoided by African Americans: "'Indiana was a slave state,' Valentine continued. 'That evil soaks into the soil. Some say it steeps and gets stronger. Maybe this isn't the place. Maybe Gloria and I should have kept going after Virginia'" (2016: 331).

In sum, it seems clear that houses, islands, fields, graveyards, ovens, towns, cities, states, or even whole countries or continents, bear with them—or *in* them—the traces of the past, and, with it, of trauma (whether it be personal or historical, collective or individual), memory and history. Different histories call for different relationships with the past and different responses to it, as well as different ways of portraying that past and the trauma embedded in it.

5 Trauma Writing/Writing Trauma[7]

> The writer's function is not without its arduous duties. By definition, he cannot serve today those who make history; he must serve those who are subject to it.
>
> ALBERT CAMUS, "Nobel Prize Acceptance Speech"

The rise of public awareness about trauma in the 1980s and 1990s, and the growing attention given to Vietnam and Holocaust survivors, gave way to the flourishing of numerous trauma narratives. Thus, trauma writing grew as a type of writing that either portrayed traumatic events or explored the workings of trauma in the minds of its victims, and its forms are nowadays manifold, ranging from memoirs to novels, including humorous literature (like Kurt Vonnegut's *Slaughterhouse 5*), children's literature (like Jane Yolen's *Briar Rose*) or even graphic novels (like Art Spiegelman's *Maus*). Appearing "at least a decade after the traumatic experience in question" (Tal 1996: 125), the resulting narratives tend to approach the effects that those traumatic events have in survivors as well as in their families and communities, and can be part of the process of recovery, not only for the victim him/herself but also for other persons affected by it. According to Desmond Harding, "literary representations of trauma attempt to help readers access traumatic experience and thus have an important place among diverse historiographic, testimonial, and representational approaches in illuminating the personal and public aspects of trauma" (2006: 9).

However, we should not equate "literary representations of trauma"—that is, fiction about trauma—with "testimonial approaches"—autobiographical narratives of traumatic experiences—or even to the type of therapeutic writing of the type used in some psychoanalytical practices. In the quote above, Harding posits that "literary representations of trauma" have "a place" among the other types of trauma writing, not that they are equal to them or that both, literary and testimonial narratives, in any way present the same types of truths. Consequently, I maintain that asking a fictional text about trauma to somehow lead to a process of psychological healing in the real world would be a rather tall order, perhaps completely unattainable, nonsensical and even unethical. My contention is that, in fictional writing, the author creates a possible world which is perhaps similar in appearance to the real one, but nonetheless artificial and therefore nonexistent outside the work of fiction itself. This created

---

7 A different and much shorter version of this section (in Spanish) appeared in the 2017 online issue of *e-cadernos ces* (27) under the title: "Demostraciones públicas del sufrimiento privado: Utilidades colectivas de la escritura del trauma."

world exists outside of, or parallel to, the factual world and therefore lacks the same kind of referential component that the therapeutic writing of memoirs have. Nevertheless, it does perform a function: keeping the memory of the real traumas of the past alive—and thus helping readers access that memory, as Harding puts it—in order for that writing to perform a variety of tasks in the present that range from giving voice to those traumas to using awareness of them to further certain socio-political agendas.

On the other hand, even if the truth-value of literary representations of trauma is not the same as that of therapeutic writings, it may be argued that, through the use of fiction, literary representations make the 'real' truth a little bit more palatable and therefore more of greater social, political or ethical value in the real world. According to Jorge Semprún, in order to tell an "unimaginable" experience in a successful way—that is, in a way in which it can be listened to—such an experience must be told through some degree of "artifice" (Semprún 1997: 124). Traumatic experiences like those of Holocaust survivors can never be completely understood by those who did not go through them; their "essential truth" can be transmissible "only through literary writing" (Semprún 1997: 125). Semprún continues: "That leaves books. Novels, preferably. Literary narratives, at least, that will go beyond simple eyewitness accounts, that will let you imagine, even if they can't let you see" (1997: 127).

Be that as it may, trauma writings, fiction or otherwise—and even though they sometimes "draw skepticism more readily than sympathy because they expose the conflict between identification and representativeness" (Gilmore 2001: 22)—often prove to be beneficial both to the victims and their cause. As Laurie Vickroy contends, the advantages of contemporary trauma narratives can be manifold, from testifying to the frequency of trauma and "its importance as a multicontextual social issue," to raising questions about "our ability to deal with loss and fragmentation in our lives," together with confronting readers with their own fears and raising the problem of the "public's relationship to the traumatized" (2002: 2).

And yet, several authors have highlighted the difficulties that can arise when narrating the traumatic experience. One of these difficulties—perhaps the most relevant—has to do with the very possibility of representing or articulating trauma. Since trauma is an event that falls outside the range of experience and distorts the victim's normal sense of memory and articulation, some scholars argue that it cannot be coherently put into spoken words, much less written ones. As Jenny Edkins puts it, "the traumatic experience is seen as something that takes place outside language. In that sense it is not experience at all, in that it cannot be made sense of or recounted in language" (2003: 213). She adds: "Trauma cannot for this reason be spoken. It is outside the realm of language, and to bring it back within that realm by speaking of it, by setting it within a linear narrative form, is to destroy its truth" (Edkins 2003: 214). Others, like Lawrence Langer, have pointed to a difference in the memories of a trauma, such as the Holocaust, and the domain of narrative memory: "[N]arrative possibility, coherence and normalization belong to *mémoire ordinaire*, whilst Holocaust accounts must always touch on the irresolvable and incomprehensible traumas of the *mémoire profonde*" (Luckhurst 2008: 65. Italics in the original). Insomuch as both practices—normal narrative and Holocaust retellings—belong to different domains of memory, they cannot be equated, and thus a coherent narrative of the Holocaust is not possible. Likewise, Elie Wiesel describes his own trauma as a Holocaust survivor as defying literature (Luckhurst 2008: 69) and expresses his own experience of post-traumatic language—and testimony writing—in the following terms:

> The word has deserted the meaning it was intended to convey—impossible to make them coincide. The displacement, the shift, is irrevocable ... We all knew that we could never, never say what had to be said, that we could never express in words, coherent, intelligible words, our experience of madness on an absolute scale ... All words seemed inadequate, worn, foolish, lifeless, whereas I wanted them to be searing. Where was I to discover a fresh vocabulary, a primeval language? The language of night was not human; it was primitive, almost animal ... A brute striking wildly, a body falling; an officer raises his arm and a whole community walks toward a common grave ... This is the concentration camp language. It negated all other language and took its place. Rather than link, it became wall. (qtd. in Tal 1996: 122)

However, other theorists have countered all these arguments that refer to trauma as something beyond narrating or even coherent wording, and favor trauma writing as an accessible, therapeutic and reliable enough process. Numerous literary and cultural critics have agreed with this use of trauma writing as a healing device and have countered those who claim that trauma cannot be represented. "[I]f trauma is a crisis in representation," Luckhurst says, "then this generates narrative *possibility* just as much as *impossibility*" (2008: 83. Italics in the original). To which he adds, "[t]rauma needs to be represented, over and over" (131), a view which is also shared by Dori Laub (1992a: 85). "The impossibility of a comprehensible story," Caruth argues, "does not necessarily mean the denial of a transmissible truth" (1995a: 154), and this is the view that several writers and trauma victims seem to favor. Jorge Semprún, himself a Holocaust survivor, would argue that "you can always say everything. The 'ineffable' you hear so much about is only an alibi. Or a sign of laziness. You can always say everything: language contains everything" (1997: 13). He also states that what victims like him lived through was not "indescribable" but "unbearable," and that the issue with trauma narratives is not one of "articulation" but of "density" (Semprún 1997: 13). As mentioned above, he claims that the only way to "reach this substance"—that is, to be able to put this unbearable experience into words—will be through "those able to shape their evidence into an artistic object, a space of creation. Or of re-creation. Only the artifice of a masterly narrative will prove capable of conveying some of the truth of such testimony" (Semprún 1997: 13).

It is my contention that trauma narratives are not only possible, but potentially beneficial, if not for the individuals themselves then at least as a means of giving voice to the injustices of the past, recognizing them as such, and offering a viable standpoint from which to work toward the halting of future repetitions of violence. In fact, in many cases even if the authors find it almost impossible to write about their experiences, they feel almost compelled to do so by the belief that certain injustices must be known and acknowledged by those who did not suffer them. An example of this could be the stance of Elie Wiesel who, despite the difficulties that verbalizing his traumatic experience posed for him, strongly believed that "[n]ot to transmit an experience is to betray it" (qtd. in Tal 1996: 120). Likewise, Jorge Semprún recounts in his *Literature or Life* that he, for many years, abandoned the idea of writing about his Holocaust experience for fear of not being able to survive the telling, but that he ultimately felt compelled to retake it after he learned of the death of Primo Levi. Even if Levi himself realized that "our language lacks words to express this offence, the demolition of a man" (1959: 21), he did write numerous volumes about his Auschwitz experience, perhaps moved by a fellow prisoner's advice that "one must want to survive, to tell the story, to bear witness" (Levi 1959: 39). Similarly, African American author James Baldwin often talks about his writing as bearing witness, and says that it is in that role—as the sole existing witness—that the people of one generation are responsible to the next (1985b: 393). Baldwin also points to the necessity of exploring the complete history of a people—regardless of its traumatic content—not only for those who were overcome by it, but also as a testimony for the ones to come, lest their vision should be externally corrupted:

> Whoever has found himself in a real Catfish Row knew he had two choices, to live or to die, and some lived. If the day ever comes when the survivors of the place can be fooled into believing that the Hollywood cardboard even faintly resembles, or is intended to resemble, what it was

like to be there, all our terrible and beautiful history will have gone for nothing and we will all be doomed to an unimaginable reality. I prefer to believe that the day is coming when we will tell the truth about it—and ourselves. On that day, and not before that day, we can call ourselves free men. (Baldwin 1985d: 181)

However, as in any communicative process, in order for that witness-bearing to take place, it is not enough to simply express the trauma, to put it into words; a listener is needed. In the case of collective traumas, such as the Holocaust or slavery, readers and listeners alike are also asked to transmit the trauma, to bear witness to it together with the survivors and their descendants. According to Laurie Vickroy, readers must be responsible and play an active role in the task of the transmission of "shocking and incomprehensible" information (2002: 218). This empathic sharing of the experience by the reader is necessary so that it cannot be forgotten and thus provide an example in order to prevent further repetition. According to Dorothy Allison, literature must serve to make people change their preconceived ideas of the world and to want to make it "more just and more truly human" (qtd. in Vickroy 2002: 146).

This impetus to change is one of the most important uses of trauma writing; to recover hidden, silenced, unacknowledged, or even repressed memories and to share them with others. Literature about trauma, Kalí Tal argues, emanates from the need to "tell and retell the story of the traumatic experience," thus making it real for both victims and communities. Trauma literature therefore serves "both as validation and cathartic vehicle for the traumatized author" (Tal 1996: 21). Likewise, Laurie Vickroy states that trauma narratives "suggest that oppression and resulting psychic vulnerability will be perpetuated unless memories are collectively articulated and shared" (2002: 113).

Sometimes, traumatic memories seem more bearable if they are shared by the collective, as Lois Lowry suggests in her novel *The Giver* (2008). Although originally intended as fiction for young adults, the novel addresses the very problematic question of collective memory and trauma. It depicts a utopian community whose members are protected from any type of evil or pain. Strict rules govern their everyday routines and interactions so that even personal relationships are carefully designed and controlled in order to avoid any confrontation, lies or personal aggression. The disadvantage is that other type of feelings and experiences such as love, color awareness, music or even carnal pleasure are also limited. Difference is eradicated, but so is anything potentially damaging to people's absolute happiness and wellbeing, including memories. The community does not hold any type of memories previous to their confinement in their present restricted area—they are naturally not aware of this confinement—which means they have no history. Knowledge of wars, pain, illness, even death, is bestowed upon the figure of the Receiver of Memory, who uses that knowledge to advise the community's council of elders in their decision-making. This Receiver of Memory is a highly honored person for he is, thanks to his historical knowledge, the wisest person in the community. Apart from this, the community is only aware that he knows things they would not want to know, and thus helps protect them from pain. However, that knowledge is too much; a single person should not bear the weight of a whole collectivity's past sufferings, just as Jonas, the Receiver of Memory's young apprentice and the boy designated to become the next Receiver quickly realizes: "But why can't *everyone* have the memories? I think it would seem a little easier if the memories were shared. You and I wouldn't have to bear so much upon ourselves, if everybody took a part" (Lowry 2008: 146. Italics in the original). To this hardship, moreover, another inconvenience is added: "The worst part of holding the memories is not the pain. It's the loneliness of it. Memories need to be shared" (194).

As Lowry's novel suggests (and the fact that the narrative is addressed to young adults is further indicative of it), memories—traumatic or otherwise—need to be shared, not only in order to share the pain they may entail but also to make them known. Pain and suffering are part of human nature, and we need to be aware of them in order to learn and attempt to construct a better world, especially when that pain and suffering have been the product of man's actions. This brings us back to issues of traumatic past experiences such as the Holocaust and the necessity of putting those experiences down in writing. An event like the Holocaust cannot be silenced and needs to be remembered for the sake of future generations. Literature offers countless portrayals of this imperative to remember and pass down the injustices of the past, and many are the memoirs and autobiographies, as well as novels, that confront their readers with the traumas of history. Some even make this necessity explicit through their characters, as in Joy Kogawa's Obasan, which tackles the time during World War Two when hundreds of Japanese-Canadians were forcefully taken from their homes, deprived of most of their possessions and put in camps, as well as the memory of those events in the minds of their descendants. In the words of one of its characters: "You have to remember [...]. You are your history. If you cut any of it off you're an amputee. Don't deny the past. Remember everything. [...] Denial is gangrene [...]" (Kogawa 1994: 60).

And yet, attempts to silence these kinds of events are common. Usually the oppressor or inflictor of the trauma attempts to silence such events in an attempt to 'leave matters behind' or simply to escape retribution. For that reason, if remembering traumatic events and histories through literature is imperative in any kind of community, it may be even more so in the case of ethnic minorities, where traumatic events—that fundamental part of their history—have been forcefully erased by those in power. In those cases, communities may feel an "injunction to remember" in order to counteract the "external distortion and censorship" (Eyal 2004: 9) that has been forced upon them. Since trauma falls outside the range of the ordinary, certain traumatic events are difficult to believe and, indeed, the fear of not being believed is commonly shared by victims of trauma (McKinney 2007: 287). Consequently, the memory of these events needs to be shared in order to establish their authenticity and to raise awareness when believability may fail. African Americans encountered a similar problem in that most slave narratives of the nineteenth century were taken as fiction, a misconception that was certainly useful for the anti-abolitionist cause. This, says Judith Herman, is common to all perpetrators, who would use secrecy and silence as their "first line of defense" and, when it fails, they would put the credibility of the victim into question (2001: 8).

In the United States, the white community traditionally exercised a similar type of cultural oppression against other ethnic communities. White cultural supremacy resulted in a silencing and suppressing of the histories of those communities that are now being recuperated in the form of narrative. Literature may be particularly instrumental in this struggle against forgetting, since, as Singh et al. argue,

> [i]n the act of reading, readers are enabled to remember things that culture has asked them to forget, to put into historical perspective the ahistoricized and commercialized sites and scenes of American conflict, to see forbidden scenes from behind closed doors and thus from hidden cultural spaces, and to experience a new sense of identity. The ethnic writer's interrogations of public memory are a reminder that all memories—individual, family, ethnic, or racial—are socially constructed and allow for their reconstruction in narratives in quest of change and new meaning. (1994: vii)

One of those silenced ethnicities in the US now making a conscious effort to retrace their silenced past is the African American community. Its history of repression and, especially, of slavery, was silenced not only by the white American community, but also by other communities in Europe whose cities benefited from the profits and products of slavery and have only recently begun to acknowledge it (Edkins 2003: 114). This was noted by Ralph Ellison when, grappling with the canon of American literature, he reflected that not only had the African American experience been silenced, but also, the African American individual had been dramatically misrepresented: "Thus when the white American, holding up most twentieth-century fiction, says, 'This is American reality,' the Negro tends to answer [...], 'Perhaps, but you've left out this, and this, and this. And most of all, what you'd have the world accept as *me* isn't even human'" (1972b: 25. Italics in the original).

It is for this reason that the African American community saw the need to recuperate its hidden past in order to make visible the traumas inherent in it and work towards eliminating the racist ideologies that caused them, even if it took generations to successfully accomplish it. Writing about that hidden past seems to be a sufficient means of accomplishing this necessary recuperation, as well as a moral imperative for writers, as Ellison argued in the 1970s, when he stated that "[n]egro writers and those of the other minorities have their own task of contributing to the total image of the American by depicting the experience of their own groups" (1972b: 43). However, merely recuperating the past is not enough; according to Gil Eyal, "[s]uch knowledge should be made public once again, in order to rehabilitate the victims and punish the wrongdoers" (2004: 24). One way of doing that is by recreating the past in literature, which is exactly what African American authors have been doing in the last few decades. Toni Morrison described it thus in an interview:

> The reclamation of the history of black people in this country is paramount in its importance because while you can't really blame the conqueror for writing history his own way, you can certainly debate it. There's a great deal of obfuscation and distortion and erasure, so that the presence and the heartbeat of black people has been systematically annihilated in many, many ways and the job of recovery is ours. It's a serious responsibility and one single human being can only do a very very tiny part of that, but it seems to me to be both secular and non-secular work for a writer. You have to stake it out and identify those who have preceded you—resummoning them, acknowledging them is just one step in that process of reclamation—so that they are always there as the *confirmation* and the affirmation of the life that I personally have not lived but is the life of that organism to which I belong which is black people in this country. (Davis 1994: 224–225. Italics in the original)

The African American community, says Morrison, has never heard the true story of their past and need to hear it in order to overcome their collective trauma. As Holloway points out, "the victim's own chronicles [of slavery] were systematically submerged, ignored, mistrusted, or superseded by 'historians' of the era" (qtd. in Wyatt 2004: 77). Slaves were prohibited from reading and writing in order to deprive them of the most distinguishable of human characteristics: the use of language as a tool. That enabled slaveholders to subjugate slaves and to treat them as mere animals intended only for reproduction and labor (Wyatt 2004: 75). As a consequence of this situation, African Americans were barred from the literature of the time. Since most slaves weren't able or permitted to write, African American writers—except for the very few who managed to write slave narratives, and whose merit must therefore be recognized—did not exist. Additionally, there were very few black characters in novels and, if they appeared at all, they were minor characters, often dull-witted and savage-like in a clear attempt to reinforce the ideology of slavery.

In *Playing in the Dark* Toni Morrison discusses—along much the same lines as Ellison—the black presence in the American literary scene and realizes that this biased representation "provided the staging ground and arena for the elaboration of the quintessential American identity" (Morrison 1993: 44). At one point talking about and taking a stand on slavery *was* necessary in the American community, and some effort was put into translating those issues into the literary production. However, the result was "a master narrative that spoke *for* Africans and their descendants, or *of* them" (Morrison 1993: 50. Italics in the original) rather than a narrative that established a dialogue through which whites and blacks could both express their points of view. Even when African Americans were permitted to express themselves in the form of slave narratives, they were being utilized to serve the purposes of white abolitionists. Slave narratives, Morrison states, although successful in many other ways, could not destroy the master narrative, that is, the story told by those in power, which they endeavored to maintain untouched (Morrison 1993: 51).

Suppression by the ruling community is not the only reason that secrecy regarding certain traumatic histories is maintained. As Bouson discussed in depth in his 2000 monograph *Quiet as it's Kept*, sometimes, that secrecy also emerges from the traumatized community on account of shame. This is what Toni Morrison seems to suggest in her 1993 afterword to *The Bluest Eye*: "It is a secret between us and a secret that is being kept from us. The conspiracy is both held and withheld, exposed and sustained. In some sense it was precisely what the act of writing the book was: the public exposure of a private confidence" (Morrison 1999b: 169). This is reflected as well in the beginning of the novel with the words "[q]uiet as it's kept" (Morrison 1999b: 4), which also serves as the title for Bouson's work. These words, as Morrison explains, are "conspiratorial" (1989: 20) and stand for "a piece of information that means exactly what it says," but that to black people implies that "a big lie is about to be told" or that "someone is going to tell some graveyard information" (LeClair 1994: 124). That is, they refer to something as a zealously guarded secret in order to bring that secret to light. The reason for this secrecy is straightforward and comprehensible enough: like many victims of traumatic events, the African American community has suppressed its memories in order to escape further harm. For Toni Morrison, this is something that the whole African American community, including herself, share:

> I thought this [*Beloved*] has got to be the least read of all the books I'd written because it is about something that the characters don't want to remember, I don't want to remember, black people don't want to remember. I mean, it's national amnesia. (Angelo 1994: 257)

Literature plays another significant role in working through past traumas by giving voice to them, or by helping "turn victims into agents by giving voice to the voiceless" (Eyerman 2001: 44). Victims, Dori Laub says, cannot "find peace in silence" and, when silence is nonetheless maintained, the repressed story becomes an "external evil" that assists the "perpetuation of its tyranny" (1995: 64). Literature is very useful in breaking this silence and promoting the agency of its victims. As Martínez Falquina points out, "literature makes silence audible, and it verbalizes pain, bringing up its hidden causes" (2009: 514). Likewise, the writing down of a traumatic experience in a coherent narrative has been known to help traumatized individuals and communities make sense of their traumatic past. Quoting Paul Ricoeur, Luckhurst states that narrative is an "act of concordance" that "grasps together" a series of "scattered events" and integrates them into a coherent story (2008: 84). To this Luchurst adds Ricoeur's definition of narrative as "the privileged means by which we re-configure our confused, unformed, and at the limit mute temporal experience" (2008: 84). Returning to Toni Morrison and her work, we can find a portrayal of this use of trauma writing as, at least, an attempt to create order and cohesion within the individual's traumatic experience. In *A Mercy* we are faced with the character of Florens who, tormented by the trauma of separation from her mother and taken to her sanity's limit by the abandonment of her lover, feels the compulsion to write down her story on the walls of her mistress's house. Regardless of the fact that she is aware that her intended addressee—the illiterate lover that abandoned her and whom she has presumably murdered—will not be able to read it, she goes on writing as a means of giving voice to her trauma and finding peace and rest at night: "What will I do with my nights when the telling stops? Dreaming will not come again" (Morrison 2008: 158). We find a similar situation in Gloria Naylor's *Linden Hills*, when, after witnessing a terrible event that just adds to his own baggage of traumatic memories, Willie feels the need to commit his experience to writing in order to find both rest and relief:

> Poetry wrote itself for him. [...] Something about Linden Hills was blocking that. And to unstop it, he would have to put Linden Hills into a poem. [...]
>
> [...] Willie knew how to do it. Just close his eyes and let the images swirl about as he emptied his mind. The first line would always come that way. [...]
>
> [...] He was almost there. At that terrifying place where his groin contracted and release was demanded before his mind went over the edge. He kept pushing himself toward that dangerous point. He couldn't stay awake forever. And those dreams would never end until he had the first line. And if he had just that one, he could sleep. He would have made peace with those night images. If they were anything, they were that: the first line unborn. It came with an expulsion, a relief that always felt like ejaculation and, more often than not, brought tears to his eyes. And once it was out of his mouth to be heard by his ears, he knew he was committed. (1985: 275–276)

Literature can also help victims recover a sense of identity that had been impaired by the traumatic experience: "It is only when the events of the past can be imagined not only to have consequences for the present but to live on in the present that they can become a part of our experience and can testify to who we are" (Michaels 1996: 7). This is related to the issue of trauma as a marker of collective identity and, in fact, it is through public representations, such as literature, that trauma can have its binding and collective identity formation power. However, in order for this to happen, communities must be aware of their hidden/repressed/silenced past because, as Jeffrey Alexander points out, identities are constructed by confronting the present and the future and by recovering the community's past (2004a: 22). Building up a collective identity through literature by making a community aware of its lost history—including the unifying sense of shared trauma— would create a sense of collectiveness that would enforce the individuals' sense of identity as pertaining to a broader, unified group. Insomuch as "cultural identities are formed and informed by a nation's literature" (Morrison 1993: 39), the recreating of the scenes of historical traumas in writing would potentially help enhance this sense of unity. And yet there is ambivalence in this. When Carmen Flys declares that ethnic writers can "contribute to forging a collective cultural identity, often by re-discovering, re-telling and re-creating the long-buried oral traditions" (1998: 367), we should pause to ponder the meaning of the verb 'to forge.' According to Merriam-Webster, the transitive verb to forge has, in addition from its first meaning alluding

to the making of objects by hammering on incandescent metal, two more meanings:
1. "To form or bring into being especially by an expenditure of effort."
2. "To make or imitate falsely especially with intent to defraud."

Therefore, when Flys refers to forging, she could either mean that writers endeavor to *form* a sense of collectiveness in their communities or that they want to *invent* one. As Eyerman points out, "[f]ounding narratives are about creating, constituting, a collective subject as much as they are about creating an 'imagined' community" (2004: 163). However, since the feeling of belonging in a broader social group that shares and understands the individual's suffering is in itself healing, whether or not the coming together of the community is a natural or an artificial process is of little relevance here. According to Desmond Harding, "the staging of trauma within the symbolic confines of a performative space makes possible the transformation of the private agonies of traumatic survival into public acts of communal healing" (2006: 14).

Toni Morrison understands this, and, even though she is aware of the mechanisms of self-imposed silencing due to shame or fear, she views recovering a people's past as significant because of its healing potential:

> And no one speaks, no one tells the story about himself or herself unless forced. They don't want to talk, they don't want to remember, they don't want to say it, because they're afraid of it—which is human. But when they do say it, and hear it, and look at it, and share it, they are not only one, they are two, and three, and four, you know? The collective sharing of that information heals the individual—and the collective. (Darling 1994: 248)

Sometimes, however, communal healing is not what the recovery of past traumas intends. Sometimes, the memory of a traumatic event or series of events is re-accessed in the hopes of turning "tragedy into triumph" (Eyerman 2001: 101). Especially in the cases in which, such as the African American history of racism and oppression, the source of the past traumas is perceived as living in the present and continuing to create new traumas there, a collective identification and sense of community emerging from a shared and ongoing history of trauma can serve to raise awareness and address past wrongs inflicted upon a community, preventing their future recurrence. According to Carmen Flys, "[m]uch of ethnic literature has itself become the battlefield, the place, for creating self and group identity and much of that stems from the struggle to make something good come out of the pain caused by ethnic strife" (1998: 72). Such a possibility has also been observed by various other critics, such as Dominick

LaCapra, who argue that the acts of bearing witness and giving testimony that working through enables are oriented to "broader sociopolitical processes [...] oriented to achieving desirable change," including the eradication of oppression and traumatization of "typically scapegoated groups of victims" (2004: 82).

In this sense, trauma writers may feel some moral responsibility for making their past known, not only to the community affected by it but also to all other communities. In the words of Laurie Vickroy, "serious trauma writers attempt to guide readers through a re-created process of traumatic memory in order that this experience be understood more widely" (2002: 8). Toni Morrison also seems to feel this responsibility since she once declared that

> all artists have either to bear witness or effect change—improvement—take cataracts off people's eyes in an accessible way. It may be soothing; it may be painful, but that's his job—to enlighten and to strengthen. [...] I think novels are important because they are socially responsible. I mean, for me a novel has to be socially responsible as well as very beautiful. [...] I mean a novel written a certain way can do precisely what spirituals used to do. It can do exactly what blues or jazz or gossip or stories or myths or folklore did—that stuff that was a common well-spring of ideas and again the participation of the reader in it as though it's not alien to him. The people he may not know, but there is some shared history. (Jones and Vinson 1994: 183)

When a novel is "socially responsible" it enables communities and individuals alike to recover and make use of the traumatic past so that change can take place in the present and influence the future. As the famous George Santayana quote suggests ("those who cannot remember the past are condemned to repeat it"), recovery of the traumatic past is necessary to prevent a repetition of those or similar traumas in the future, as well as to "halt the transgenerational transmission of trauma" (Schwab 2009: 298). This is the aim of many museums and memorials dedicated to atrocities such as the Holocaust, for example (promotional buttons for the United States Holocaust Memorial Museum read both "remember" and "never again" (Kidd 2005: 122)), but also of several authors of trauma writings. In this line of thought, Laurie Vickroy claims that "[a]nother significant aim of trauma narratives is to reshape cultural memory through personal contexts, adopting testimonial traits to prevent and bear witness against such repetitive horrors" (2002: 5). After all, as Ricoeur says, "for tomorrow, one must not forget ... to remember" (2006: 30).

All this, of course, has a very clear political intention. Moving from "the retribution of past wrongs" to the "persecution of perpetrators" (Eyal 2004: 12), trauma and the unearthing of historically denied truths can be used as socio-political tools. This is more ostensibly so in the case of minorities with a collective history of shared trauma and oppression trying to gain access to more equal treatment by the dominant society. In those cases, the unearthing of trauma can be seen as pernicious by the dominant society, who will try to keep it silenced. It is then that the victimized minority needs to "retain control over the interpretation of their trauma" in order to prevent its appropriation by the dominant culture and promote a change in the status quo (Tal 1996: 7). As Milan Kundera pointed out, "the struggle of man against power is the struggle of memory against forgetting" (qtd. in Eyal 2004: 20). This is still more integral, LaCapra argues, in cases of inherited traumas in which the victims are not direct survivors. In those cases, working through would not only imply that victims regain a more or less coherent and trauma-free psychological state, but also achieve some kind of social or political retaliation in the present: "[W]orking through problems for one born later is itself distinctive and closely linked to ethical, social, and political demands and responsibilities" (LaCapra 2001: 212). Since trauma writing is a highly convenient tool to recover memory, its use for political purposes—or what Luckhurst calls "identity politics" (2008: 62)—is also of high value. Just as Flys states, "art becomes a way of increasing awareness, challenging the *status quo*, or reordering the master narrative: in short, a political tool" (1998: 53). In this sense, Herman argues, "[t]estimony has both a private dimension, which is confessional and spiritual, and a public aspect, which is political and judicial" (2001:181). This potential of literature as a political tool gained prominence in recent years and was used by all sorts of previously oppressed groups, as Luckhurst points out: "[T]he identity politics that emerged in the 1970s and established itself institutionally in the 1980s supported an explosion of memoirs and commentary on memoir in post-colonial, African, Latin American, feminist, gay and lesbian writing" (2008: 120). Likewise, the African American community has also made use of trauma writing as a political tool, as Eyerman suggests when he notes that it was through a recovery of the trauma of slavery during the flourishing of African American literature that took place under the auspices of Booker T. Washington and W.E.B. Du Bois that organizations such as the NAACP could see the light (Eyerman 2001: 2; 2004: 163–164).

However, even if trauma writing can potentially offer all the aforementioned benefits, it does not necessarily need to do so. Sometimes, the purpose of trauma writing—especially fictional trauma writing—is not to offer a solution, or a coherent narrative, or even to make sense of past traumas or prevent their repetition. Sometimes, the purpose of trauma writing is simply to present trauma and its experience in all its complexities and dichotomies, and in its incoherence. Perhaps voicing the silence, the unspeakability of trauma—oxymoronic as the idea may be—is a narrative's sole intention, and it is by focusing on that ambivalence, on the value of silence and indefinition, that some of those trauma narratives achieve their purpose and effect. One could not argue, for example, that Kurt Vonnegut's *Slaughterhouse 5*, despite its incoherencies, time lapses, and raw irony—or precisely *because* of them—does not manage to portray the impact, unexpectedness and nonsense of trauma. Nor could one argue that Primo Levi's *If This is a Man* is not an accurate and extremely unsettling narrative of his experience at Auschwitz. Nevertheless, in that narrative, Levi offers few reflections and little to no overt morality teachings (whatever lessons the reader might extract from reading *If This is a Man* is an altogether different issue). Instead, he simply presents the facts of his experience in a crude way and lets them speak for themselves, which is yet another way of giving testimony; perhaps, as some critics maintain, the only ethical one. Some victims of trauma decide to remain silent either because they cannot find the words to express their experiences or because they feel that they should remain silent, others feel a need to give voice to and narrate those experiences. Some fictional authors feel they must address the traumatic past of their communities, others do not. And even those authors who do feel they must address the traumatic past are moved by different agendas or by no specific agenda at all. It is not the purpose of the present volume to argue which position is the 'correct' one or to determine whether trauma can or should be narrated and how; the purpose is precisely to point out that trauma *is* narrated, and that, in some cases, those narratives can serve a purpose, whether the authors intended their work to serve such a purpose or not. Literature makes readers think—which is why books are often banned in dystopian novels, and why books have been often burned by totalitarian regimes—and if thinking about an atrocity makes people empathize with the victims, question their own moral values or inspires them to work towards the avoidance of a repetition, then trauma writing has a clear and undeniable value to society.

6   Trauma Fiction

> Stories, [...] we are made up of stories. And even the ones that seem the most like lies can be our deepest hidden truths.
> JANE YOLEN, *Briar Rose*

The very idea that non-direct survivors identify with the experience of a traumatic past that they did not suffer themselves, and can use it to achieve communal agency in the present, suggests that collective trauma is, in a sense, distinctly fictive. Clearly, this kind of identification is not factual; the traumatic experience in question did not happen to the non-survivor individual, yet this does not prevent non-survivors from testifying to the truth of the event or events in question. This is the reason that this type of trauma presents itself as so accessible to writers of fiction, because 'fiction,' like inherited memories of a traumatic past, does not necessarily mean 'not true.' Dominick LaCapra suggests this when he highlights the fictive element of trauma by saying that the processes of "vicarious experience" that make non-survivors appropriate the trauma of others present "fiction as if it were testimony or historical memoir" (LaCapra 2004: 132). Therefore, he concludes, "[t]he experience—real, 'really' phantazised, simulated, or some combination thereof—becomes enough for the postulation of the event" (LaCapra 2004: 132).

In light of this, I maintain that something that is not factual may, nevertheless, be true to the essence of what actually happened. Indeed, Linda Hutcheon points out that scholars like Fredric Jameson or Hayden White question our capacity to actually know the *real* past, since our only way to it is by means of textualized and interpreted accounts (1988: 143). Therefore, all historiography can, in a way, be considered fiction, which in turn, Paul Ricoeur says, "permits historiography to live up to the task of memory" (1990: 189). Moreover, memory can be—and is—unavoidably distorted by time and retelling. If we add to this the fact that, in collective trauma, we are not dealing with the memory of a person that directly experienced the traumatic event but with the collective depiction of the event that a community has been transmitting over centuries, we find ourselves not with an exact account of the experience but with a constructed image of it. That, however, does not necessarily mean that the resulting depiction is a lie or that the built-up version of the traumatic event is completely unrelated to the actual event. In the same way, writers of fiction do not sell lies, but rather 'substitute realities' or metaphors that may be based on real facts: "Narrative structures may involve truth claims, either in terms of 'correspondence' to lived narrative structures [...] or in terms of references" (LaCapra 2001: 13). If we take, for example, Toni Morrison's *Beloved*, we can clearly see that she is not claiming to be giving us the factual account of exactly what happened to one specific real person in real life—that real person being Margaret Garner, whose story of infanticide inspired Morrison—but instead is giving us an account of what slavery was like, to the point that the novel could be "used to teach American history classes" (Horvitz 1989: 157). As Furman puts it,

> the difference between slave autobiography and *Beloved* is the difference between autobiography and fiction. [...] She [Morrison] does

acknowledge that her work is imaginative, but more important, it is also truthful. Truthful does not mean recounting verifiable details of specific events, places and people as in the approach which Morrison calls the 'oh, yes, this is where he or she got it from school.' It does mean absolute fidelity to the subject. In *Beloved* it means fidelity to the slaves' experiences. The truth of slavery is its contamination of humanity, its agency of evil, and that truth lies beyond the specific details of suffering of any individual. Truth transcends time, place, and audience, and it gives universal insight. (1996: 78)

Clearly, when writing about founding traumas that happened centuries ago, a novelist cannot rely on his/her memories, or on the memories of his/her family members. Even though it has been argued above that memories of the past can pervade subsequent generations and, in that way, survive for centuries, it is undeniable that those memories must have been distorted both by the traumatic experience itself and by the passing of time. "Retrieved memories," Hartman argues, "often include a fanciful intervention to fill in details, even to create a sort of phantom reminiscence of what happened" (2004: 3). Recovered memory, in sum, is always revised memory, which calls for a focus on the representation thereof rather than on its validity as truth claims.

Insomuch as, when talking about the recovered memory of a past event, there are no longer any direct witnesses of it, imagination and reconstruction must be necessarily employed when retelling that past. In the case of the African American heritage of slavery and continued racist oppression, we are talking about a series of traumatic memories of racial inequality that have not only have been taking place over centuries, but have been being transmitted, constructed upon, and inherited through generations as well, each generation adding their own experience of trauma to their predecessors' and passing it on to the next. When contemporary authors try to access and re-represent the memory of the most distant events—take slavery, for example—they naturally find that those who directly witnessed the events and suffered from the trauma first-hand are long dead. Their history was not told either, as they were barred from literacy, and, moreover, the master narrative written by the oppressor did not address the events from their point of view. All that remains are distorted memories passed on through oral stories and the incomplete and biased account of history books. Writers, therefore, have no resort but to use their imagination to 'fill in the blanks.' Still, the unearthing and retelling of these events is crucial, if not for the collective working through of the trauma, then for the community's agency in the present, as evidenced by what Craps, following Fred D'Aguiar's 1996 article "The Last Essay about Slavery," calls "a compulsive need to revisit slavery for every succeeding generation of black writers" (2010: 472).

As well as a degree of imagination, authors usually employ several narrative techniques when representing or recreating the memory of a traumatic past. A vast majority of those literary works dealing with trauma attempt, to a greater or lesser extent, to reproduce the disruptions and workings of trauma not only in their plots and characterizations, but also in their narrative techniques. As Laurie Vickroy explains,

> [t]rauma narratives go beyond presenting trauma as subject matter or character study. They internalize the rhythms, processes, and uncertainties of traumatic experience within their underlying sensibilities and structures. They reveal many obstacles to communicating such experience: silence, simultaneous knowledge and denial, dissociation, resistance, and repression, among others. (2002: 3)

Instances of fragmentation in time and language, multiple narrative voices, repetitions, gaps, omissions and open endings are common in writings dealing with trauma and they require special attention. The first, fragmentation, is widely used in trauma narratives in order to convey to the reader not only the disruption that trauma causes in the victim's mind, but also the unsettling effect that a past trauma can cause in a community. A traumatic past of repeated violence and oppression upon a community is often difficult to make rational sense of even—or especially—by the members of that community. In order to represent that sense of unintelligibility, some contemporary trauma novels choose to disrupt the linearity of time and place and construct their plots around a series of flashbacks and flashforwards that, moreover, highlight the consequences that traumatic past events can bear across time and into the present. In order to get a clear image and make sense of the written story, the reader must learn to differentiate the past from the present and put the pieces in order, which in turn helps him/her understand how the past bears into the present. In what follows, we will see how African American narratives like *Mama Day*, *Beloved*, or *The Chaneysville Incident* present a notably disrupted storyline told by means of repeated flashbacks, characters' recollections of past events or pieces of character's diaries, for instance, that help to convey the idea of the necessity of recovering the past in order to form a coherent new narrative of it that can help in the present and future.

However, breaking the narrative line is not the only way that this effect can be achieved. Broken and fragmented speech is another device often used. In Morrison's *A Mercy*, this technique surfaces particularly when Florens speaks.

Her train of thought often jumps from one topic to the next with no apparent coherent link and she speaks in short, disconnected sentences that are sometimes even ungrammatical:

> Lina twitchy as fresh-hook salmon waits with me in the village. The wagon of the Ney brothers does not come. Hours we stand then sit roadside. A boy and a dog drive goats past us. He raises his hat. That is the first time any male does it to me. I like it. A good sign I am thinking but Lina is warning me of many things, saying if you are not in your place I must not tarry. I must return at once. I cannot handle a horse so I must seek return on the next day's horse cart, the one that hauls fresh milk and eggs to market. Some people go by and look but do not speak. We are female so they have no fright. They know who is Lina yet look as if we are strange to them, we wait more and so long that I do not save my bread and codfish. I eat all the cod. Lina holds her forehead in her hand, her elbow on her knee. She gives off a bad feeling so I keep my thoughts on the goatherd's hat. (36)

Notice the ungrammaticality and lack of coherence in the quotation above. According to Wyatt, this fragmentation approaches the "unintelligibility of trauma" in that it tends to return to the victim's mind in an array of intrusive images with no apparent logic or connection (2004: 78). Although perfectly applicable to *A Mercy*, or to *Jazz* (Bouson 2000: 166), Wyatt is referring here to Toni Morrison's other great novel about trauma, *Beloved*, whose representation of trauma through fragmentation has not escaped the notice of other theorists (Bouson 2000: 136). In this novel, speech is also highly fragmented, which is especially noticeable when Beloved speaks. Beloved, a character who, unlike Florens, cannot be described as a traumatized mind, but rather as the embodiment or incarnation of somebody else's trauma—her mother's. As such, Beloved can be understood as standing in for trauma itself. The excited state of mind typically caused by trauma is reflected precisely by having the character that embodies the trauma speak through a series of disconnected, at times irrational, tirades in which pauses are typographically marked by spaces rather than by full stops:

> I am Beloved and she is mine. I see her take flowers away from leaves she puts them in a round basket   the leaves are not for her   she fills the basket   she opens the grass   I would help her but the clouds are in the way   how can I say things that are pictures   I am not separate from her   there is no place where I stop   her face is my own and I want to be

there in the place where her face is and to be looking at it too a hot thing (Morrison 2005: 248)

These gaps are reminiscent of the cracks in the mind of a traumatized individual, reflected in the victim's language. They are holes in perception caused by the fragmentariness of trauma that disrupts and adulterates any attempt at narrating the experience and are consequently replicated in fictional accounts of trauma. The representation in literary form of this effect in the mind of the victim parallels the effect that silenced parts of a community's past can have on the collective unconscious of that community, which highlights the necessity of recovering that silenced and unsettling past.

This same idea lies behind the use of multiple narrators. The resultant multivocal narratives mimic the passing on of memory from one generation to another through different accounts of the same traumatic event or else through the accounts of different events that are perceived to be similar because they were produced by the same oppressive system and frame of mind. In African American literature, both *A Mercy* and *Beloved*—among many others—make use of this technique: they are narrated by third-person narrators and, simultaneously, by different first-person narrators. Accordingly, the novels allow each character, in turn, to narrate his/her own history—albeit often in an elusive and broken way—which provides the reader with a fragmented narrative that mirrors the fragmentary quality of traumatic memory as well with a myriad of different stories and angles to be placed together in order to reconstruct the whole narrative. Similarly, Ernest Gaines's *A Gathering of Old Men* is also narrated through several different voices, portraying not only the fragmentariness of trauma, but also the communal aspect of its collective form such that each character's painful experience is added to the next in the community's shared memory of injustice and oppression.

Having several narrators give different accounts of the same story not only helps illustrate the fragmentariness of trauma but also conveys a sense of repetition, which is another characteristic trait of trauma. Much as the victim of trauma is often bombarded with flashbacks and reminiscences of the traumatic event, trauma narratives tend to repeat—often elusively—certain key scenes in the development of the narrative and the protagonists' personal traumas. Frequently, too, writers try to imitate the victim's manner of speech, which usually tends to repeat certain words or expressions. Authors, therefore, reiterate "narratively dissociative but affectively overdetermined" words, phrases or motifs in order to create the aforementioned sensation (Vickroy 2002: 30). A clear example of this is the constant repetition in *Beloved* of the phrase "I am Beloved and she is mine" and variations thereof, as well as the recurrence of the phrase "you are mine" that, like a chorus, is repeated several times in the course of two pages (Morrison 2005: 255–256). Additionally, repetition can sometimes be felt by the victim as a haunting, a revenant of the past that never leaves and that is usually equated with a ghost in literature. As already pointed out, contemporary trauma literature has been replete with ghosts; examples of their presence in trauma novels are many. These ghosts, Luckhurst argues, embody "the idea of the persistence of traumatic memory, the anachronic intrusion of the past into the present" (2008: 93), and can be made to disappear when that past is coherently voiced and silence and repression are broken.

Silence and repression are undeniably two of the most distinguishable psychological traits of trauma, and are therefore fairly well portrayed in literature. Silence, Vickroy argues, represents "the loss, repression, inarticulateness, and shock associated with trauma" (2002: 102). She continues,

> [s]ilence can represent a traumatic gap, a withholding of words because of terror, guilt, or coercion; it characterizes traumatic memory as wordless, visual, and reenactive rather than cognitive/verbal when facing the unspeakable. Silence at times is textually represented with page or section breaks, but most often in what is not said, what the characters avoid saying or cannot say. (Vickroy 2002: 187)

Similarly, in order to represent trauma's uncertainty and resistance to closure, open endings are highly common in trauma literature. All of the novels analyzed here, for instance, end with different degrees of aperture, either in terms of plot, character development or explanation of events. For instance, it is not clear, at the end of *Paradise*, how many—if any—of the convent women die, nor, in *Mama Day*, if Cocoa will ever reach the complete understanding of events that she so desperately needs. We do not know where Beloved goes, in the eponymous novel, nor do we know the outcome of Milkman and Guitar's confrontation at the end of *Song of Solomon*. *The Chaneysville Incident*, likewise, leaves an open door for the hope of a communion between races, yet ends with the main protagonist wondering if that understanding is really possible. These are but a few examples, but numerous other novels with similarly open endings testify to this narrative technique as one more way to reflect the uncertainty of trauma on paper.

However authors choose to portray it, it seems clear that the representation of trauma whether individual or collective can be mastered in an artistic manner that, while exploring the dramatic consequences that a traumatic experience can have in the minds and lives of its survivors, can help achieve a degree of social agency in the present. Whether memoirs or fictional accounts, as long as the narration of the traumatic experience maintains a degree of fidelity to the historical truth, trauma writing can help readers explore and be instrumental in the remembrance—albeit not necessarily the overcoming—of historical traumas that have survived generations, sometimes embedded in places that still bear the resonances of the atrocities committed. Operating as *lieux de mémorie* in their active retrieval, rewriting and memorialization of the historical African American trauma, the novels analyzed in the following chapters call attention to the throbbing scar of slavery while, at the same time, soothing its pain through the potential sociological and ideological applications of their recuperation of the past.

CHAPTER 2

History, Roots and Myth: Toni Morrison's *Paradise* and Gloria Naylor's *Mama Day*

1   History and Traumatic Memory

> I know of no way of judging the future but by the past.
> PATRICK HENRY. March, 1775

> The best prophet of the future is the past.
> LORD BYRON

At the opening session of a 2011 conference on trauma and literature,[1] plenary lecturer Cathy Caruth eloquently addressed the problem of the erasure of history and the Derridean notion of "archive fever" from the perspective of trauma studies. She used Freud's concepts of "return" and "departure" to illustrate the way in which history is constituted by a continuous drive to write and erase itself, leaving only archival traces that can themselves be misleading or altogether silenced—erased—by the very passing of time (Caruth, 31st March 2011). She spoke of the historian's role as a psychoanalyst in order to bear witness to a history that is otherwise in ruins—or in ashes, as the title of her address states—and to prevent that erasure. Since memory—traumatic memory—in Caruth's reading of Freud originates precisely from the forgetting and deferral of that memory, she is able to demonstrate how history and trauma are two discourses that are inextricably linked in their conception and treatment.

Although trauma studies are currently turning away from this psychoanalytical view of history and are focusing more on context-based, collective references in order to expose "the failure of the psychoanalytic method to account for the traumatic events that occur in the context of a long-term pattern of oppression or persecution based on group identity, including race, gender and class" (Tal 2003: n.p.), it is true that history—like trauma—tends to repeat itself. This is also particularly relevant for the transmission of history (Ramadanovic 1998: 58), and is connected to the issue of communities' identity formation and collective trauma. Especially in cases in which a traumatic history is placed at

---

[1]   "After the End: Psychoanalysis in the Ashes of History." University of Zaragoza, Spain, 31st March 2011.

the core of the formation of a group's identity, the repetition of that history, of that foundational trauma and its passing on, will become fundamental to that collectivity and would result in the existence of an intergenerational trauma. History will become more than merely an account of past deeds and events; it will be catechized into the collective unconscious until it becomes a living memory of the past.

And yet, 'history' and 'memory' have often been taken as somewhat different concepts. Actually, in recent writing on history and historicity the two terms have often been used as antonyms—although LaCapra believes they should "neither be opposed in binary fashion nor conflated" (2004: 67) and Paul Ricoeur would rather resist both "a claim on behalf of memory in opposition to history" and "the inverse claim to reduce memory to a simple object of history" (2006: 87). This opposition between history and memory is clearly seen in Pierre Nora's text "Between Memory and History: Les Lieux de Mémoire," wherein he establishes the basis for the distinction between a hierarchical, institutionalized, silencing history, and the ever-changing, ever-returning memory:

> Memory is life, borne by living societies founded in its name. It remains in permanent evolution, open to the dialectic of remembering and forgetting, unconscious of its successive deformations, vulnerable to manipulation and appropriation, susceptible to being long dormant and periodically revived. History, on the other hand, is the reconstruction, always problematic and incomplete, of what is no longer. (Nora 1989: 8)

It is not my intention, however, to suggest a blind adherence to Nora's view of history and historiography as a hierarchical and monolithic way of recording the past, nor to suggest that historiography must always fail to tackle the issue of truth in an acceptable way. Indeed, I am aware of the widespread debate in the field of historiography and the new ways of understanding the practice of history writing to which historians and scholars like Hayden White, Robert Berkhofer or Gabrielle Spiegel, among others, have contributed. If I reproduce Nora's argument, it is precisely because I agree with the need to oppose what used to be the widespread notion of 'history'—as based on documents rather than recollections, on the archive and verifiable proof rather than on oral history—to his notion of 'memory'. In other words, Nora points to a particular practice of the discipline of historiography, perhaps no longer widely accepted by theorists or even carried out by historians, that goes against what I understand to be at the core of any successful practice of trauma writing: the active re-creation and re-presentation of the past that allows for an active memorialization and working through rather than a stagnant repetition of past events.

When past events are repeated and perpetuated without allowing for any growth or transformation—as they are in Morrison's *Paradise*—they can be understood to become 'history,' according to Nora's conception of the term, whereas when they are allowed to evolve and change, such as through other readings and understandings of the same events—as they are in Naylor's *Mama Day*—they can be taken to become 'memory' as Nora defines it, or perhaps the newer conception of 'history' brought about by the aforementioned historians and scholars. If in what follows I use the terms 'history' and 'memory' according to Nora's distinction, it is to avoid having to specify whether I am referring to the 'old' or the 'new' conception of history and history writing. That is, I adhere to Nora's perhaps manichaeistic distinction not out of an unquestioning belief in his view of history, but out of a need to differentiate these concepts through terminology.

In light of this distinction, and to return to my argument, several scholars have come to understand history as referring exclusively to the account of past events as recorded by those in power traditionally used to exclude those silenced minorities mentioned in the previous chapter. Memory, on the other hand, would refer to minorities' versions of the same events kept alive, in many cases, through oral transmission, since their past "may not have left sufficient traces in official documents and histories" (LaCapra 2004: 3) and around which they construct their collective identities. Although this binarism may sound slightly over-analogical—there is an implication that dominant cultures do not produce memory, which is clearly not true—several authors have chosen to abide by it and express it in terms such as these: "History is modernism, the state, science, imperialism, androcentrism, a tool of oppression; memory is postmodernism, the 'symbolically excluded,' 'the body,' 'a healing device and a tool for redemption'" (Klein 2000: 138). In some spheres, consequently, memory has been accepted as more worthy of study than the old-fashioned sense of history and historical research, which is why historians and historicists are now turning more to these forms of collectively shared memory than to the formerly accepted 'truth' imposed by the dominant power structures.

Yet another difference between history and memory is that "[m]emory attaches itself to sites, whereas history attaches itself to events" (Nora 1989: 22), which enables us to talk about *sites of memory* in relation to trauma rather than *sites of history*. In Nora's definition, the sites of memory (or *lieux de mémoire*) are those "moments of history torn away from the movement of history, then returned; no longer quite life, not yet death, like shells on the shore when the sea of living memory has receded" (1989: 12). In other words, they are objects, sites, monuments, etc. that those communities with a suppressed history have invested with a commemorative, symbolic meaning providing the necessary tangible proof of their hidden pasts. They exist, Nora says, to "block the work of forgetting" (1989: 19) that is, to serve as a collective reminder of the past that needs to be recuperated.

Paul Ricoeur suggests a further differentiation, not between history and memory, but between 'reminiscing' and 'reminding.' Whereas the process of reminding is exerted by external objects (photographs, objects, even sites of memory) in order to prevent individuals from forgetting what must be remembered, reminiscing is a much more active process in which communities can attempt to make "the past live again by evoking it together with others, each helping the other to remember shared events or knowledge, the memories of one person serving as a reminder for the memories of the other" (Ricoeur 2006: 38). This points to the existence of a somehow collective memory among individuals within a community whereby the memories or recollections of one become the recollections of the other by way of oral transmission and collective sharing. However, the notion of a collective memory has also been contested. For James Young, the term 'collective memory' could be, to say the least, arguable, since "individuals cannot share another's memory any more than they can share another's cortex" (1993: xi). We are faced here with a similar situation to that of the notion of transmitted or inherited trauma. Although it is true that memories (in their strictest sense of mental images of the past processed and stored in one's brain) cannot magically travel through the air and be implanted in somebody else's head—much in the same way as non-survivors cannot genetically inherit their parent's psychological illnesses—this argument can be contested by referring to the notion of memory as "a collection of practices or material artifacts" (Klein 2000: 135). In this sense, we are drawn to Halbwachs's argument that "[i]t is in society that people normally acquire their memories. It is also in society that they recall, recognize, and localize their memories" (qtd. in Olick 1999: 334). This means that memory, in its selectivity, is inherently collective, for it is only the consensual truth that is reinforced through sites of memory and passed on as part of the group's identity. In other words, although it is only individuals who remember, they cannot do so coherently outside the socially accepted and collectively transmitted context. Likewise, collective memory exists only insomuch as there is a group of individuals that commit themselves to a socially engaged—yet, by force, individual—remembrance: "There is no individual memory without social experience nor is there any collective memory without individuals participating in communal life" (Olick 1999: 346). Additionally, it is through this collective experience of memory that groups can "produce memories in individuals of events that they never 'experienced' in any direct sense" (Olick 1999: 335). Through repetition and transference in its more psychoanalytical sense, it is possible that memories one has never fabricated—that is, memories of events that one never experienced first-hand—are nevertheless present in our minds and accessible through conscious or unconscious recall. In Gayl Jones's *Corregidora* we find a clear example of this in the Corregidora women, a family in which traumatic memories have been orally transmitted from one generation to the next to the point that they have been appropriated and felt by each of the women as their own. Ursa, the protagonist, realizes this after a conversation with her mother when she concludes that "[i]t was as if she had *more* than learned it off by heart, though. It was as if her memory, the memory of all the Corregidora women, was her memory too, as strong with her as her own private memory, or almost as strong" (Jones 1975: 129). It is, therefore, my argument that if a memory of the past is perceived as sufficiently relevant or significant to the group in question for whatever reason, it is bound to be appropriated by all the members of the group, regardless of their having been present at the event or not—this is much in the same vein as the concept of 'false memories' that appears in Philip K. Dick's *Do Androids Dream of Electric Sheep?* or in the 80s popular film *Blade Runner*, loosely based on it.

This brings us back to the issue of collective memory and its relationship with the formation of cultural identity. As Jan Assmann noted: "Cultural memory preserves the store of knowledge from which a group derives an awareness of its unity and peculiarity" (1995: 130). Since it is memory and not history, as defined by Nora, that is transmitted and collectively agreed upon rather than being imposed from above, we should agree that it is on memory and not history that group distinctiveness is based: "History is the remembered past to which we no longer have an 'organic' relation—the past that is no longer an important part of our lives—while collective memory is the active past that forms our identities" (Olick 1999: 335). If, moreover, we are to understand history as the hierarchical and non-reliable construct that some theorists declare it to be, it seems only logical that minority groups should resort to their shared memories rather than to the broadly accepted version of the past in order to construct their collective identities. Just as Fei-hsuan Kuo puts it in relation to ethnic identity, "[m]emory serves as a mirror that reflects ethnicity—to define who we are and provide a memory of connectedness of which cultural group we belong to. Collective memory functions to support the identity of a race or a group of people" (2009: 91).

Obviously, when talking about memory, trauma, repressed communities and identity, the term 'identity politics' is never far off. In fact, one of the reasons that Klein gives for the displacement of attention from history to memory in the US is the cultural context prevalent after the 1960s, when a number of previously silenced minorities—African Americans included—began their fight for civil rights (2000: 143). Jeffrey Olick agrees with this appreciation, and provides the term 'political culture' as the merge between cultural memory and identity politics initiated in the 1950s and 1960s by, among others, Gabriel Almond, Lucien Pye and Sidney Verba (1999: 337).

If, for political purposes, the memory of the past needs to be recovered and perpetuated in a more permanent form than orally shared memories, narrative and—more specifically for permanency purposes—writing are very useful tools:

> Perhaps the clearest demonstration of the genuinely collective nature of remembering is the degree to which it takes place in and through language, narrative, and dialogue. Language, for instance, is commonly used as the quintessential example of a supra-individual phenomenon [...]. And it is not merely that individuals remember in language, coding their experiences as language and recalling them in it. Language itself can be viewed as a memory system. (Olick 1999: 343)

As discussed before, narrative—and language—helps perpetuate, pass on and give voice to previously silenced (traumatic) experiences. This aspect, of course, is particularly relevant for the present volume, and may explain today's proliferation of memoirs, trauma narratives, testimonies and the like. But, despite the current abundance of said genres, the transmission of memory is nothing new. It has already been noted that storytelling has always been a very important part of the transference of knowledge and memory in communities, as well as a social bonding practice (Flys 1998: 502), and the African American community is no exception. Toni Morrison, for instance, in a 1983 interview conducted by Nellie McKay recalls how she was encouraged to participate in "the business of story-telling" even as a child (1994: 141), and how, in later years, she tried to catch its sound and structure in her novels (152). Writing, in its emphasis on becoming a bearer of the past and preventing its erasure, becomes, therefore, a site of memory in the strictest sense of Nora's definition. "Because of what writing counters, parallels, responds to, repeats, negates, and affirms," Ramadanovic argues, "even if writing does not mark any event external to itself, but solely itself, we who read and write are marked by what text, writing, and language carry over: an (unremembered) memory" (1998: 65).

The past is, after all, part of us and, as such, it is present in all our actions. In the words of James Baldwin, "[h]istory [...] is not merely something to be read. And it does not refer merely, or even principally, to the past. On the contrary, the great force of history comes from the fact that we carry it within us, are unconsciously controlled by it in many ways, and history is literally *present* in all we do" (1985f: 410). When that history, that past which is at the same time our present, bears the marks of trauma, it needs to be acknowledged both by the perpetrators and by the victims or their descendants in order to prevent its repetition, promote understanding and move towards the completion of the process of working through. The present chapter is dedicated fully to the presence and importance of the past in any of its forms in two contemporary African American novels: Toni Morrison's *Paradise* and Gloria Naylor's *Mama Day*.

Firstly, my analysis of *Paradise* will illustrate how the past plays a significant role in the lives of the inhabitants of Ruby, a small town deep in Oklahoma. For these people, or at least for part of them—hence the novel's central conflict—the past, embodied in the uncontestable presence of 'the oven,' becomes the sole center of their collective identity, and they are devoted to impeding any modification of that previously accepted version of the past. However, that version, produced by the elders' consensual agreement, is not (if we abide by the definition of the term above) what we could call 'memory' but, precisely because of that imposition, a 'history.' As such, this history is, quite predictably, contested and resisted by the younger generations.

In *Mama Day*, however, we find the opposite situation. The novel centers on the evolution of a community's memory of a founding event; a memory that changes through time and becomes almost forgotten only to reappear in the form of myth. As a much more complex piece than *Paradise*, *Mama Day* intertwines the story of this memory with some of the main characters' personal traumas, creating an incredibly moving and enthralling narrative that speaks of the individuals' most intimate relationships with the past, its significance and its effect on everyone's lives.

2 *Paradise*: The Perils of Sublimated History

> How can they hold it together, [...] this hard-won heaven defined only by the absence of the unsaved, the unworthy and the strange? Who will protect them from their leaders?
>
> TONI MORRISON, *Paradise*

2.1 History Revisited

Like *Beloved* and *Jazz*, the two previous installments of Toni Morrison's trilogy, *Paradise* is a novel intent on revisiting the past and the traumas embedded in it. Whereas *Beloved* and *Jazz* dealt with the Emancipation and Reconstruction periods and with the Harlem Renaissance respectively, *Paradise* concerns itself with the era of the Vietnam War and the fight for Civil Rights. *Paradise*, thus, offers a return to the—traumatic—past not only of the African American community but of the whole of the US. In depicting the story of a group of families escaping from a history of oppression and lack of liberties in order to settle and found their own, separate community in a new world, Morrison is equating the fictional history of the inhabitants of Ruby with that of the founding fathers of the US. As Marni Gauthier argues, "the mechanisms of nationhood endemic to Ruby echo and illustrate those of the US" (2005: 406). Moreover, the narrative alludes to several US historical events, from the Declaration of Independence to the assassinations of John F. Kennedy, Malcolm X and Martin Luther King, and passes through the American Revolution, the Civil War, the Reconstruction and the Vietnam War. What is more, the fact that the novel's narrative present is set in July 1976, the time of the American Bicentennial, further highlights the revision and criticism of US history that Morrison executes throughout the novel.

Morrison has repeatedly claimed that African Americans have consistently been erased from America's Master Narrative (see *Playing in the Dark*), and that her novels intend to put that erased history of her community back in its proper place, to make it known. However, one could argue that although this is part of *Paradise*'s intention, the novel goes a bit further in its rewriting of history in that it warns precisely against the dangers of *not* rewriting history. Maintaining the now obsolete claim that there is one valid version of history—that of the ruling classes—is clearly untenable because it often shows just one very restricted side of the events in question. The parallel work of recovering the, often silenced, lateral (hi)stories must be done in order to provide a multifaceted and more accurate version of events. Therefore, by portraying in *Paradise* the gradual failure of a community in which great pains have been taken to maintain a single master narrative—and prevent any internal or external distortion of it—and by linking it to the master narrative of American Exceptionalism, Morrison seems to offer a harsh critique of the mainstream view of American history as well as to warn readers against the danger of losing themselves in never-ending cycles of repetition.

2.2 *This, You Must Learn: the Elders' Exaltation of History*

As mentioned above, in *Paradise* Morrison takes as a structural frame of reference the narrative of American Exceptionalism in order to tell the story of the members of the community she portrays. This is made clear through the description of how Zechariah Morgan (a.k.a. Big Papa)—one of the integrants of the original group of nine families of ex-slaves that founded the town of

Haven—decided on that location. After having wandered—like the Jews in the desert—for some time, and being near the point of exhaustion, Zechariah woke his son up one night and made him pray with him. When they had passed the whole night kneeling on the ground in prayer, they were both startled by a vision of a man walking away from them and seemingly leading the way. This vision gives the group faith and a feeling of having been chosen that encourage them to continue marching until they arrive at what would later be the location of Haven, where the man in the vision makes his last appearance:

> It was September by then. [...] Rector was lying in tall grass, waiting for a crude trap to spring [...] when just ahead, through a parting in the grass, he saw the walking man standing, looking around. Then the man squatted, opened his satchel and began rummaging in it. Rector watched for a while, then crawled backward through the grass before jumping up and running back to the campsite where Big Papa was finishing a cold breakfast. Rector described what he had seen and the two headed toward the place where the trap had been set. The walking man was still there, removing items from his satchel and putting others back. Even as they watched, the man began to fade. When he was completely dissolved, they heard the footsteps again, pounding in a direction they could not determine: in back, to the left, now to the right. Or was it overhead? Then, suddenly, it was quiet. Rector crept forward; Big Papa was crawling too, to see what the walker had left behind. [...] Not a thing in sight. Only a depression in the grass. Big Papa leaned down to touch it. Pressing his hand into the flattened grass, he closed his eyes.
> 'Here,' he said. 'This is our place.' (Morrison 1999a: 98)

The clearly biblical note of this passage is consistent with the parallelism between Morrison's book and the history of some of the first settlers in America: a group of Puritans that, having escaped persecution in England and, following the command of their leader John Winthrop, finally found a place in which to settle, free from persecution, in the New World. Those pilgrims considered themselves to be chosen by God, and based their exceptionalist identity on the concepts of the Chosen People and the Chosen Land that appear in the biblical books of Genesis and Exodus.

Apart from this clear allusion to the Old Testament and the Puritan set of beliefs, Morrison's text makes at least two more specific allusions to the Bible. One lies in the fact that Zechariah—that messianic figure—named himself (his original name was Coffee); notably, this is an otherwise rather frequent practice among members of the African American community that refuse to bear the names given to their ancestors by slaveholders. However, while he could have chosen any name, he chose the name Zechariah: a name with clear biblical resonances. Such biblical references in naming are highly common among African Americans. Yet, such a name may actually fit within the imposed narrative that Zechariah/Coffee and his descendants imposed upon the whole community until the last generation, as Patricia (Pat) Best, the daughter of one of the town elders, realizes:

> Zacharias, father of John the Baptist? or the Zechariah who had visions? The one who saw scrolls of curses and women in baskets; the one who saw Joshua's filthy clothes changed into rich ones; who saw the result of disobedience. The punishment for not showing mercy or compassion was a scattering among all nations, and pleasant land made desolate. All of that would fit nicely for Zechariah Morgan: the curse, the women stuffed into a basket with a lid of lead and hidden away in a house, but specially the scattering. The scattering would have frightened him. The breakup of the group or tribe of consortium families or, in Coffee's case, the splitting up of a contingent of families who had lived with or near each other since before Bunker Hill. He would not have trouble imagining the scariness of having everyone he knew thrown apart, thrown into different places in a foreign land and becoming alien to each other. He would have been frightened of not knowing a jawline that signified one family, a cast of eye or a walk that identified another. Of not being able to see yourself re-formed in a third- or fourth-generation grand-child. Of not knowing where the generations before him were buried or how to get in touch with them if you didn't know. (192)

In order to prevent this scattering—or miscegenation, as we will later see—Zechariah and the other members of the founding families constructed a master narrative that, just as in the case of the Puritans, would perpetuate their exclusiveness and their 'chosenness.' In order to do that, they would inscribe that narrative with biblical resonances such as the abovementioned passage or the nativity scene in which seven pairs of boys and girls impersonating as many holy families parade in front of a table designated as an inn where four children wearing yellow and white masks sit counting oversized dollar bills. When the innkeepers are asked for shelter they throw pictures of food to the holy families, laugh, and tell them to go. Obviously, as one of the characters realizes, the multiplication of holy families and innkeepers is not done to "please as many children as possible" (211), but in order to equate the story of the community's rejection—what they have termed 'the Disallowing'—with the rejection of the holy Family in Nazareth. By conflating the history of their own people with that of the biblical characters—first Moses and the Jews and then Jesus himself—the founding fathers of Haven and Ruby have mystified their narrative, sublimating it into a quasi-religious narrative of identity formation that cannot be touched. In the words of Gauthier, "[m]arrying myth to their collective history, Ruby's citizens [...] perpetuate a mythic history that carries a tremendous weight and moral authority, as evidenced by the dire consequences suffered by those who transgress its moral code" (2005: 405).

That history includes, however, not only the mystified narrative of the community's Disallowing, but also the whole history of repression and oppression suffered by the African American community. In a way that seems to validate the idea of concatenated traumas proposed here, *Paradise* embodies the whole traumatic history of African Americans, from slavery to the rejection of black soldiers after their return from the Second World War, which, in the case of the citizens of Haven, re-opened old scars and propelled their next relocation:

> The rejection, which they called the Disallowing, was a burn whose scar tissue was numb by 1949, wasn't it? Oh, no. Those that survived that particular war came right back home, saw what had become of Haven, heard about the missing testicles of other colored soldiers; about medals being torn off by gangs of rednecks and Sons of the Confederacy—and recognized the Disallowing, Part Two. It would have been like watching a parade banner that said WAR-WEARY SOLDIERS! NOT WELCOME HOME! So they did it again. (Morrison 1999a: 194)

What the elders in Ruby are trying to protect is the memory of all those concatenated traumas and rejections and, above all, the community's pride in its power of survival. Their ancestors survived slavery and, with their psychological baggage on board, managed to become free men and set out to establish themselves some other place. However, to their already existing traumas, produced by slavery, they had to add "the shame of seeing one's pregnant wife or sister or daughter refused shelter" (95) as a series of already established communities refused to accept them. And yet, once more, they emerged triumphantly—if psychologically disturbed—when they managed to found their own town of Haven and live there peacefully until the Depression made them move and begin again. What in reality is a string of never-ending humiliations and exclusions is equated with biblical suffering and thus sublimated into a narrative of proud, chosen, victorious people that succeed even in the most antagonistic of environments. In order for this narrative to be effective in the formation of the collective exceptionalist narrative maintained by those in power, it needs to be repeated over and over until it is accepted by all as the only possible truth.

Of course, the most repeated story is that of the Disallowing, which is "seared in the memories of the Old Fathers" (Bouson 2000: 196) and becomes central to the construction of their master narrative. It is this event that forms their collective identity by distinguishing the community of Haven—and ultimately Ruby—from the rest of the African American community, some of whose members participated actively in that disallowing by refusing to allow Ruby's Old Fathers to settle in their already formed communities because of their darker skin color:

> They [the Old Fathers] must have suspected yet dared not say that their misfortune's misfortune was due to the one and only feature that distinguished them from their Negro peers. Eight-rock. In 1890 they had been in the country for one hundred and twenty years. So they took that history, those years, each other and their uncorruptible worthiness and walked to the 'Run.' Walked from Mississippi and Louisiana to Oklahoma and got to the place described in advertisements carefully folded into their shoes or creased into the brims of their hats only to be shooed away. This time the clarity was clear: for ten generations they had believed the division they fought to close was free against slave and rich against poor. Usually, but not always, white against black. Now they saw a new separation: light-skinned against black. Oh, they knew there was a difference in the minds of whites, but it had not struck them before that it was of consequence, serious consequence, to Negroes themselves. [...] The sign of racial purity they had taken for granted had become a stain. The scattering that alarmed Zechariah because he believed it would deplete them was now an even more dangerous level of evil, for if they broke apart and were disvalued by the impure then, certain as death, those ten generations would disturb their children's peace throughout eternity. (Morrison 1999a: 193–194)

This is how Haven came into being: as a place in which the inhabitants' racial purity, scorned by others, would become cherished, a place where the younger generations could be properly protected from the "humiliations they did not have to face" (93). As the source of those humiliations, the elders identify anything and everything from outside their community, and, although only whites are blamed for their misfortunes—certainly, in the bigger picture, whites are to blame for most of the African Americans' misfortunes—light-skinned blacks are also held responsible. Citizens in Ruby are prohibited from marrying outside their eight-rock color, a term that refers to a particularly black type of coal found in mines at a certain profundity and with which Morrison probably became familiar through her grandfather, a coal miner in Kentucky (Peach 1995: 3). In Ruby, a town where the words "outsider" and "enemy" "mean the same thing" (Morrison 1999a: 212), this threatening world, this danger of contamination through impurity, this peril of miscegenation, is qualified in the novel as the "Out There" (16):

> Ten generations had known what lay Out There: space, once beckoning and free, became unmonitored and seething, became a void where random and organized evil erupted when and where it chose—behind any standing tree, behind the door of any house, humble or grand. Out There where your children were sport, your women quarry, and where your very person could be annulled; where congregations carried arms to church and ropes coiled in every saddle. Out There where every cluster of whitemen looked like a posse, being alone was being dead. (16)

In order to keep that racial purity intact, three generations of elders used the threat of the Out There, together with their mythologized history, until it became catechized through the generations and imbued in the memories of each and every one of Ruby's citizens, to the point that they accepted and glorified the memory as their own: "The twins were born in 1924 and heard for twenty years what the previous forty had been like. They listened to, imagined and remembered every single thing because each detail was a jolt of pleasure, erotic as a dream, out-thrilling and more purposeful than even the war they had fought in" (16). In fact, as Morrison continues, "Steward remembered every detail of the story his father and grandfather told, and had no trouble imagining the shame for himself" (95).

Surely, Steward can identify himself with the shame of his ancestors because he has suffered his own share of shame and trauma at the hands of white men. Nevertheless, instead of falling into a constant commiseration process of self-pity—and instead of trying to work through their traumas—he and the others chose to pass on the history of their past suffering and invest it with an aura of sacredness so that the trauma became a community binder in the sense that Kai Erikson ascribes to it. Nicola King has talked about similar elevations of a people's past for political purposes both in the rise of fascist nationalisms—like the Nazis—and in the claims of "compensatory and exclusive possession" of the Serbians with the battle of Kosovo (2000: 5). A similar use of the past is at play in *Paradise*, for, as Fei-hsuan Kuo argues, "[i]n Ruby, the trauma of being rejected and despised maims the manhood of the communal leaders who in response to the racist rejections they have endured build an exclusively all-black town whose stability and memorialization of the past wound are carefully maintained" (2009: 169). This passing on of a traumatic memory through oral storytelling has taken place at the least of opportunities, being repeated and reinforced after every little threat to that memory. "A trained memory is," Ricoeur claims, "on the institutional plane an instructed memory; forced memorization is thus enlisted in the service of the remembrance of those events belonging to the common history that are held to be remarkable, even founding, with respect to the common identity" (2006: 85). This instruction is evident not only in the yearly Christmas representation of the Disallowing but also, as Misner (an outsider) realizes, in the town's daily life: "Over and over and with the least provocation, they pulled from their stock of stories tales about the old folks, their grands and great-grands; their fathers and mothers. Dangerous confrontations, clever maneuvers. Testimonies to endurance, wit, skill and strength. Tales of luck and outrage" (Morrison 1999a: 161).

And yet, naturally, this endlessly repeated tale is but a controlled and edited version of the community's history; not a truly reliable account—far from it—of that history. In the words of Ricoeur, it is possible to "account for the express abuses of memory on the level of the effect of distortion belonging to the phenomenal level of ideology" (2006: 85). That is, even in founding memories (perhaps even more so in founding memories) there exists a certain level of distortion whose extent depends on the group that is using—always for their own purposes—the narrative in question. In the town of Ruby the elders—most specifically the Morgans—use their own version of their forefathers' past traumas in order to maintain their supremacy within the town, and they use it to silence any sign of rebellion from the younger generations. After all, as Ricoeur realizes, "[e]ven the tyrant needs a rhetorician, a sophist, to broadcast his enterprise of seduction and intimidation in the form of words. The narrative imposed in this way then becomes the privileged instrument of this twofold operation" (2006: 85). This narrative, of course, in order to serve its purpose, must be carefully controlled and maintained in a certain way, without allowing for any type of addition, change or editing so that it becomes an "imposed memory [...] armed with a history that is itself 'authorized,' the official history, the history publicly learned and celebrated" (Ricoeur 2006: 85). The Morgan brothers are aware of the mechanisms of power and they are determined not to admit any rewriting of their imposed narrative. Indeed, when conflict erupts around the renaming of the oven—an embodiment of the Disallowing founding history, a true site of memory—one of them, Deacon (Deek) Morgan, offers a passionate speech that makes clear their complete refusal of change:

Well, sir, I have listened, and I believe I have heard as much as I need to. Now you all listen to me. Real close. Nobody, I mean nobody, is going to mess with a thing our grandfathers built. They made each and every brick one at a time with their own hands. [...] They dug the clay—not you. They carried the hod—not you. [...] They mixed the mortar—not a one of you. They made good strong brick for that oven when their own shelter was sticks and sod. You understand what I'm telling you? And we respected what they had gone through to do it. Nothing was handled more gently than the bricks those men made. Tell, them, Sargeant, how delicate was the separation, how careful we were, how we wrapped them, each and every one. Tell them, Fleet. You, Seawright, you, Harper, you tell him if I'm lying. Me and my brother lifted that iron. The two of us. And if some letters fell off, it wasn't due to us because we packed it in straw like it was a mewing lamb. So understand me when I tell you nobody is going to come along some eighty years later claiming to know better what men who went to hell to learn knew. Act short with me all you want, you in long trouble if you think you can disrespect a row you never hoed. (Morrison 1999a: 85–86)

The oven thus becomes the embodiment of the community's controlled memory and the symbol for their unity and pride in what their forefathers had to undergo in order not only to build it but to reach the place in which they could build it as free men. It is, therefore, the symbol of their suffering and the reminder of their past lives. A community kitchen, it was built to give the group cohesion and a sense of togetherness and to serve as, Bouson argues, yet another wink at their precious racial eight-rockedness (Bouson 2000: 198). Insomuch as it was built for women who had never "worked in a whiteman's kitchen" (Morrison 1999a: 99), a job which would often entail being raped by their masters, the oven also stands as public praise to their racial purity. It is all this that Deacon is asking the younger generations to respect in the passage above, the previously edited and almost sacred memory of their forefathers. Moreover, through his speech and his passionate defense of the care he and his brother took in the packing, transfer and reconstruction of the oven, he is also setting them up as bearers of the official, controlled version of memory, as befits them in their role as direct descendants of Zechariah Morgan. Out of respect for that memory and the suffering it stands for, Deacon claims, no one else should be allowed to change, rewrite, or have any part in it. Moreover, they claim that, if the memory has somehow changed—or if, reading between the lines, the power is slowly slipping from the elders' hands—it is not their fault but a consequence of the influence from the outside of which Zechariah was so afraid.

2.3 Not *the Truth, After All: Archival Work and the Unearthing of the Secret*

Even though the elders have endeavored to establish and maintain a clear-cut version of history—as it is discovered by the town's self-taught historiographer, Pat Best[2]—this zealously guarded memory presents several inaccuracies or, rather, gaps and omissions. As these are gradually revealed throughout the narrative, they allow the reader to uncover the true history of Ruby or, rather, the "shameful family and community secrets" it conceals (Bouson 2000: 199). It is through Pat's archival work that we discover, for example, that Zechariah Morgan had a brother who was disowned and crossed out from the family's bible. As follows, the official history of the town only takes Zechariah into account: "His foot was shot through—by whom or why nobody knew or admitted, for the point of the story seemed to be that when the bullet entered he neither cried out nor limped away" (Morrison 1999a: 189). However, behind the glorified and glorifying story of this mythic figure with superhuman capacities to endure both physical and psychological pain without evident distress, there is the true one, the one that no one knew, or rather, the one that nobody admitted. That long-awaited true version is revealed—yet only to Misner—only when Deacon Morgan is filled with enough remorse to make him seek help after a violent and gratuitous attack against an innocent group of women living on a nearby convent with which the novel opens. In his confession to Misner, Deacon discloses the truth of Zechariah's story:

> Few knew and fewer remembered that Zechariah had a twin, and before he changed his name, they were known as Coffee and Tea. [...] One day, years later, when he and his twin were walking near a saloon, some whitemen, amused by the double faces, encouraged the brothers to dance. Since the encouragement took the form of a pistol, Tea, quite reasonably, accommodated the whites, even though he was a grown man, older than they were. Coffee took the bullet in his foot instead. From that moment they weren't brothers anymore. Coffee began to plan a new life elsewhere. He contacted other men, other former legislators who had the same misfortune as his—Juvenal DuPress and Drum Blackhorse. They were the three who formed the nucleus of the Old Fathers. Needless to say, Coffee didn't ask Tea to join them on their journey to Oklahoma. (302)

---

2 Pat Best was married to a Cato, surprisingly enough, the name of the "most famous American slave reparations lawsuit to date," which highlights the character's peculiar search for historical truth (Yukins 2002: 223).

Behind this account lies the true reason for Zechariah's foot injury and, what is more important, the real history behind the formation of the Old Fathers and their migration to Oklahoma before the Disallowing. Although Deacon does not make it explicit—even in his hour of remorse he does not betray the biggest of the town's secrets—the reader can easily extract it from what he says: Zechariah, Juvenal DuPress and Drum Blackhorse were all 'eight-rock' blacks, which is why they were expelled from their statehouse jobs. That is, in his own words, they all "had the same misfortune" (302). However, although the story portrays Coffee and Tea as twins, like Deacon and his brother Steward, it somehow implies that they might not have been. The fact that Coffee's brother's name in the story is Tea, points to the idea that the name might not be, as Pat thinks, "a misspelling of Kofi," (192) but a reference to skin color. As Marni Gauthier points out, "Coffee brewed is a shade darker than brewed tea" (2005: 410) and, therefore, the story might be suggesting that Tea actually had lighter skin than Coffee. That must have bothered Coffee, especially when he lost his job because of his skin color, and Tea's unheroic compliance with the white bullies would have been the last straw. Coffee decided to part with his traitorous brother, change his name—choosing one with clear messianic resonances, as aforementioned—and, together with other eight families carefully chosen for their 'eight-rock' qualities, move on. And, like the Pilgrims—or Jews—they established their own separate kingdom where they could idealize what others despised. Tea is therefore disowned by his own brother not—or not only—because he danced in front of the whites instead of bravely taking the shot, but because he was a symbol of the miscegenation, of the 'racial impurity,' that the elders in Haven and Ruby would later reject.

This story is, of course, kept from public knowledge as is the reason that two families are eventually dropped from the special designation reserved to those of the Old Fathers, those nine original families that traveled to Oklahoma whose "names were legend" (Morrison 1999a: 188). However, after some years, during the Nativity scene portrayed every year by the schoolchildren that stands for yet another repetition of the founding narrative, there are only seven Holy Families to stand for the original nine. The reason for this is that the other two families violated the blood rule. "The one nobody admitted existed. The one established when the Mississippi flock noticed and remembered that the Disallowing came from fair-skinned colored men. Blue-eyed, gray-eyed yellowmen in good suits" (195). The first person to do it was Roger Best, who secretly married a fairer woman and, although he was allowed to keep her and their child—Pat—because the deed was already done, the family was no longer considered pure, was dropped from its former privileged position and despised by the whole town to the point that they let Delia, his wife, die of childbirth rather than helping her. The second, Menus Jury, was persuaded not to marry the woman he had met while in Vietnam, but he received the town's scorn nonetheless.

Yet, although the whole town somehow knows, deep down at least, this rule, no one actually admits it. When Reverend Misner recognizes the discrepancy between the number of families represented in the school's performance and the number in the original story and asks Pat about it, even she—despite being intent on discerning precisely this type of riddle—offers him only a vague response: "You don't know where you are, do you?" (211). This can be explained in the words of Paul Ricoeur who, dealing with the ways in which a master narrative can be appropriated, modified and imposed by those in power, says that, in this situation, "[a] devious form of forgetting is at work [...], resulting from stripping the social actors of their original power to recount their actions themselves" (2006: 448). This dispossession, he continues, is achieved unwittingly by those social actors that, in a "semi-passive, semi-active behavior," have forgotten by avoidance "the expression of bad faith and its strategy of evasion motivated by an obscure will not to inform oneself, not to investigate the harm done by the citizen's environment, in short, by a wanting-not-to-know" (Ricoeur 2006: 448–449).

Such is the case of the citizens of Ruby who, with the exception of Misner and Pat, seem never to have asked themselves the above-mentioned question referring to where they live—or any others, for that matter. This is also the reason that Pat's genealogy was not readily admitted by the citizens of Ruby: on the one hand, they feared she would discover the truth, and, on the other hand, because they themselves did not want to know or have anything to do with the truth. They would very much prefer to believe the ritualized version of their traumatic history rather than face the truth hidden beneath which would impede their ability to convert the shared trauma into the basis for their collective identity. This, ultimately, is what motivates Pat's compliance with the majoritarian version rather than her discoveries. This is also the reason that she is deeply ashamed of her skin color, inherited from her mother, and passed onto her daughter, Billie Delia, whom she blames and whom she once even tried to kill. Finally, this willful not-knowing is the reason that she would not answer Misner's questions about the nativity scene as well as the reason that she ends up burning her alternative historical account. Unfortunately, her act of witnessing is never completed, and her destructive act mirrors the consistent erasure of traces undertaken by those who write the official story, be it the dominant culture or, in the case of *Paradise*, the town elders (Yukins 2002: 236).

By making Pat's act of resistance unsuccessful and her role as a witness invalid, Morrison seems to be advising against any such destructive practices of archive writing. Alternative histories must be written, she seems to suggest, in order to give voice to past traumas and injustices. This is what African American writers should do; this is what she claims is necessary. Pat's private work in pointing out and filling in the gaps and omissions in the official history of Ruby functions, Gauthier argues, as a counter-historical narrative parallel to all those other ethnic US histories that were never included in the country's master narrative and that are only now, through the works of writers like Morrison, coming to light: "Pat's alternative histories serve as clues for the reader to constitute, in fact, a true story embedded in, between, and outside of Ruby's official story in the same way that the African American history narrated by *Paradise* (like other Morrison novels) makes truth mean outside of dominant, traditional US histories" (2005: 408).

Those African American hidden counter-histories to which Gauthier refers are made explicit within the very text of *Paradise*, because, as mentioned above, it references issues of the African American traumatic past such as slavery, lynchings, segregation and racism and the rejection of black war veterans. However, it also references all those small stories of private suffering and heroism behind those traumatic events even as it acknowledges that they will go unnoticed by the greater historical accounts:

> What could not be gainsaid, but would remain invisible in the newspapers and the books he [Richard Misner] bought for his students, were the ordinary folk. The janitor who turned off the switch so that the police couldn't see; the grandmother who kept all the babies so the mothers could march; the backwoods women with fresh towels in one hand and a shotgun in the other; the little children who carried batteries and food to secret meetings; the ministers who kept whole churchfuls of hunted protesters calm till help came; the old who gathered up the broken bodies of the young; the young who spread their arms to protect the old from batons they could not possibly survive; parents who wiped the spit and tears from their children's faces and said, 'Never mind, honey. Never you mind. You are not and never will be a nigger, a coon, a jig, a jungle bunny nor any other thing white folks teach their children to say. What you are is God's.' Yes, twenty, thirty years from now, those people will be dead or forgotten, their small stories part of no grand record or even its footnotes, although they were the ones who formed the spine on which the televised ones stood. (Morrison 1999a: 212)

2.4 "An Endless Cycle of Repetition": Inverted Racism and Violence[3]

The archival work that writers such as Morrison carry out in order to recuperate these hidden histories of trauma—that archival work that Pat so recklessly destroys—is paramount in order to escape from the repetitive force that trauma—and history, insomuch as it is formed by and through trauma—has. In order to throw some light on this affirmation, let us go back to the history of the Pilgrims that *Paradise* mirrors. The Pilgrims, the founders of the US, arrived in the New World escaping religious oppression and a lack of freedom. They dreamed about a kind of paradisiacal land; a 'city upon a hill' where they vowed to establish themselves in order to be free and equal. However, it does seem ironic that precisely those Pilgrims that escaped persecution would be the very same ones that persecuted and almost exterminated the native population of their newly acquired land, not to mention the events in Salem or their treatment of the African Americans that were imported there. To an impartial observer of history—if such a thing could ever exist—it would seem that historical events tend to repeat themselves, especially if those events are the tragic result of violence and oppression. This has to do with the recurrent aspect of trauma and, of course, with human nature. It often seems that those who have been touched by trauma—who have suffered in their persons and collectivities both the pain and the suffering that discrimination and cruelty at the hands of other human beings entails—are inclined to repeat that cruelty by inflicting it upon others. Cathy Caruth highlights the way in which history seems to be formed as "the endless repetition of previous violence" and equates it with Freud's idea of the death drive (1996: 63). Indeed, it is not uncommon to find that children who have suffered abuses at home or that have witnessed their fathers' abusive treatment of their mothers during childhood are more prone to become abusers themselves than those who grew up in healthy environments. As Bouson argues in reference to Morrison's novels—particularly in regard to the violent treatment Pecola (*The Bluest Eye*) receives from her traumatized and abused father—"humiliated individuals can temporarily rid themselves of their shame by humiliating others" (2000: 25). In other cases, it seems that those individuals or communities that should more easily empathize with other traumatized groups do not always do so, as Merle ponders in *The Timeless Place, the Chosen People*: "[I]t seems suffering doesn't make people any better or wiser or more understanding. They used to say it did, that it

---

3 A previous and shorter version of this section appeared in 2013 under the title: " 'It's Black, It's White, It's Hard for you to Get By': Discourses of Race, Color, and Ugliness in Contemporary African-American Novels." *DISCOURSES THAT MATTER: Selected Essays on English and American Studies*. pp. 233–247. Newcastle upon Tyne: Cambridge Scholars Publishing.

was—how did they put it?—an ennobling experience. Ha! I haven't seen much evidence of that, my dear" (Marshall 1969: 262).

This is precisely what happens to people in Ruby, especially to its elders, who, by dint of repeating the stories of the past have "internalized the shame and hatred they experienced and, through storytelling, passed on a determination to their descendants to become even more exclusive and intolerant than their persecutors" (Romero 2005: 418). When, after a scene of unbearable violence against a group of innocent women at a nearby Convent, the whole town goes back home, they do so thinking "[h]ow hard they had worked for this place; how far away they once were from the terribleness they have just witnessed. How could so clean and blessed a mission devour itself and become the world they had escaped?" (Morrison 1999a: 292). Reverend Misner has a ready answer:

> Whether they be the first or the last, representing the oldest black families or the newest, the best of the tradition or the most pathetic, they had ended up betraying it all. They think they have outfoxed the whiteman when in fact they imitate him. They think they are protecting their wives and children, when in fact they are maiming them. And when the maimed children ask for help, they look elsewhere for the cause. Born out of an old hatred, one that began when a kind of black man scorned another kind and that kind took the hatred to another level, their selfishness had trashed two hundred years of suffering and triumph in a moment of such pomposity and error and callousness it froze the mind. Unbridled by Scripture, deafened by the roar of its own history, Ruby, it seemed to him, was an unnecessary failure. (305–306)

Indeed, over the generations, the members of the founding families of Haven have been systematically putting into practice "an inversion of the US's one-drop rule" (Gauthier 2005: 397), which is nothing more than a perpetuation of the exclusion that their own community suffered. Instead of having opened their minds to the cruelty of racism based on skin color and difference, the trauma suffered by their predecessors has been utilized as an excuse for poorly considered retribution; having been wronged in the past, they see themselves as entitled to do wrong in their turn. Of course, they would not accept that maintaining this hatred towards outsiders, lighter-skinned African Americans and white people, is as much a form of racism and segregation as the one imposed on them. Instead, they argue that it is nothing more than a protective measure against the evils of Out There. This is due to a lack of useful rewriting and organic retelling of their traumatic past. The citizens of Ruby are stuck in the cyclical repetition of the traumatic memory of the past with no intention of extracting from it any valid meaning for their own present and future lives. Such stagnation is not only not helpful, but also completely counterproductive, for it may result in cycles of repeated violence due to the coalescence of shame and rage, as Bouson maintains (2000). In the words of Channette Romero, "[i]n its portrayal of Ruby, *Paradise* suggests that until it comes to terms with its traumatic past, a community created in opposition is destined to repeat exclusions similar to those of the community it is reacting against" (2005: 423).

It is clear by now that the past action that marked the development of the citizens of Haven and later Ruby was the Disallowing. After they are rejected by the citizens of Fairly—note the suggestion of light skin-tone in the town's name—they

> became a tight band of wayfarers bound by the enormity of what had happened to them. Their horror of whites was convulsive but abstract. They saved the clarity of their hatred for the men who had insulted them in ways too confounding for language: first by excluding them, then by offering them staples to exist in that very exclusion. Everything anybody wanted to know about the citizens of Haven or Ruby lay in the ramifications of that one rebuff out of many. But the ramifications of those ramifications were another story. (Morrison 1999a: 189)

It is precisely "the ramifications of those ramifications" to which we need to pay attention now. Importantly, although the quote above specifically mentions whites as the object of their horror, it also points out that those they feel hatred for are "the men who had insulted them" that is, the light-skinned African Americans in the town of Fairly. It was among those same light-skinned African Americans that, they realized, "their daughters would be shunned as brides; their sons chosen last; that colored men would be embarrassed to be seen socially with their sisters" (194). This is the reason that they make a point of living in complete separation from them. It is not—or, at least, not only—whites to whom they so strongly react; they also shun the company of those fair-skinned blacks that once despised them. This is what, as mentioned above, lies behind the disagreement between Coffee and Tea, and this is what explains why Patricia Best and her daughter Billie Delia are scorned. Their mother was not white, but "cracker-looking" (196), and so are they, which means that, in spite of their being both half eight-rocks, their lighter skin tone sets them apart and provokes the disdain of their fellow citizens in Ruby.

This question of skin color and color racism (or colorism) among African Americans runs deeper than it may at first appear, and it merits closer attention. The issue of skin color and the positive or negative connotations attached to it has very deep roots that can be found even before the period of African American slavery. In the western tradition, the color black has been associated with impurity, degradation, evil, etc. In contrast, the color white has often served as a symbol of purity, beauty and virtue. In a Petrarchan sonnet, for instance, the ideal of beauty in women hinges on the whiteness of their skin which was often compared to alabaster, ivory, marble or snow. Thus, in Renaissance England, Queen Elizabeth was praised for the paleness of her skin, which was also implicitly associated with her designation as 'the virgin queen' in reference to her supposed purity. Similarly, Shakespeare adopted the Petrarchan trope in relation to women's beauty and morality in most of his sonnets, while portraying Othello—a black moor—as a jealousy-driven murderous madman. Later on, as the slave trade became increasingly profitable and landowners sought cheap and abundant labor after the introduction of cotton or cane crops in puritanical Virginia, attitudes toward slave labor began to evolve around the notion of race and skin color. Even though slavery was not initially racially marked, some slave holders began to realize the utility of a visible mark that would separate slaves from free men, and made use of several of the aforementioned preconceived ideas about the moral wickedness and inherent inferiority of black people—together with a few other strategically interpreted passages from the Bible such as Noah's curse on Ham (Baker 1970: 433) or the dualism between the "Black Satan" and the "snow-white Lamb of God" (Peach 1995: 100)—to justify and institutionalize slavery. In an environment in which fellow human beings truly believed in their moral and mental inferiority as indicated by their darker skin color and operating within a belief system that made them accept without question that western white beauty was natural and black beauty nonexistent (Heinze 1993: 17), African Americans developed a series of mixed feelings of pride and shame regarding their skin color. As Heinze points out, "[t]hose blacks who are light-skinned often assume, or are perceived to assume, a superiority based solely on the relative absence of melanin from their skin, while dark-skinned people take such overblown pride in their African heritage as to label light-skinned blacks Uncle Toms" (1993: 18). Blackness would be either overvalued—as it was, for instance, during the age of the Harlem Renaissance or the Black Power Movement—or consistently devalued, even by the African Americans themselves (Bouson 2000: 77). Some African American women, for instance, tried beauty products in hopes of lightening their skin, wore blue contact lenses (Heinze 1993: 20) and those who could 'pass' as whites were usually both envied and despised, as exemplified in Nella Larsen's novel *Passing* (1929).

Also significant in this debate—even more so if we keep in mind that it shows children's views and feeling on the issue—are the increasing number of doll tests that are being carried out nowadays. These are replicas of the 1940s experiment carried out by Kenneth Clark in which a number of African American children were shown two dolls identical in everything but skin color. When asked which doll they preferred to play with, 63% of the children chose the white doll, and—perhaps even more alarmingly—a total of 60% also chose the white doll when asked which doll they identified with (Clark and Clark 1947: 175). A variety of tests like Clark's are nowadays being done in countries like the United States, Mexico, Brazil and Denmark and the results are—even today—shocking. In a 2010 CNN report carried out for the Anderson Cooper 360° program, called "Black or White: Kids on Race,"[4] a team of psychologists designed a similar experiment in which they showed a number of black and white children from different backgrounds five drawings of a little girl or boy that varied only in terms of the child's skin color shade. The results showed that we "still live in a society where dark things are devalued and light things are valued" as Dr. Margaret Beale Spencer, from the University of Chicago eloquently puts it in the report (CNN 2010a (Video 3 of 8): 5'04"–5'10"). This is perceived to be so by white and black children alike as we can see from the results: 70.59% of the older black children interviewed chose the two darkest skin colors when asked which skin color looked 'bad' on a boy or girl. Similarly, 53.57% of the younger black children chose the two darker shades when asked which was the 'ugly' child. When asked about personal attributes, 75.86% of the younger white children chose the two darkest pictures when asked which was the 'dumb' child, 65.52% when asked which was the 'mean' child, and 59.38% of the older white children also chose the two darkest drawings when asked which was the 'bad' child (CNN 2010b: 16–40). This shows that white children were mostly 'white biased,' but it also shows a clear tendency on the part of black children to similarly prefer the white over the black. Moreover, when asked to identify their skin color, several of the black children chose a lighter shade than that of their own skin and picked a still lighter one when asked which skin color they would prefer to have, some of them showing clear signs of distress when making the choice.

---

4   The full video report can be accessed at the following YouTube playlist: https://youtu.be/wYkUMqxr_o8?list=PLfmVNxXV6-8En6AgVD-yfKPw4wyV5a1eS, while the full test results can be accessed through the CNN's ac360°'s webpage at http://i2.cdn.turner.com/cnn/2010/images/05/13/expanded_results_methods_cnn.pdf.

Instances of this mixture of feelings abound in African American literature, from the 1930s novel *Black No More* in which George S. Schuyler toys with the notion of the blacks' desire to become white and the sociological consequences that such a conversion could have, to more recent works. For instance, one of the main protagonists of Gloria Naylor's *Mama Day* receives her nickname Cocoa because of her light skin-tone, yet she often uses the wrong foundation color in an attempt to look darker. Likewise, in *The Women of Brewster Place,* Naylor presents us with the character of Kiswana (originally Melanie), a young 'golden' girl involved in the Black Movement who goes to great pains in order to wear an afro (not quite succeeding, and very much envying her twin, 'ebony,' brother for it). Kiswana is scolded by her mother for needing "to reach into an African dictionary to find a name to make [herself] proud" (Naylor 1983: 86) and disrespecting her own cultural and family heritage as well as her skin color. Similarly, in Paule Marshall's short story "Reena," the eponymous character of Reena, who has been despised for her dark skin color several times, "was always being plastered with Vaseline so [she] wouldn't look ashy" (1983b: 78), and whenever she had her picture taken as a child "they would always pile a whitish powder on [her] face and make the lights so bright [she] always came out looking ghostly" (1983b: 78). She explains the situation in the following terms: "We live surrounded by white images, and white in this world is synonymous with the good, light, beauty, success, so that, despite ourselves sometimes, we run after that whiteness and deny our darkness, which has been made into the symbol of all that is evil and inferior" (Marshall 1983b: 79).

But if any African American contemporary writer has dealt with the issue of colorism and African Americans' ambivalence towards skin color, it is Toni Morrison. Morrison has often despised "[t]he concept of physical beauty as a *virtue*," critiqued the Black is Beautiful slogan as "a white idea turned inside out" (qtd. in Stern 2000: 77) and has portrayed both sides of the debate in her novels. In Morrison's work, we find characters who actively desire white characteristics and resent those who don't, like Pecola in *The Bluest Eye*, who desperately wishes for blue eyes and hates her own dark skin color, or Violet in *Jazz*, who is convinced that the reason her husband had an affair with the creamy Dorcas is because of her lighter skin color, and even attempts to defile Dorcas's face during her funeral. Likewise, in *Song of Solomon*, Milkman's grandfather on his mother's side not only behaves like a white man and calls his darker-skinned neighbors "cannibals" (Morrison 2006: 71), but he also becomes increasingly anxious about his grandchildren's skin color after his fair-skinned daughter marries a darker man. In her last novel, *God Help the Child*, Morrison returns to the issue of colorism through her portrayal the character of Bride, the protagonist, who must shape her identity and individuality

HISTORY, ROOTS AND MYTH

against the backdrop of the preconceived ideals of beauty. Bride's mother was born to a "high yellow" mother (Morrison 2015: 3) whose own mother could have passed as white but chose not to and whose grandmother actually did pass as white and deliberately cut off all contact with her children in order to do so. When Bride turns out to be darker than expected, her mother is utterly disappointment and despairs:

> It didn't take more than an hour after they pulled her out from between my legs to realize something was wrong. Really wrong. She was so black she scared me. Midnight black, Sudanese black. [...] I hate to say it, but from the very beginning in the maternity ward the baby, Lula Ann, embarrassed me. Her birth skin was pale as all babies', even African ones, but she changed fast. I thought I was going crazy when she turned blue-black right before my eyes. I know I went crazy for a minute because once—just for a few seconds—I held a blanket over her face and pressed. (Morrison 2015: 3-5)[5]

As a consequence of Bride's black skin, her father leaves them and her mother refuses to ever touch her, let alone show any sign of love or care. Such unmotherly behavior leaves Bride traumatized forever, always yearning for love and approval, and willing to go to any lengths (even falsely accusing and sending an innocent woman to prison) in order to achieve it.

On the other hand, in Morrison's works we also have various instances of the kind of racial pride prevalent in *Paradise*. Bride herself, Morrison's last protagonist, despite her parents' rejection due to her skin color, and unlike Pecola in *The Bluest Eye*, learns not to despise her own black skin, but actually works it to her advantage, highlighting it by always dressing in all-white clothes. She even extracts some personal satisfaction from it, a satisfaction, nonetheless, intricately linked to her past race-related traumas:

> So I let the name-calling, the bullying travel like poison, like lethal viruses through my veins, with no antibiotic available. Which, actually, was a good thing now I think of it, because I built up immunity so tough that not being a 'nigger girl' was all I needed to win. I became a deep dark beauty that doesn't need Botox for kissable lips or tanning spas to hide deathlike pallor. And I don't need silicon on my butt. I sold my elegant

---

5 Lula Ann is Bride's given name. She changed it later and only her mother calls her by that name in the narrative.

blackness to all those childhood ghosts and now they pay me for it. I have to say, forcing those tormentors—the real ones and the others like them—to drool with envy when they see me is more than payback. It's glory. (Morrison 2015: 57)

In *Sula* too, for example, there is a clear concern about skin tone, for its lightness could even endanger its bearer:

> Nel was the color of wet sandpaper—just dark enough to escape the blows of the pitch-dark truebloods and the contempt of old women who worried about such things as bad blood mixtures and knew that the origins of a mule and a mulatto were one and the same. Had she been any lighter-skinned she would have needed either her mother's protection on the way to school or a streak of mean to defend herself. (Morrison 1982: 52)

Moreover, in the same narrative, we find the case of a whole town's animosity towards the protagonist, Sula, not only because she has put her grandmother in a filthy home for the elderly, because she has stolen her best friend's husband or because of her loose morals, but because word got out that she had slept with white men, something equated with "crossing the line between good and evil" (Heinze 1993: 163):

> But it was the men who gave her the final label, who fingerprinted her for all time. They were the ones who said she was guilty of the unforgivable thing—the thing for which there was no understanding, no excuse, no compassion. The route from which there was no way back, the dirt that could not ever be washed away. They said that Sula slept with white men. It may not have been true, but it certainly could have been. [...]
>
> Every one of them imagined the scene, each according to his own predilections—Sula underneath some white man—and it filled them with choking disgust. There was nothing lower she could do, nothing filthier. The fact that their own skin color was proof that it had happened in their own families was no deterrent to their bile. Nor was the willingness of black men to lie in the beds of white women a consideration that might lead them toward tolerance. They insisted that all unions between white men and black women be rape; for a black woman to be willing was literally unthinkable. In that way, they regarded integration with precisely the same venom that white people did. (Morrison 1982: 112–113)

Both the citizens of Medallion in *Sula* and the citizens of Ruby in *Paradise* have the same fear of blood contamination and repeat the segregationist pattern imposed upon them by whites. Although they fear and strongly dislike whites, their hatred is reserved for those who betrayed their racial purity and allowed their blood to be mixed with whites'—the exact opposite position to the one that whites around the United States were taking at that time with respect to blacks whereby "black women came to represent sexual immorality and were compared to prostitutes" (Heinze 1993: 17) and a black man could be lynched for so much as looking at a white woman. And yet, the colorists in *Paradise* and *Sula* seem oblivious to the fact that most of those 'betrayals' were the product of white slaveholders raping or forcing their female slaves to have sexual intercourse with them and that, therefore, they could not be held responsible for it—much less so, their descendants. Nevertheless, as Rob Davidson puts it, "[s]kin color trumps morality every time in Ruby" (2001: 365).

However, the great, unspoken pureblood rule that the elders have established in Ruby has some terrible consequences, not the least of which is the aforementioned repetition of historical traumas. Four consecutive children were born "broken" (Morrison 1999a: 142), that is, with some unspecified mental and/or physical incapacities. This is clearly the result of repeated incest—and therefore, "ingrowth and degeneracy" (Dalsgárd 2001: 242)—to which the inhabitants of Ruby have been driven as a result of their racial purity rule, as Pat Best realizes: "Since Bitty Cato married Peter Blackhorse, and since her daughter, Fawn Blackhorse was wife to Bitty's uncle, and since Peter Blackhorse is Billy Cato's grandfather—well, you can see the problem with blood rules" (Morrison 1999a: 196).

All this pressure, together with the younger generations' new scope of interests and insistence on contesting the old rules, finally erupts in the scene of brutal and completely uncalled for violence against a group of unarmed, innocent women with which the novel opens. According to Marni Gauthier, "[t]he founding fathers of Ruby reproduce the logic of discrimination endemic to the nation's history by intercalating their own repressed fears and inability to live up to the austere moral code of their haven into their perception of occurrences in town and at the Convent" (2005: 398).

In the convent women, the men see a representation of the Out There they have so feared for generations as well as a threat to their racial purity (Deacon Morgan has already had an affair with one of the women there) and they use these women as scapegoats "to vent their anger on racial inequality" (Kuo 2009: 167), and as a way to assert their dominance. What is more, the fact that "[t]hey shot the white girl first" (Morrison 1999a: 3)—although who the white girl was is never stated in the narrative—seems to point to the fact that, conceptually, "[t]he ultimate targets of these black men's attacks and killing are not the women but the white men" (Kuo 2009: 170). However, although there has indeed been a history of African Americans openly professing to despise whites and their desire for violence against them (Kuo 2009: 178–179; 188–193), I maintain that what the inhabitants of Ruby really hate and seek to eradicate from their midst are not only white men and white looking blacks but also the influence of the Out There, the danger of miscegenation and loss of racial purity as well as the degradation of their sacred history.

2.5   Wind of Change: When the Out There Reaches Paradise

This degradation of their history results from the influence that the Out There has on the youngsters at Ruby. They did not experience firsthand their sacralized history, yet they have been catechized and "repetitively informed" of a history that they need to rewrite in order to make it theirs, but that rewriting is seen as a betrayal by the elders (Yukins 2002: 239). Moreover, due to their increased exposure to the world outside Ruby and the Black Power Movement (Yukins 2002: 239–240), they see that things have changed, are changing and need to change, a process in which they want to take part. Just as Morrison herself puts it in an online interview for amazon.com,

> [t]hese people have an extraordinary history, and they were sound people, moral people, generous people. Yet when their earlier settlement collapsed, and they tried to repeat it in Ruby … well, the modern generation simply couldn't sustain what the Old Fathers had created, because of the ways in which the world had changed. The Ruby elders couldn't prevent certain anxieties about drugs, about politics. And their notions of women—particularly about controlling women—left them very vulnerable, precisely because they had romanticized and mythologized their own history. It was frozen, in a sense. (Marcus n.p.)

In spite of their "extraordinary history," the elders will not allow any change to take place in Ruby because, for them, "past heroism was enough of a future to live by" (Morrison 1999a: 161), and they preferred to stick to their solidified, 'frozen' version of history. This is something that Misner does not understand since, given their baggage of oppression and exclusion, he thinks they should be more comprehending of the present fights: "Why such stubbornness, such venom against asserting rights, claiming a wider role in the affairs of black people? They, of all people, knew the necessity of unalloyed will; the rewards of courage and single-mindedness. Of all people, they understood the mechanisms of wresting power. Didn't they?" (161). As discussed previously, their past trauma has not opened them to understand the needs of others but instead has closed them in themselves and, as a result, they want nothing to do with whatever lays Out There in a world that, they feel, is nothing but a threat to their self-made paradise and that, furthermore, is filled with all those who treated them wrongly in the past. Therefore, when the younger people in Ruby ask for change in their customs, in their way of seeing themselves, and in the Oven; the embodiment of the town's exceptionalist narrative, the elders shut themselves off completely and are incapable of understanding a word of what has been said:

> When Royal and the other two, Destry and one of Pious Du Pres's daughters, asked for a meeting, it was quickly agreed upon. No one had called a town meeting in years. Everybody, including Soane and Dovey, thought the young people would first apologize for their behavior and then pledge to clean up and maintain the site. Instead they came with a plan of their own. A plan that completed what the first had begun. Royal, called Roy, took the floor and, without notes, gave a speech perfect in every way but intelligibility. Nobody knew what he was talking about and the parts that could be understood were plumb foolish. He said they were way out-of-date; that things had changed everywhere but in Ruby. He wanted to give the Oven a name, to have meetings there to talk about how handsome they were while giving themselves ugly names. Like not American. Like African. [...] And he talked about white people as though he had just discovered them and seemed to think that what he'd learned was news. (104)

Change is understandably not in the elders' plans because change would undermine the control that they have over the rest of the citizens of Ruby. Any modification to their master narrative—or to the symbol thereof, the Oven—is deemed unnecessary, as Deacon Morgan ultimately shouts at Roy, one of Ruby's youngsters: "That Oven already has a history. It doesn't need you to fix it" (86). So fixated are they on their official account of history that they consider the young rebels as blasphemous traitors to their roots and to their forefathers: "Imagine," Deacon thinks, "what Big Papa or Drum Blackhorse or Juvenal DuPres would think of those *puppies* who wanted to alter words of beaten iron" (99. Emphasis added).

What those 'puppies' want is precisely a rewriting, not only of what is written on the Oven's lip but of history. As E.L. Doctorow says,

> There is no history except as it is composed. There are no failed revolutions, only lawless conspiracies. All history is contemporary history, says Benedetto Croce in *History of Liberty*:

'However remote in time events may seem to be, every historical judgment refers to present needs and situations.' That is why history has to be written and rewritten from one generation to another. The act of composition can never end. (qtd. in Davidson 2001: 358)

History has been kept static in Ruby for over three generations, and now it is high time for a rewriting. The history of a community cannot survive separated from the outer, broader history, and it cannot be kept apart from any outer influence, for it would be bound to end in disaster: "[A] town or belief system that allows no difference, new ideas, or new members is bound to destroy itself from within. The resentments against the rigid code of behavior established by the wealthiest patriarchs of Ruby have built up so greatly that the town needs an outlet for its hostility" (Romero 2005: 419).

2.6   Breaking the Cycle of Repetition: Sharing Trauma

What the outlet for the town's hostility was, we already know: the massacre at the Convent. However, what remains to be discussed is whether or not there was any possibility of avoiding such a dramatic ending. Since the tragedy was provoked by a fixation on a traumatic past, instead of an acceptance and internalization of the trauma in order to be able to start a process of working through, a more efficient and healthy way of dealing with the community's painful history might have been beneficial, and might have avoided the bloodshed. As important as history is, communities, if they want to avoid the repetition of past traumas, must try to extract their present identities from the whole picture, without editing any part of it, as the citizens in Ruby do. The character of Saul in *The Chosen Place, the Timeless People* expresses precisely this same idea when he ponders the history of his people (the Jews), the history of African Americans and the people at Bournehills:

> [P]eople [...] who've truly been wronged—like yours, like mine all those thousands of years—must at some point, if they mean to come into their own, start using their history to their advantage. Turn it to their own good. You begin, I believe, by first acknowledging it, all of it, the bad as well as the good, those things you can be proud of [...] and the ones most people would rather forget [...]. But that's part of it too. And then, of course, you have to try and learn from all that's gone before—and again from both the good and the bad—especially that! Use your history as a guide, in other words. Because many times, what one needs to know for the present—the action that must be taken if a people are to win their right to live, the methods to be used: some of them unpalatable, true, but

again, there's usually no other way—has been spelled out in past events. That it's all there if only they would look ... (Marshall 1969: 315)

Surely the reclamation of a (traumatic) past can be beneficial for a community in that it foments bonding and the creation of a sense of belonging. However, the use of history as a mechanism for identity formation—especially if that identity formation is rooted in the experience of a shared or founding trauma—should not become stagnant as it did for the citizens of Ruby. Both history and identity, in the sense that they are inextricably linked, should remain in flux, admitting the ever-changing influences of the outside and the passing of time.

In the case of Ruby, this malleability of history and collective identity has not taken place thanks to its leaders' determination to adhere to a set of rules and imperatives more appropriate to an old-fashioned narrative. By controlling that narrative, keeping it safe from change and, especially by hiding certain telling aspects of it and offering to the public only what they deemed necessary, they have prevented their traumatic past from being productively integrated into a collective identity and becoming a positive foundation for their present and their future. This prevention has taken place due to a mistaken form of respect for their predecessors, the original victims of the trauma. Characters such as Deacon and Steward Morgan are afraid of a rewriting of their traumatic past and refuse any suggestion of change by claiming respect for their elders and their history. They believe that, if their restricted version of the past is not properly—that is, utterly unchanged—passed onto the next generations, the members of those new generations will forget the magnificent history of their community and end up betraying the memory of their forefathers' suffering. They are mistaken however, for as King states, "[t]he lives of the marginalized [...] need to be remembered, acknowledged and reconstructed, but not preserved like monuments or relics in a museum case" (2000: 59). The latter would mean stagnation and a probable repetition of the trauma. Through the former, however, communities can hope to achieve healing which, as Peter Kearly indicates, "does not mean forgetting but recovering what has been repressed and ignored in order to make historically viable options for what people can choose to make their lives meaningful" (2000: 14).

As a counterpoint to this situation stand the women at the Convent who could be seen as "Morrison's ideal alternative" (Dalsgård 2001: 243). In fact, according to the narrative, "unlike some people in Ruby, the Convent women were no longer haunted" (Morrison 1999a: 266). This clear separation between the outsiders that are able to find peace in their personal traumas and the people from the town that cannot move towards a healing of their collective past suffering is due to the fact that, unlike the Ruby community, the Convent women have taken the necessary steps towards a proper working through. Under the guidance of Consolata, a Native American working as a maternal figure for the rest of the women, they all engage in a collective voicing of their personal traumas both in words and through art-making:

> In the beginning the most important thing was the template. First they had to scrub the cellar floor until its stones were as clean as rocks on a shore. Then they ringed the place with candles. Consolata told each to undress and lie down. [...] When each found the position she could tolerate on the cold, uncompromising floor, Consolata walked around her and painted the body's silhouette. [...]
>
> That is how the loud dreaming began. How the stories rose in that place. Half-tales and the never-dreamed escaped from their lips to soar high above guttering candles, shifting dust from crates and bottles. And it was never important to know who said the dream or whether it had meaning. In spite of or because their bodies ache, they step easily into the dreamer's tale. [...]
>
> In loud dreaming, monologue is no different from a shriek; accusations directed to the dead and long gone are undone by murmurs of love. So, exhausted and enraged, they rise and go to their beds vowing never to submit to that again but knowing full well they will. And they do.
>
> Life, real and intense, shifted to down there in limited pools of light, in air smoky from kerosene lamps and candle wax. The templates drew them like magnets. It was Pallas who insisted they shop for tubes of paint, sticks of colored chalk. Paint thinner and chamois cloth. They understood and began to begin. First with natural features: breasts and pudenda, toes, ears and head hair. [...] They spoke to each other about what had been dreamed and what had been drawn. (263–265)

This sharing of traumas, this collective pouring out of pain both in words and in drawings clearly helps the convent women start the process of recovery instead of, like the citizens of Ruby, becoming stagnant in an endless repetition of static memories. "*Paradise*," Romero says, "suggests that the individual and communal acknowledgment of past histories and the recognition of others' similar traumas frees humans to move on, to focus on the endless work of healing and community building" (2005: 423). And, as such, she continues, it "attempts to bring out material change by encouraging its readers to view themselves as part of a collective history of oppression and resistance that extends beyond the boundaries of the novel, the ethnic community, and the nation-state"

(Romero 2005: 425–426). The description of the 'loud dreaming' is, according to Bouson, a dramatization of Morrison's "long-held view of the ideal reader-text transaction as one in which the reader-participant is open and receptive to the text" (2000: 210) from which, Morrison seems to suggest, we readers can benefit as much as the Convent women did. This healthy form of community building through storytelling and the sharing of traumas that the women at the Convent—and, according to Romero, also Morrison herself through her novel—practice is something that the rest of the inhabitants of Ruby do not accomplish. "Only supportive communities," Schreiber suggests, "provide the healing necessary for future generations to grow and move beyond ancestral or firsthand trauma" (2010: 53). This is what the Ruby community—unlike the women at the Convent—fail to achieve. Insomuch as their method of community building is the strict opposite of that of the women at the Convent, a circle of shame-hate is generated and eventually scapegoated on the Convent women, whom the citizens of Ruby come to regard as "the repository of the scandalous secrets of the respectable 8-rocks" (Bouson 2000: 203) and therefore as dangerous for their carefully manipulated, endlessly repeated founding story. The citizens of Ruby eventually fail in their attempt to build a strong, united community because they are not willing—or able—to "utilize collective memory to preserve the past yet live fully in the present" (Schreiber 2010: 53). Instead they exhaust their ancestors' history by their refusal to allow an integration of alternative narratives into their own out of fear of taint from the Out There. The history becomes stagnant and, when threatened, their only recourse becomes the infliction of violence and the repetition of traumatizing practices.

3 Know thy Roots: *Mama Day* and the Significance of the Past[6]

> She talks about what she knows, not what she's afraid to remember.
> GLORIA NAYLOR, *Mama Day*

Gloria Naylor's *Mama Day* presents a completely opposite vision of the past and the building up of communities of that depicted in Morrison's *Paradise*. In the latter, we found a collective history that had become mystified by means of an imposed devotion to a unique, controlled version of it and that had resulted

---

6 A previous and much shorter version of this section appeared in 2013 under the title: "The Trauma behind the Myth: The Necessity to Recover the Past in Gloria Naylor's *Mama Day*." Is This a Culture of Trauma? An Interdisciplinary Perspective. pp. 77–84. Oxford: Inter-Disciplinary Press.

in a fragmented and violent community. In *Mama Day*, however, although the community's collective identity has likewise been formed around one distinctive event in the past, its narrative has been allowed to evolve through time to such a degree that its original version has become almost erased—not hidden, as in *Paradise*—from the collective memory of the community.

3.1   Dynamic Memory vs. Stagnant History

The catalyst for the collective history of the community depicted in *Mama Day*, and the event that is celebrated and passed on as the foundation for the community's identity is the story of Sapphira Wade, a former slave to Bascombe Wade, a slaveholder and owner of the whole fictive island of Willow Springs. According to legend, Bascombe Wade had been in love with Sapphira, and may have fathered at least some of her seven sons. However, Sapphira, also believed to have magical powers, did not love him back and only took advantage of his love in order to persuade him to deed the entire island to his slaves prior to murdering him. Nevertheless, although this story is understandably held as the uniting, common source of the community, it is not continually repeated and stubbornly maintained unaltered in the strict and highly manichaeistic way in which Coffee's story was preserved and passed on in *Paradise*. On the contrary, many of its details were lost to the general population of Willow Springs, and there exist several parallel stories of which, although collectively they provide a broader picture of how the community of Willow Springs came into being, none seems to take prevalence over the others, thus transforming the story not into history but into legend:

> Everybody knows but nobody talks about the legend of Sapphira Wade. A true conjure woman: satin black, biscuit cream, red as Georgia clay: depending upon which of us takes a mind to her. She could walk through a lightning storm without being touched; grab a bolt of lighting in the palm of her hand; use the heat of lightning to start the kindling going under her medicine pot: depending upon which of us takes a mind to her. She turned the moon into salve, the stars into a swaddling cloth, and healed the wounds of every creature walking up on two or down on four. It ain't about right or wrong, truth or lies, it's about a slave woman who brought a whole new meaning to both them words, soon as you cross over here from beyond the bridge. And somehow, some way, it happened in 1823: she smothered Bascombe Wade in his very bed and lived to tell the story for a thousand days. 1823: married Bascombe Wade, bore him seven sons in just a thousand days, to put a dagger through his kidney and escape the hangman's noose, laughing in a burst of flames.

1823: persuaded Bascombe Wade in a thousand days to deed all his slaves every inch of land in Willow Springs, poisoned him for his trouble, to go on and bear seven sons—by person or persons unknown. (Naylor 1988: 3)

And indeed it is this legend-like tinge that lives on in the collective memory of the inhabitants of Willow Springs, which is enhanced by the fact that this story has not been intentionally used for any private purposes, as the forefathers of Ruby did with the story of Coffee and the foundation of Haven. In fact, the story of Sapphira Wade has not been passed on by means of repetition and storytelling, for "the *name* Sapphira Wade is never breathed out of a single mouth in Willow Springs" (4. Italics in the original). As Eckard argues, "[t]he legend of Sapphira wade is passed along not by re-tellings, but through intuitive, transcendent ways of listening and knowing" (1995: 129). In the following quote we can see how this re-telling and passing on has taken place over the years and has inevitably changed the original meaning behind certain 'traditions' as well as the knowledge of the community's history:

Over here nobody knows why every December twenty-second folks take to the road—strolling, laughing, and talking—holding some kind of light in their hands. It's been going on since before they were born, and the ones born before them.

This year is gonna be a good one, 'cause the weather's held and there ain't no rain. A lot of the older heads can bring out their candles, insisting that's the way it was done in the beginning. They often take exception to the younger folks who will use kerosene lamps or sparklers, rain or no rain. They say it's a lot more pleasant than worrying about hot wax dropping on your hands. The younger ones done brought a few other changes that don't sit too well with some. Used to be when Willow Springs was mostly cotton and farming, by the end of the year it was common knowledge who done turned a profit and who didn't. And with a whole heap of children to feed and clothe, winter could be mighty tight for some. And them being short on cash and long on pride, Candle Walk was a way of getting help without feeling obliged. Since everybody said, 'Come my way, Candle Walk,' sort of as a season's greeting and expected a little something, them that needed a little more got it quiet-like from their neighbors. And it weren't no hardship giving something back—only had to be any bit of something, as long as it came from the earth and the work of your own hands. A bushel of potatoes and a cured side of meat could be exchanged for a plate of ginger cookies, or even a cup of ginger toddy.

It all got accepted with the same grace, a lift of the candle and a parting whisper, 'Lead on with light.'

Things took a little different turn with the young folks having more money and working beyond the bridge. They started buying each other fancy gadgets from the catalogues, and you'd hear ignorant things like, 'They ain't give me nothing last Candle Walk, so they getting the same from me this year.' Or you stop by their place, and taking no time to bake nothing they got a bowl of them hard gingersnaps come straight from a cookie box. A few in this latest bunch will even drive their cars instead of walking, flashing the headlights at folks they passed, yelling out the window, drunk sometimes, 'Lead on, lead on!'

There's a disagreement every winter about whether these young people spell the death of Candle Walk. You can't keep 'em from going beyond the bridge, and like them candles out on the main road, time does march on. But Miranda, who is known to be far more wise than wicked, says there's nothing to worry about. In her young days Candle Walk was different still. After going around and leaving what was needed, folks met in the main road and linked arms. They'd hum some lost and ancient song, and then there'd be a string of lights moving through the east woods out to the bluff over the ocean. They'd all raise them candles, facing east, and say, 'Lead on with light, Great Mother. Lead on with light.' Say you'd hear talk then of a slave woman who came to Willow Springs, and when she left, she left in a ball of fire to journey back home east over the ocean. And Miranda says that her daddy, John-Paul, said that in his time Candle Walk was different still. Said people kinda worshipped his grandmother, a slave woman who *took* her freedom in 1823. Left behind seven sons and a dead master as she walked down the main road, candle held high to light her way to the east bluff over the ocean. Folks in John-Paul's time would line the main road with candles, food, and slivers of ginger to help her spirit along. And Miranda says that her daddy said *his* daddy said Candle Walk was different still. But that's where the recollections end—at least, in the front part of the mind. (Naylor 1988: 110–111. Italics in the original)

This quote, though lengthy, is necessary in its entirety in order to show the way in which Willow Spring's memory is a dynamic memory, open to the mental interpretation of each of its bearers, rather than a stagnant, monolithic fixed version of past events controlled by particular interests. This dynamism of memory permeates all aspects of communal life in Willow Springs, for even what the community terms 'traditions' like the celebration of Candle Walk, inevitably change over the years, as the quote above shows. And yet, although change is seen by some as potentially destructive to the maintenance of traditions, those aware of the previous mutations—like Mama Day—realize that not only do youngsters not "spell the death" (111) of Candle Walk, but introduce the dynamism necessary to keep history and memory alive and vital. Miranda—unlike the elders of Ruby—acknowledges that history and tradition need to evolve if a community wants to healthily maintain itself. She does not make the same mistake as the Malcolm brothers in *Paradise* because she understands that a community cannot permanently stand protected from the Out There and the passing of time. After all, "You can't keep 'em from going beyond the bridge, and like them candles out on the main road, time does march on" (111). Both *Mama Day* and *Paradise* suggest, albeit in different ways, that cultural memory is better constructed through "active reconstruction and recreation of tradition, rather than a passive acceptance and transmittal" (Lamothe 2005: 164).

It becomes clear in the above excerpt that the 'true' story of Sapphira Wade has not been intentionally preserved through generations, rather the opposite, for, with the passing of time, each generation knows less and less of it just as they maintain less and less of the original phrase spoken at Candle Walk. In fact, nobody actually remembers how it all started, as its true meaning and history has only been preserved in the Day family and, more specifically, in the memory located past the "front part" (Naylor 1988: 111) of the mind of Mama Day, a direct descendant of Sapphira who is said to have inherited her great-grandmother's magical powers:

> My daddy said that his daddy said when he was young, Candle Walk was different still. It weren't about no candles, was about a light that burned in a man's heart. And folks would go out and look up at the stars—they figured his spirit had to be there, it was the highest place they knew. And what took him that high was his belief in right, while what buried him in the ground was the lingering taste of ginger from the lips of a woman. He had freed 'em all but her, 'cause, see, she'd never been a slave. And what she gave of her own will, she took away. (308)

This final version deprives the story of all the fantastic and mythical elements that are evident in the other, less informed, subsequent editions, such as the alleged magical powers of Sapphira (her ability to walk through a thunderstorm or to grab lightning bolts and use them to her advantage). It also explains the reason behind the presence of light and ginger in Candle Walk as well as the actual name of the family descended from Sapphira: the Days. Once more, we have a significant story for an African American community mixed with a story from the Bible, more specifically, in this case, from Genesis. "God rested on the seventh day and so would she," we are told in the novel's front matter, which references to the fact that she bore seven sons and then stopped altogether. This equation of an important historical figure of a particular community with a biblical character or deity is consistent with the mystification that any collective identity building narrative inevitably endures. However, in this case, the collective history of Willow Springs does not stop at this, but, perhaps thanks to its lack of dissemination, includes also those mythical and magical elements that make Sapphira Wade a witch/goddess with the power to influence even the lives of her descendants.

This distinction between memory—the dynamic, unstable, distorting yet perpetuating side of history—and history itself is made clearer in the expression '18 & 23,' which, for people of Willow Springs is "just our way of saying something" (7). What that something is, is part of memory. It is a reference to 1823, the historical year in which Bascombe Wade deeded his land to his slaves and Sapphira allegedly murdered him. But it also refers to "the curve in [Cloris's] spine that came from the planting season when their mule broke its leg, and so she took up the reins and kept pulling the plow with her own back" (8); to "the hot tar that took out the corner of [Winky's] right eye the summer [they] had only seven days to rebuild the bridge so the few crops [they] had left after the storm could be gotten over before rot sat in" (8); to "the fields [they] had to stop farming back in the '80s to take outside jobs [...] 'cause it was leave the land or lose it during the Silent Depression" (8); as well as to the story of Cocoa and her first husband, George (the novel's main plotline). In sum, it refers to the whole of the traumatic memory embedded in Willow Springs and, in the minds and hearts of its inhabitants, to the part of history that is never recorded in books but passed on through storytelling and memory-work. Therefore, any attempt to fully explain what 18 & 23 means would entail telling and understanding what those traumatic memories have done to the collective identity of the inhabitants of Willow Springs, their meaning and significance as well as their present consequences. When an estranged child of a Willow Springs native returns to his mother's homeland with the intention "to put Willow Springs on the map" (7), he becomes determined to find out the meaning behind the expression 18 & 23. However, he is unable to understand the particular character of the expression because, being a stranger to his community, he lacks his share in the collective understanding of the term and the memory related to it and also because he is not willing to listen. Memory in this case is not recorded and, therefore, has to be passed on orally. Just as with trauma therapy, if there is to be communication with and understanding of the telling party, there must exist in the listener the willingness to listen and understand. Only then can the sharing and passing on take place.

However, the unnamed foreigner—he is always referred to by his only link to the Willow Springs community and therefore only named "Reema's boy" (7)—does not want to listen properly and therefore he does not understand. He, in his attempt to rationalize and historicize memory, comes up with a convoluted explanation of 18 & 23 that has nothing to do with the reality behind it and which earns him the scorn and animosity of people in Willow Springs:

> [Y]ou see, he had come to the conclusion after 'extensive field work' (ain't ever picked a boll of cotton or head of lettuce in his life—Reema spoiled him silly), but he done still made it to the conclusion that 18 & 23 wasn't 18 & 23 at all—was really 81 & 32, which just so happened to be the lines of longitude and latitude marking off where Willow Springs sits on the map. And we were just so damned dumb that we turned the whole thing around.
>
> Not that he called it being dumb, mind you, called it 'asserting our cultural identity,' 'inverting hostile, social and political parameters.' 'Cause, see, being we was brought here as slaves, we had no choice but to look at everything upside-down. And then being that we was isolated off here in this island, everybody else in the country went on learning good English and calling things what they really was—in the dictionary and all that—while we kept on calling things ass-backwards. And he thought that was just so wonderful and marvelous, etcetera, etcetera … (7–8)

The obvious irony in this passage is clearly directed towards the works of countless historiographers that, in their western-bound ideology, attempt to convert memory, its orality, and subjectivity into rationalized, fixed and rigidly-structured history. This also coincides with the recent accusations of Eurocentrism against some trauma theorists that appear to be not only "almost exclusively concerned with traumatic experiences of white Westerners," but also, in analyzing those experiences, "solely employ critical methodologies emanating from a Euro-American context" (Craps and Buelens 2008: 2). This could mean, as in the case of Reema's boy's failed explanation of 18 & 23, that "by ignoring or marginalizing non-Western traumatic events and histories and non-Western theoretical work, trauma studies may actually assist in the perpetuation of Eurocentric views and structures that maintain or widen the gap between the West and the rest of the world" (Craps and Buelens 2008: 2). As a critique of the one sided-focus of these types of practices, and in the words of Daphne Lamothe, "Naylor privileges the dynamism of the island's living memory over the representations of the past attempted by inhabitants of the Western-oriented mainland.

History, ethnography and other institutionalized discourses prove to be little more than what historian Pierre Nora has called 'sifted and sorted historical traces'" (2005: 155).

18 & 23, therefore, is not just some mixed up set of coordinates, neither is it merely a date. It is the shorthand by which the people of Willow Springs refer to their traumatic past, and, by extension, the shorthand by which Gloria Naylor refers to the African Americans' history of trauma, oppression and hardship. It is the record of what has not been recorded in the official accounts of history and of what people like Reema's boy failed to understand. Through the pages of *Mama Day*, Gloria Naylor highlights the significance of memory, myth, tradition and, above all, personal experience in the account of the African American past. Consequently, the resulting image is not what has already been told about issues like slavery, reconstruction and segregation, but a recreation of what real African Americans actually experienced. For instance, when talking about segregation and how job offers in the newspapers were marked as colored or white, and how, after segregation was abolished thanks to the fight for Civil Rights and equal opportunities were supposed to exist, not everything was as straightforward as historical accounts have made us believe. Accordingly, while looking for a job during the 1980s, Cocoa offers the following—controversial—opinion:

> Where had it [segregation] gone? I just wanted to bring the clarity about it back—it would save me a whole lot of subway tokens. What I was left to deal with were the ads labeled *Equal Opportunity Employer*, or nothing—which might as well have been labeled *Colored apply* or *Take your chances*. And if I wanted to limit myself to the sure bets, then it was an equal opportunity to be what, or earn what? That's where the headwork came in. (Naylor 1988: 19. Italics in the original)

Similarly, in the following quotation, the narrator offers a brief review of the African American experience and traumatic history, and a possible explanation of how African Americans came to survive it all:

> Now, I'm gonna tell you about *cool*. It comes with the cultural territory: the beating of the brush drum, the rocking of the slave ship, the rhythm of the hand going from cotton sack to cotton row and back again. It went on to settle into the belly of the blues, the arms of Jackie Robinson, and the head of every ghetto kid who lives to a ripe old age. You can keep it, you can hide it, you can blow it—but even when your ass is in the tightest crack, you must never, ever LOSE it. (102)

3.2 *The Day Family: a Trauma within the Folds of Memory*

Mama Day is, however, not only about the story of a people, nor of a community, it is the story of a family, the Day family. Descending from the original Sapphira Wade and, arguably, from Bascombe Wade's seventh son, the only survivors—Miranda (Mama) Day, her sister Abigail and Cocoa, the latter's granddaughter—bear the weight of the family's traumatic past. The early death of Peace—Abigail and Miranda's sister—the suicide of their mother, the death of another Peace—Abigail's daughter—and, later, of Grace—Cocoa's mother—haunt the two elder survivors of the Day family like a ghost. This is intertwined with the legend of Sapphira Wade, for, even though it is never openly discussed, its essence pervades the Day family in the credence that the Day women are bound to break their men's hearts. Bascombe Wade's pain in losing his love is passed on like a curse through the subsequent generations of Days with such a force that it seems to keep repeating itself without giving the protagonists the chance to avoid its impact. This apparent curse is behind the death of Miranda and Abigail's mother and the pain of John-Paul, the seventh son of the seventh son of Sapphira Wade. All this pain and trauma is rooted in "the other place;" the family home where most of these traumatic events took place: the house that Bascombe Wade built and where the well down which Peace fell lies; the place that Abigail refuses to visit; and the place to which, accosted by Cocoa's impending death, Mama Day retires to think and seek a solution. It is in this site of trauma that Mama Day realizes the force of the curse, the parallels between Sapphira and her mother and between Bascombe and her father and that is what, seen in this perspective, transforms their respective stories into replicas of each other.

> A woman in apricot homespun: Let me go with peace. And a young body falling, falling toward the glint of silver coins in the crystal clear water. A woman in a gingham shirtwaist: Let me go with Peace. Circles and circles of screaming. Once, twice, three times peace was lost at that well. How was she ever gonna look past all that pain?
>
> And then she opens her eyes on her own hands. Hands that look like John-Paul's. Hands that would not let the woman in gingham go with Peace. Before him, other hands that would not let the woman in apricot homespun go with peace. No, *could* not let her go. In all this time, she ain't never really thought about what it musta done to him. Or him either. It had to tear him up inside, knowing he was willing to give her anything in the world but that. And maybe he shoulda, 'cause he lost her anyway. But she wasn't sent out here for that—the losing was the pain of

her childhood, the losing was Candle Walk, and looking past the losing was to feel for the man who built this house and the one who nailed this well shut. (284–285)

In this novel we have the same pattern as in *Paradise*: traumatic history and repetition. However, in this case, the repetition does not come on account of a stagnation of memory that has been converted into history instead of been allowed to naturally flow and transform itself, but from a stagnation in the process of recovery as a result of repression and silencing of memories. These processes will be covered more in depth in the following chapter, but suffice it to say that such a denial of remembrance inhibits a proper working through of trauma and favors its inherent capacity of repeating itself. In this novel, even though all three remaining members of the Day family are, in different degrees, aware of their forefathers' legend, only the two oldest know about the more recent repetition of the story in their parents' lives. In a—retrospectively—very telling scene, in which Mama Day is sewing a quilt for Cocoa and her new husband out of rags belonging to the different members of the family, we see, already, a hint of the similarities between the two dramatic stories in the Day family. For a moment Mama Day seems to realize the force of the curse, and how it may affect Cocoa and George, but she nonetheless thinks that there is nothing she can do to help it:

> The front of Mother's gingham shirtwaist—it would go right nice into the curve between these two patches of apricot toweling, but Abigail would have a fit. Maybe she won't remember. And maybe the sun won't come up tomorrow either. I'll just use a sliver, no longer than the joint on my thumb. Put a little piece of her in here somewhere.
>
> The gingham is almost dry rot and don't cut well, the threads fraying under her scissors. She tries and tries again for just a sliver. Too precious to lose, have to back it with something. Rummaging through the oranges, she digs up a piece of faded homespun, no larger than the palm of her hand and still tight and sturdy. Now, this is real old. Much older than the gingham. Coulda been part of anything, but only a woman would wear this color. The homespun is wrapped over and basted along the edges of the gingham. She can shape the curve she needs now. [...] Miranda feels a chill move through the center of her chest. She doesn't want to know, so she pushes the needle through and tugs the thread down—tugs the thread up. [...] She tries to put her mind somewhere else, but she only has the homespun, the gingham, and the silver flashing of her needle. [...] It doesn't help to listen to the

clock, 'cause it's only telling her what she knew about the homespun all along. The woman who wore it broke a man's heart. Candle Walk night. What really happened between her great-grandmother and Bascombe Wade? How many—if any—of them seven sons were his? But the last boy to show up in their family was no mystery; he had cherished another woman who could not find peace. Ophelia. It was too late to take it out of the quilt, and it didn't matter no way. Could she take herself out? Could she take out Abigail? Could she take 'em all out and start again? With what? (137–138)

Surely they cannot take themselves out of the quilt—or of the family's history—but Miranda is wrong when she believes there is nothing she can do to prevent tragedy from recurring. Just as in the previous case of *Paradise*, tragedy is bound to reappear unless the traumatic memories of it are actively acknowledged and incorporated into the family's story to be available to its present and future members. By maintaining secrecy about the past—or by stubbornly fixating on the past—individuals and communities alike are prevented from moving forward and thus favor repetitive patterns. History, after all, has to be known in order to learn from it and use it to our advantage in the present time and in order to promote a better future for the next generations. In the case of *Mama Day*, it is Abigail who refuses to deal with the past. She does not want to set foot in 'the other place,' the site of so much trauma and suffering, and it is she that does not want to remember or tell Cocoa about her grandmother's story. It is Miranda, in relation to their mother's old sewing basket, who realizes that "[w]e can get rid of the basket. But you can't burn away memories" (95), a very sensible approach, and she is also the one to insist on the potential benefits that could be extracted by telling Cocoa about her troubling history:'

> [...] And we ain't even told Baby girl about ... And we should, you know, Abigail. It ain't nothing to be ashamed of, it's her family and her history. And she'll have children one day.
> There's time before you saddle her with all that mess. Let the child live her life without having to think on them things. Baby Girl—
> That's just it, Abigail—she ain't a baby. She's a grown woman and her *real* name is Ophelia. We don't like to think on it, but that's her name. Not Baby Girl, not Cocoa—Ophelia.
> I regret the day she got it. (116. Italics in the original)

Abigail is reluctant to let the secret be known and is thus perpetuating the silence and allowing for the repetition to take place, but she is nonetheless aware of the potential danger in which Cocoa and George are, reflected in Cocoa's true name. In the narrative, it seems as if, in addition to the power of Sapphira Wade's curse, naming is also equally important in the repetition of tragedy; it is as if the bearer of a name is somehow predestined to follow the same tragic path as their namesake—which could also account for the name Sapphira Wade having been silenced in Willow Springs. It happened with Abigail's first daughter, Peace. Although Miranda begged her not to name the baby after their deceased sister (39), Abigail felt she had to, out of a debt to her mother (95). Unfortunately, the baby followed its namesake to the tomb, and now Abigail fears that Cocoa, named after her grandmother Ophelia, will, as her predecessor did, break her husband's heart. And so does Cocoa herself, for, despite her grandmother and great-aunt's secrecy, she is somehow—although not fully—aware of the terrible fate hanging over her head and, failing to understand, also tries to block it, as she later explains to her—by now deceased—husband:

> Yes, George, you tried hard. But it would have been too much to ask for you to understand those whispers as we passed through my family plot. As soon as I put the moss in my shoes, I could hear them all in the wind as it moved through the trees and stirred up dust along the ground. That's what upset me so the day we first sat right here, looking at the water. A beautiful day like this. I knew I wasn't the best of wives, but I gave it my personal best and you—or any man—would have to accept that or nothing at all. And I was lucky enough to have found someone who often accepted much less than the best from me. So how—I wanted to scream at all those silent whispers—how would I break his heart? Instead of screaming at them, and having you think I'd lost my mind, I snapped at you. And you probably thought I was in one of my uglier moods. Well, it was the lesser of two evils.
>
> No, you didn't know this place. And you didn't know my people. I was sorry I had brought you—on that walk, to Willow Springs period. And if what they said held any truth, then I was sorry I had married you. But I'd never allow myself to think that, so I told myself it had all been a figment of my imagination. (223)

Yet, it turns out not to be merely a figment of her imagination, and George dies dramatically at the end of the novel, literally, of a broken heart. In one of the novel's most fantastic parts—so much so that it almost reads as magical realism—Miranda asks him to go to the old chicken coop and bring her back whatever he finds there in order to magically save Cocoa's life, which is at risk due to a mysterious illness. What she means is his blood, just his scarred and bitten hands—for she knew the hens would protect their eggs—but he, lacking the family's mystical knowledge and non-Western frame of mind, misunderstands her and not only does he massacre the hens and break all the eggs, but he also ends up dying from a heart attack due to the effort. Miranda realizes how this could happen; George, like Reema's boy, does not share the same roots, customs, traditions and knowledge as she does and therefore could never have understood her real intentions. In spite of this, she still refuses to tell him the secret of the family, when speaking clearly could have spared his life and the repetition of tragedy:

> Miranda fights back a heavy inner trembling. She needed George—but George did not need her. The Days were all rooted to the other place, but that boy had his own place within him. And she sees there's a way he could do it alone, he has the will deep inside to bring Baby Girl peace all by himself—but, no, she won't even think of that. (285)

3.3 *The Need for Roots: George and Cocoa*

Indeed George lacks the Days' roots, and he has his own, which is the reason that he fails to understand the island's peculiar ways and, ultimately, what Mama Day is actually asking of him. As Daphne Lamothe suggests, George is a "cultural orphan" (2005: 160) that envies Cocoa not only her connection with a homeland and her apparent rootedness—he does not know about Cocoa's imperfect knowledge of her family history—but also the fact that she has a family at all. The son of an anonymous prostitute raised in an institution that imprinted in his mind all the principles and behavioral codes of western civilization, he deeply resents the fact of his rootlessness:

> New Orleans. Tampa. Miami. None of those cities seemed like the real South. Nothing like the place you came from. I was always in awe of the stories you told so easily about Willow Springs. To be born in a grandmother's house, to be able to walk and see where a great-grandfather and even great-great-grandfather was born. You had more than a family, you had a history. And I didn't even have a real last name. I'm sure my father and mother lied to each other about even their first names. How would he know years later that I might especially wonder about his? When the arrangement is to drop twenty bucks on a dresser for a woman, you figure that's all you've left behind. I had no choice but to emphasize my nows, while in back of all that stubbornness was the fear that you might think less of me. (Naylor 1988: 129–130)

It seems ironic that, within this couple, it should be the rootless character that pays more attention to roots and the individual's, the family's, and the community's past. It is because he knows nothing of his personal past that he is interested in his people's past, and because he was raised in the western frame of mind that, as a reaction, he is prouder of his community's culture and racial identity than Cocoa. This is made evident in the fight they have over Cocoa's make up; their "worst fight ever" (230). She, probably proving that she is indeed the descendant of Bascombe Wade, has a peculiarly light skin tone, which earned her the nickname cocoa. However, she seems to be ashamed of it and tries to cover it with a darker shade of foundation than she would really need. This type of shame about one's mixed origins is reminiscent, once more, of the theme of skin color predominant in African American literature and, more specifically, in Toni Morrison's *Paradise*, whose characters, in their obsession with 'eight-rockedness,' shun those with a lighter skin color. George, however, because of his lack of ancestors, is much more appreciative of them, regardless of their skin color or their past actions and deeds and does not like Cocoa's attempt at disguising her real roots. That is, since George does not have roots and is ashamed of this fact, he is highly appreciative of Cocoa's, while, on the other hand, Cocoa, having an incredibly rich yet traumatic family history does not make the effort to connect with it until it is too late. She, moreover, cannot understand George's refusal to share his highly limited past life with her for fear of her scorn:

> Oh, you'd hold a conversation—and you could make me laugh with the stories about some of your clients, about your partner's offbeat relatives and the niece who put chewing gum in the filing cabinet.
>
> And when I pressed you for *your* life, you'd say that you grew up in a boy's shelter, that it was hard, working your way through Columbia and getting set up in your own business. You'd mention a woman named Mrs. Jackson sometimes, the world lost a lot when she died, you said. But you'd never talk about your *feelings* surrounding any of that. 'Only the present has potential' is how you'd brush me off. Deal with the man in front of you. I was trying, George. But what you didn't understand is that I thought you didn't trust me enough to share those feelings. A person is made up of much more than the 'now.' (126–127. Italics in the original)

A person is made up of much more than the 'now,' indeed, but not George. For him, only the 'now' counts because he has no 'then,' which is what Cocoa, who takes her 'then' for granted, does not understand. However, her 'then' is not made fully accessible to Cocoa until after George's death. It is through the understanding of the reason that he died that she will eventually learn how to listen to those whispers in her family plot, how to interpret them and extract from them the true nature of her family's history. And because George's ashes have been spread on the sea below that same family plot—gaining, at last, his long-searched connection with the ancestral—he will serve as the intermediary. Moreover, Cocoa will not be the only one that will find meaning through George's death. Even though Miranda was more aware than Cocoa of the significance of the past in their present lives, it is only after his death that she is finally reconciled with her past traumatic memories and overcomes repression. She ponders this one Candle Night walk after George's demise:

> George done made it possible for all her Candle Walks to end right here from now on; the other place holds no more secrets that's left for her to find. The rest will lay in the hands of the Baby Girl—once she learns how to listen. But she's grieving for herself too much now to hear, 'cause she thinks that boy done left her. He's gone, but he ain't left her. Now, another one who broke his heart 'cause he couldn't let her go. So she's gotta get past the grieving for what she lost, to go on to the grieving for what was lost, before the child of Grace lives up to her name. (307–308)

Cocoa needs to become aware of her traumatic past, of the pain and suffering embedded in the true history of her family in order to start grieving or, in other words, to start the process of working through as a means to overcome the trauma and put an end to the repetition. She is grieving now, Miranda says, over her present loss: the loss of her husband. But when that grieving finishes—and it will finish in the healthy, gradual, accustomed length of time, since the trauma has not been avoided or repressed—she will have to start the process of recovering the memories that were repressed and avoided. That will take longer, but, once she learns how to listen, it will be accomplished. She will learn about Sapphira Wade, about the true story that is hers as well, and will unlock all the secrets buried in the whispers over the burial ground:

> I can't tell you her name [Sapphira's], 'cause it was never opened to me [Miranda]. That's a door for the child of Grace to walk through. And how many, if any, of them seven sons were his? Well, that's also left for her to find. And you'll help her, won't you? She says to George. One day she'll hear you, like you're hearing me. And there'll be another time—that I won't be here for—when she'll learn about the beginning of the Days. But she's gotta go away to come back to that kind of knowledge. And

> I came to tell you not to worry: whatever roads take her from here, they'll always lead her back to you. (308)

Miranda, once more, is right. Almost fifteen years later, Cocoa returns to her family's graveyard to talk with George. It is then that we realize that George has been dead for the whole narrative and that it is this conversation that we have been reading. At this point we also discover that Cocoa has remarried, has two sons—one of them named after her first husband—and that she has been periodically coming to the graveyard to talk to George. It is through these conversations that she ends up "finally opening her mind to the stories that she refused to hear while George was alive" (Donlon 1995: 24). However, the recovery process has not been fully completed. She is starting to understand, but she does not yet have the whole picture and, therefore, cannot find the words to explain it to her son:

> I guess one of the reasons I've been here so much is that I felt if we kept retracing our steps, we'd find out exactly what brought us to this slope near The Sound. But when I see you again, our versions will be different still. All of that would have been too complicated to tell a child. Mama Day was right—give him the simple truth. And it's the one truth about you that I hold on to. Because what really happened to us George? You see, that's what I mean—there are just too many sides to the whole story. (Naylor 1988: 310–311)

It is indeed necessary to find out and understand all the sides to one story, to be in touch with one's roots and history, because, in failing to do so, the individual risks losing that part of their personal identity that is linked to the collective and communal past. There are several examples of characters who, for one reason or another, fail to be connected to their group's identity through their shared past and the sense of rootedness that emanates from it. In Toni Morrison's *Tar Baby*, for example, Jadine fails to identify herself with the group with which she ought to identify. This poses problems for her identity as well as for her social relationships with members of that group. She sees herself as not belonging to the African American collectivity and, therefore, different from Son, her aunt and uncle and all the people in Eloe, where she feels excluded and out of place. Failing to see her own personal history as connected to that of her people distances her from her cultural sources and leaves her in a state of rootlessness, of personal instability that she is unable to overcome. In the words of Toni Morrison, Jadine is "cut off [from] her ancient properties" (qtd. in Wyatt 2004: 95), which is already a trauma in itself, materialized in the haunting presence of women holding their breasts. Jadine needs to work through her own personal trauma of rootlessness, but she cannot do so until she comes to terms with the traumatic memories of her community's history and how those memories are connected to her identity, both personal and collective.

It is left for the readers to discern whether Cocoa will finally get to the whole truth or if she will fail and, by doing so, if the repetition of the curse will be perpetuated. There is hope, but, in a highly typical move in trauma narratives, the author leaves an open ending, for, at the end of the narrative, she has not yet come to all the sides of the story. Unveiling all of these different sides is necessary—yet difficult—for the completion of the recovery process, as Miranda once tells George:

> [E]verybody wants to be right in a world where there ain't no right or wrong to be found. My side. He don't listen to my side. She don't listen to my side. Just like that chicken coop, everything got four sides: his side, her side, an outside, and an inside. All of it is the truth. But that takes a lot of work and young folks ain't about working hard no more. When getting at the truth starts to hurt, it's easier to turn away. (Naylor 1988: 230)

This multiplicity of sides to a (hi)story is reminiscent of Michael Rothberg's concept of multidirectional memory, which he qualifies as "meant to draw attention to the dynamic transfers that take place between diverse places and times during the act of remembrance" (2009: 11). This understanding of memory as "shared memory, memory that may have been initiated by individuals but that has been mediated through networks of communication, institutions of the state, and the social groupings of civil society" (Rothberg 2009: 15) highlights the several sides of stories and histories alike. It also counteracts what he calls "competitive memory," articulated around the notions "of the public sphere as a pregiven, limited space in which already-established groups engage in a life-and-death struggle" (5), and "that the boundaries of memory parallel the boundaries of group identity" (5). That is, instead of assuming that the memories that may be central to the formation of collective identities must compete among themselves for public recognition based on their perceived uniqueness (like the memory stubbornly maintained by the Ruby elders), Rothberg posits that all memories can coalesce and work towards setting "the very grounds on which people construct and act upon visions of justice" (Rothberg 2009: 19).

Although Rothberg is trying to counteract with his notion the lately widespread argument that an attention to the memory of the Holocaust has often obscured and perhaps prevented attention to other postcolonial traumas, his concept of multidirectional memory can also be applied to the two novels analyzed in this chapter. Both in *Paradise* and in *Mama Day* we are confronted with examples of competitive memories that do not allow for a recognition of the multidirectionality of memory "as subject to ongoing negotiation, cross-referencing, and borrowing; as productive and not privative" (Rothberg 2009: 3). That is, whereas the Ruby elders have imposed a strict repetition of one version of memory not allowing the creation and sharing of others, the citizens of Willow Springs—and more specifically, the Day family—have allowed for the development of a myriad of parallel remembrances but failed to maintain and transmit their recollection of the original memory. In both cases, therefore, there has been a failure to construct "a malleable discursive space in which groups do not simply articulate established positions but actually come into being through their dialogical interactions with others" (Rothberg 2009: 5), which has resulted in the repetition of violence and tragedy. The recovery and retelling of history and memory, consequently, should be done not in a competitive and hierarchical way, but in a manner that allows individuals, as well as communities, to move forward instead of stalling in the past and look upon the future in order to improve that future. The contrary reaction—that of repression/suppression—and its consequences will be analyzed in the following chapter.

CHAPTER 3

The Dangers of Repression/Suppression: Toni Morrison's *Beloved*

1   Trauma and Hidden Memory

> Rien ne fixe une chose tellement intensément dans la mémoire comme souhait pour l'oublier.
> MICHEL E. DE MONTAIGNE[1]

How does memory work? Do we, as McCarthy argues in his novel *The Road*, "forget what [we] want to remember and [...] remember what [we] want to forget" (2009: 11)? Or do we appear to forget what in truth we have always remembered? Are Billy Pilgrim's memories in *Slaughterhouse 5* real or just fantastic rewritings of his war experiences? Why is Lianne so obsessed with memory and Alzheimer's in DeLillo's *Falling Man*? Is Gemma in Jane Yolen's *Briar Rose* truly unaware of her concentration camp experience or only feigning to be? Why should a society be so afraid of memories and yet give such reverential importance to the only person possessing them in Lowry's *The Giver*? Is Than, the mother in Lan Cao's *Monkey Bridge*, right in hiding the true memory of the past from her daughter or in disclosing it to her? Or both? Are our memories loyal accounts of the past? And if not, to what extent? If memory is, on its own, infinitely complex, when the disruptive force of trauma comes into play, the result can be a hauntingly intricate mechanism of opposing and, at the same time, complementing forces that can work in a myriad of ways and provide a myriad of answers to questions like those posed here.

When talking about trauma, special attention needs to be paid to the issue of memory, how experiences are encoded in it, if and how they are recovered by it, and how it affects the formation of individual and collective identity. Memory in its multiple forms—recurrent, unexpected, unwelcome, fading or even hidden—is a constant presence in any comprehensive work on trauma, especially works that, as in this case, intend to deal with the traumatic past. Moreover, given its psychological and sociological relevance, numerous scholars have devoted entire volumes to memory and its workings. Paul Ricoeur, for

---

1   Nothing fixes a thing so intensely in the memory as the wish to forget it.

example, in his extensive work *Memory, History, Forgetting*, has provided a full account of the mechanisms of memory, its uses and abuses, its relation to history, and the processes of forgetting and forgiving. Similarly, Michael Rothberg, in his *Multidirectional Memory*, proposes an interesting approach to memory from the point of view of postcolonial studies, trauma and the formation of collective identity. These are but two examples of the abundance of recent work devoted to memory, its workings and its relation with other spheres of the human experience, which testify to its standing in current psychological, cultural and theoretical debates.

However, memory is by nature unreliable. In addition to their natural tendency to gradually disappear and become modified with the passing of time, memories can be tampered with and even implanted, which makes the claim that they are faithful to the past at least disputable. Numerous studies (McNally 2003) have shown how memories can be modified or created in laboratory trials and subject studies, but we need not go into artificial environments to witness the malleability of human memory. The more an imagined event is thought about and repeated in a person's mind, the more likely it is for that person to actually believe it occurred (McNally 2003: 43). Indeed, examples of people that have come to believe their own lies by force of repeating them are abundant. In the same way, there are also instances in which a person can have a very clear memory of something that did not happen or that he/she did not witness—as in the case of groups of friends that tell the same anecdotal incident so often that another friend who was not present at the time may actually believe that he/she was.

Still, despite its inaccuracies, both individuals and societies tend to have a very strong hold on memory. It is highly significant in the formation of individual and collective identity, and it is very often the object of careful preservation. When a person's memory begins to fail, it is always considered a terrible loss, even feared as an illness and always resisted—at least initially in cases of dementia or Alzheimer's—by the individual in question. Moreover, individuals and communities alike maintain a somewhat ambivalent relationship with memory. As Ricoeur puts it, "memory defines itself [...] as a struggle against forgetting [...] [b]ut at the same time [...] we shun the specter of a memory that would never forget anything" (2006: 413). This is where trauma comes into play.

Surely all individuals would like to preserve memories of their happy moments so that they can revisit them whenever they want and experience again the pleasurable feeling associated with them. However, when dealing with painful or traumatic experiences, the response varies. When confronted with experiences of trauma and terror, extreme physical or psychological pain and fear for one's life and personal integrity, individuals might very much prefer to "banish" those experiences (Herman 2001: 1), to forget them in such a way that they never have to deal with them again. Sometimes, however, the individuals affected by traumatic experiences may feel that the memories resulting from them are branded on their minds, and, try as they might, they cannot shed them. In any case, what is clear is that reliving traumatic experiences and the feelings they bring up is not normally welcome to those who went through them; often the persons in question avoid or attempt to avoid such memories.

In light of this we must pose the following questions: can victims of trauma ever obtain complete erasure of their painful experiences? Does repression really exist? And, if it does, is this the same as forgetting? What roles do the respective wills of the individual and the collective play in all this? To begin with the first set of questions, we must turn to an ongoing debate in the field of trauma studies. Although traditional accounts of trauma (Freud, Caruth, Herman, etc.) argue in favor of the existence of a series of mechanisms of repression that attempt to hide the impact of trauma in the unconscious in order to protect the psyche from its blunt force, new voices have recently arisen that attempt to refute this idea. In his work *Remembering Trauma* Richard McNally postulates the following conclusions:

> First, people remember horrific experiences all too well. Victims are seldom incapable of remembering their trauma. Second, people sometimes do not think about disturbing events for long periods of time, only to be reminded of them later. However, events that are experienced as overwhelmingly traumatic at the time of their occurrence rarely slip from awareness. Third, there is no reason to postulate a special mechanism of repression or dissociation to explain why people may not think about disturbing experiences for long periods. A failure to think about something does not entail an inability to remember it (amnesia). (2003: 2)

In addition to offering ample proof extracted from numerous clinical and psychological experiments with different traumatized and non-traumatized subjects that, in his view, support his claim that traumatic memory becomes forever present in the mind of its victims and disprove other previous experiments that seemed to suggest the contrary, McNally provides a number of examples in which memories of traumatic experiences remain accessible to conscious recall. In disproving Caruth's and other trauma theorists' claims that a traumatic event cannot be recorded and, therefore, remembered properly due to its sheer impact in the mind of its victim (claims strongly based on the works of influential psychiatrists like Judith Herman and Bessel van der Kolk),

McNally forces us to consider the difference between an incapacity to remember and a preference not to do so, as well as to establish a clear terminology to refer to either process.

As McNally points out, the concept behind the term 'repression' has evolved in a way that has detached itself from the original Freudian idea of an automatic response of the psyche in order to protect the ego—thus conferring to it an unmistakable psychoanalytical sense—in order to be understood as "the mundane notion of 'trying not to think about something unpleasant'" (McNally 2003: 170). As a consequence, a variety of terms have evolved as an attempt to establish a differentiation between the different modes of blocking traumatic memories. Most of these differentiations in terms revolve around the idea that there exist two types of blockages: conscious and unconscious. Whereas the former would be willingly exerted by the individual him/herself in an attempt to bar painful memories from entering conscious recall—that is, the aforementioned 'trying not to think about something unpleasant'—the latter would deal with the more Freudian concept of a psychic, automatic mechanism of self-preservation. Sigmund Freud himself maintained that repression could be either conscious or unconscious (McNally 2003: 169), although he used the concepts of repression and suppression interchangeably. Later on, several theorists agreed in establishing a distinction between the two and apply the term repression to the unconscious act and the term suppression to the more conscious one willingly exerted by the individual.

Nevertheless, it is important to differentiate not only repression (unconscious blockage, if we accept that such a mechanism exists) from suppression (the willful effort not to remember something), but also from forgetting. Memory, McNally cautions, is not a perfect recording mechanism, like a video camera, and, with the passing of time, we tend to naturally forget things, without the need for repressive or suppressive forces. What McNally posits is that the human mind is a highly complex mechanism, and a multitude of factors influence the way in which we encode and recover events. Consequently, there are several types of dysfunctions that can occur due to as many possible reasons and we should be careful when we ascribe names to what we or other people experience. Not every type of amnesia is suppressive or traumatic, and not every trauma necessarily entails amnesia. A correct differentiation in terms is necessary if we want to properly deal with these issues.[2]

---

2   Other terms have been suggested by several theorists and scholars to account for these and similar concepts. Accordingly, we have Abraham and Torok's 'introjection and incorporation,' Freud's 'dynamic' or 'constitutive repression' or the more widespread 'dissociation.' However, for the sake of clarity, I will be using 'repression' to refer to unconscious blockages

To return to the questions posited above, once we have established the difference between repression, suppression and forgetting, we must ponder to what degree are any of these processes completely conscious or unconscious. As has been mentioned before, the most psychoanalytically-inclined branch in trauma studies embodied by Cathy Caruth, Shoshana Felman and Geoffrey Hartman, among others, argue that repression is always automatic yet not necessarily complete because traumatic memories, in their view, are bound to reappear after a period of latency. In a somehow more radical view of the matter, Richard McNally refers to unconscious repression as "a piece of psychiatric folklore devoid of convincing empirical support" (2003: 275). He maintains that when an event is traumatizing enough, the most common psychological response would tend more towards unavoidable remembering and fixation than towards forgetting. Similarly, he also argues that voluntary attempts to forget are likewise inefficient, for there is a marked difference between attempting to block an experience or a memory and actually succeeding in doing so (McNally 2003: 152).

In the middle of this spectrum we find the positions of other scholars who posit that perhaps both mechanisms—conscious suppression and unconscious repression—are at play in the face of a traumatic impact. As Kalí Tal argues, human beings present "a sort of subconscious but intentional ignorance," which makes us "not notice a great deal of what we do not want to notice" (1996: 133–134). This, as will be seen during my analysis of *Beloved*, is precisely my position. Although I agree with McNally in that the apparent forgetting behind many non-verbalized memories of trauma may be due, for the most part, to willing attempts at suppression rather than to an automatic inability to record or remember the traumatic event in question, I argue that that decision to not remember something may also stem from a natural and therefore innate instinct for self-preservation, hence my use of the repression/suppression dichotomy.

Similar to this is the process of conscious denial. In conscious denial, the subject not only attempts to block the thoughts and memories surrounding his/her unpleasant experiences, he/she intends to convince him/herself—or at least to outwardly project the impression—that they never actually happened by means of a process of constant and systematic negation. Some trauma victims may maintain that they never suffered any trauma, that they never were at the site at which the traumatic event they survived took place, or they

---

of traumatic memories, 'suppression' for willing avoidance of memories and 'forgetting' as a neutral term strictly meaning a failure to bring a memory into conscious recall.

consistently deny having any memories of it. They build up a strong façade in order to keep the curiosity or pity of others, as well as their own pain, at bay. In this case, what we encounter is not a refusal to remember, but the conscious denial of the trauma itself. This of course, has its own negative consequences that can be summed up in an inability to work through the trauma. If the victim does not want to recognize that something traumatic occurred, he/she will not want to face the necessity of coming to terms with it and will refuse any treatment or help.

This denial, this refusal to acknowledge the loss, is therefore inextricably linked to the silence that many victims maintain regarding their traumas. Either driven by a fear of not being understood or listened to, by shame, by a sheer inability to put a traumatic experience into coherent wording, or by the necessity of ignoring the memories of a painful event, a trauma survivor might choose to remain silent about his/her experience. This silence, as is the case in the African American context, may also be connected to shame, as Bouson has described in depth and as was detailed in the first chapter of this volume. In any case, the existence of silence with regard to a particular traumatic memory or set of memories does not mean that either the individual or the community is *unable* to talk about his/her experience, it is rather that they are not *willing* to do so or, more accurately, that by means of willingly refusing to voice the trauma, the victims have rendered themselves incapable of doing so. This, as mentioned before, is deeply connected to the inarticulatedness of trauma and Toni Morrison's 'the unspeakable,' which is especially present in her novel *Beloved*.

If we maintain, as explained before, that experiences of trauma—regardless of how dramatically impacting they are—are never forgotten but, conversely, imprinted forever in an as yet indeterminate place within the tissues of the brain, then we find that even if the individual or the community manages to keep them at bay for some time, they are bound to reappear sooner or later. The past, Ricoeur says, "once experienced is indestructible" (2006: 445), and this is the reason that it must be recognized and converted into a more or less coherent narrative that not only testifies to the traumas of the past but also helps individuals and communities work towards some degree of agency in the present and future.

When this recuperation and rewriting fails, as we saw in the previous chapter, the cycles of traumatic violence—or, as in the case of the African American traumatic history, the mechanisms that put that violence in place—are bound to repeat themselves. This could be perceived as a repetition of the traumatic experiences themselves, as if history was repeated and repeated, almost as a form of haunting; a ghostly presence intent on constantly reminding the victim and the affected communities of the suffering and trauma experienced in their pasts. This is what Freud referred to as "the uncanny" (Kuo 2009: 86), and defined as "the once familiar that was defamiliarized through repression and that induced a compulsive return to the same place" (LaCapra 1998: 38). Several other authors have also dealt with this repetitive aspect of traumatic memory by means of different names (ghostly presences, the phantom, etc.) yet, in essence, they all refer to the same thing: "[S]omething which is secretly familiar [...], which has undergone repression and then returned from it" (Kuo 2009: 86). In this sense, the phantom, or the ghost, does not have the popular meaning of the spirit of a loved one trapped at some point during the afterlife and returned to haunt the living in order to deal with some unfinished business. Rather, it is understood as the gaps in memory created by the silencing of stories of trauma. "[W]hat haunts are not the dead," Abraham says, "but the gaps left within us by the secrets of others" (1994: 171). This is all very relevant for the discussion of Toni Morrison's *Beloved*, as we will see in due course, for in that novel we see how the ghostly presence—the phantom of suppressed, unvoiced past traumatic memories—makes itself visible in the form of Beloved and comes back to haunt the living and remind them of what they have attempted to forget.

But before launching into the discussion of *Beloved*, one more aspect of traumatic repression that is significant for our understanding of Morrison's text needs to be mentioned: the issue of collective repression. If the idea of collective trauma was controversial, this is even more so, and it is only with great consideration that it is mentioned here. The idea of a community or even a small group of people suffering from automatic repression of exactly the same memories is indeed ludicrous, but it may seem slightly more reasonable if repression—or rather suppression, denial or silence—is understood in its broader sense of 'trying not to think about something.' Collective suppression would then be a kind of implicit pact, a secret that all the members within a community have tacitly agreed to maintain. If remembering painful events is potentially damaging for an individual and thus tends to be resisted, it seems reasonable to think that it could work similarly for communities. Though not a widely accepted idea, the issue of collective repression, or rather the collective repercussions of repression, does appear in the work of several authors. In his work on history, memory and the processes of forgetting, Paul Ricoeur states the following: "[I]ndividual manifestations of forgetting are inextricably mixed with its collective forms, to the point that the most troubling experiences of forgetting, such as obsession, display their most malevolent effects only on the scale of collective memories" (2006: 443–444). In other words, the consequences of individual repressions/suppressions of the same or similar events—as in the case of individual experiences during slavery—affect, in their aftermath, the whole community and the memory that gets passed on. It makes sense: if a person refuses to speak about a particular event or set of events (denial/silence), it is unlikely that his/her memory of them will be passed onto his/her descendants. However, this is not to say that those descendants are not aware of them. They may not know the specific details, but, in the case of an atrocity committed against a whole people—such as slavery—they can infer the gist of the story. The memory, therefore, *is* passed on, though in an imperfect form, which is what allows for the resurfacing of the hidden trauma in later generations.

Although psychoanalyst Nicolas Abraham does not explain it in these terms, he seems to come to a similar conclusion when he says that "[t]he phantom is a formation of the unconscious that has never been conscious—for good reason. It passes—in a way yet to be determined—from the parent's unconscious to the child's" (Abraham and Torok 1994: 173). This transmission is seen as the consequence of silence (Rand 1994c: 168) and, Abraham continues, keeps repeating itself but with diminishing force from generation to generation until it disappears. Except—and this is especially relevant in the case of the African American community—"when shared or complementary phantoms find a way of being established as social practices along the lines of *staged words*" (Abraham and Torok 1994: 176). That is, except in the cases in which the knowledge of a shared traumatic past becomes appropriated as the fundamental aspect of a collective identity formation.

Toni Morrison's *Beloved* offers a powerful example not only of the current recovering of the traumatic past as a pillar for the formation of collective identity, but also of the representation in literature of the numerous aspects of trauma and the various forms of traumatic repression/suppression and their consequences and perils for both the individual and the community.

2   *Beloved*: The F/Hateful Power of Repressed Trauma

> For a baby she throws a powerful spell
> No more powerful than the way I loved her.
> TONI MORRISON, *Beloved*

Much has been written, said and discussed about this particular piece of fiction by Toni Morrison. In fact, it may be said that it is this story about haunting, about a love that turned out to be "too thick" (Morrison 2005: 193), and about revenge, that has made her the world-renowned author that she is today. It is not the purpose of this volume to gather all the criticism that this novel has received or to repeat the countless analyses that it has elicited.[3] Moreover, with such a vast critical production as this particular book has generated, it seems especially difficult to attempt to provide something fully innovative or as of yet unsaid on the matter. As a consequence, my intention here is not to provide a compilation of what others have written about *Beloved*, nor to offer an astonishing new approach to it, for, indeed, the view of this novel as a representation of unresolved trauma that I present here has already been accounted for by various critics. What has not been done, however, is to place it alongside the other two sides of the spectrum comprising the different attitudes of various communities towards collective memory. My reading of Beloved as the return of the repressed/suppressed serves as a middle ground between the substitution and subsequent forgetting of a traumatic past by means of a myth—as analyzed in chapter two—and the benefits that a willful recovering of that forgotten or suppressed past may have for individuals and communities alike—as analyzed in chapter four. That is, I contend that communities may feel the necessity to disguise the memories of their traumatic past or to silence them, but that neither of these two positions is favorable in terms of the recovering, sharing and rewriting of those memories that is advisable in the work of giving voice to trauma and attempting to put a stop to the perpetuation of the conduct and structures that brought those traumatic experiences into being in the first place.

2.1   *"The Unspeakable": Repressive Signs in* Beloved's *Characters*

Beloved was once defined as "the ghost in America's collective memory" (Kuo 2009: 87), and this definition seems to be particularly accurate for it stands for all those "sixty million and more" to whom the novel is dedicated; all those unknown and unaccounted for slaves who perished during the middle passage and whose bodies were mercilessly dumped into the sea. This atrocity, this big, black stain on the history of the United States of America lies hidden and scarcely mentioned or recognized in the collective unconscious of its inhabitants; banned from their master narrative, and still remembered with shame, it has been, by all accounts, repressed from America's collective consciousness.

Repression and suppression, therefore, are at the core of this narrative, which is the reason that their analysis will be dealt with in this section of the

---

3   James Phelan, for example, has discussed in depth the narrative techniques employed in the novel, and connected them to the experience of the reader and to how Morrison dictates the ethical position that he/she may take towards the events and character portrayed there. See Phelan 1993 and 1998.

present book. Clear signs of psychological repression, conscious suppression/silence, or both, are shown—albeit in different degrees—in all four of the main (human) characters of the novel. To them, we could add a fifth, more abstract character: that of the collective. Thus, Sethe, Paul D, Baby Suggs, Denver and the community of Cincinnati, Ohio, all show in their own peculiar ways the marks of an overwhelmingly tragic past, slavery, which, in most cases, is mixed with their own, personal, unacknowledged stories of loss and pain. For Sethe these two different types of memories are so interwoven that to recall one type is to bring about the other. Both are equally unwelcome, yet both are unavoidable. She is equally haunted by the memories of her past life as a slave; of her mother's absence, abandonment and tragic death; of the brutality suffered at the hands of her last owner and his two nephews; and of the circumstances surrounding her dramatic escape into freedom.

Yet, the book seems to ask, how can freedom ever reach a slave, or even an ex-slave? It does not. For Sethe, at least, it does not, because, after twenty-eight days of almost complete happiness and in spite of the unexplained absence of her husband, her past catches up to her and moves her to drastic and unthinkable action. Cornered by her master, one of his despicable nephews and a slave catcher, she decides to slay all her children rather than see them returned to the horrific institution of slavery. The two eldest boys survive, as does the younger girl. Her sister, however, does not and from that point on, there is no rest for Sethe or the other inhabitants of 124 Bluestone Road. They are now bound to another type of slavery, an equally cruel and relentless bondage: trauma and traumatic memory.

As mentioned above, the first and most typical impulse towards self-preservation against the shattering force of trauma is some degree of unconscious repression or conscious suppression: banning the traumatic experience from consciousness and burying it deep in a place where its pain cannot be felt. This is precisely what Sethe attempts to do after she murders her own child. As Sethe herself once tells Paul D, she manages to "get along" because she does not "go inside" (Morrison 2005: 55), that is, she does not dwell on her traumatic past if she can help it. Consequently, a drastic form of blockage ensues in which every reminder of what both she and Baby Suggs—Sethe's mother-in-law—wordlessly agree to call the "unspeakable" (69) is consistently rejected. One peculiar way in which this is accomplished is by means of a striking, to say the least, form of color vision deficiency:

> Sethe looked at her hands, her bottle-green sleeves, and thought how little color there was in the house and how strange that she had not missed it the way Baby did. Deliberate, she thought, it must be deliberate,

because the last color she remembered was the pink chips in the headstone of her baby girl. After that she became as color conscious as a hen. Every dawn she worked at fruit pies, potato dishes and vegetables while the cook did the soup, meat and the rest. And she could not remember a molly apple or a yellow squash. Every dawn she saw the dawn, but never acknowledged or remarked its color. There was something wrong with that. It was as though one day she saw red baby blood, another day the pink gravestone chips, and that was the last of it. (46–47)

As a contrast to Baby Suggs, who, in the last years of her life, retreated to her room to "think about the colors of things" (208)—yet another "covert reference" to the problem of skin color and racism prevalent in Morrison's novels (Bouson 2000: 159. See also Pérez-Torres 1993: 693–694)—Sethe becomes "as color conscious as a hen" (Morrison 2005: 46). After 'the unspeakable' happened, Sethe willfully banishes all trace and knowledge of color tones both from her—grey—house and from her mind in an attempt to block any "visual reminders" (Offut Mathieson 1990: 7) of her most traumatic memory which, in turn, will be forever inextricably linked to two other colors: red and pink.

However, this blockage of reminders of the past does not restrict itself to merely her murderous act, it extends to, basically, her whole past before that and her experience of racism and its terrible conditions. Surely, her existence before such a dramatic outcome was spent in bondage, which, in itself is a highly traumatizing experience. As a consequence, her memories of that period are also unavoidably tinted by tragedy and trauma, and are so disturbing and painful that they eventually lead her to slay her own child. Insomuch as "every mention of her past life hurt" (Morrison 2005: 69), Sethe decides to avoid thinking, remembering or talking about it as much as she can and turns her future into "a matter of keeping the past at bay" (51). This way, 'the unspeakable' becomes not only the circumstances surrounding the death of her "crawling-already? baby" (110) but her whole history suffering from racist discrimination and slavery as well. Her daughter, Denver, who is aware of this, has in her turn learned to understand the pain that remembering the past causes her mother and agrees not to press for more information than what Sethe voluntarily offers: "Denver knew that her mother was through with it—for now anyway. The single slow blink of her eyes; the bottom lip sliding up slowly to cover the top; and then a nostril sigh, like the snuff of a candle flame—signs that Sethe had reached the point beyond which she would not go" (45).

This behavior is likewise mirrored by the rest of the town's neighbors. Though intent on giving Sethe the cold shoulder after the incident, the rest of the community has, at least, the decency not to mention it to her, even if it is the current gossip behind her back. Stamp Paid, one of the few—or rather, the only person—that still holds Sethe and her family in some esteem, ponders on the way in which an event as widely known as Sethe's infanticide is treated as a secret and the possible reasons for this: "How did information that had been in the newspaper become a secret that needed to be whispered in a pig yard? A secret from whom? Sethe, that's who" (199).

However, on closer examination, it is not so strange that this should be so. Rather, violent events like this one are frequently kept secret from the perpetrators, even by outsiders. Slavery, though not analogous to Sethe's crime—her actions, after all, were motivated by this very institution of which she was a victim—offers an interesting point of comparison. In the same way that Sethe's actions, though well known by all, were not openly discussed by the inhabitants of Cincinnati, a persistent silence has been kept in America and Europe over the issue of slavery. This is what Morrison termed "national amnesia" (Angelo 1994: 257) and what Kaplan refers to as "national forgetting" (2005: 66). In the cases of collective traumas such as the Holocaust or slavery the differentiation between oppressor and oppressed makes the act of forgetting much more complex, and one could wonder who it is that does the forgetting: the oppressed or the oppressor? Surely the traumatized group, just like traumatized individuals, may prefer to forget the traumatic experience or to hide it due to shame, but it seems even more convincing that that silence would be imposed by the perpetrator, who would also resist its later unveiling (Kaplan 2005: 67). This seems to be the case with African American slavery. Even though its atrocity and terrible consequences were commonly known, very little was said of them. For a long time, shame and guilt prevented it from entering the master narrative and it is only recently that the topic was approached in its crudest form and dealt with in books like *Beloved*, where such an imposed silence is symbolized by the repressive measures—Paul D's iron bit, Sethe's lashing that causes her to bite off her own tongue, etc.—that schoolteacher forces upon the people of Sweet Home (Turner 1992: 86–87). Notably too, schoolteacher is writing the 'official' history in ink made by Sethe. Surely the perpetrators of the institution of slavery would not want to acknowledge the existence of such a dark shadow in the history of the country, but outsiders (Europeans) might well have pointed it out. Yet, "the most incredible story of these events is that mass murder was not a story" (Garbus 1999: 59). If we extrapolate the behavior of the fictional community in *Beloved* towards the 'incident' in the yard to that of the real American and European society towards slavery, we can infer a series of reasons for this silence: disdain, fear, guilt at allowing it to happen or, quite simply, pity. In any case, slavery, like the murder of the infant in *Beloved*, still needs to be properly acknowledged and laid to rest before its memory can cease haunting the present.

Once again silence—in this case collective silence—is to blame for this lack of resolution. To different degrees, American society, *Beloved*'s fictive community of Cincinnati and Sethe are all engaged in a process of willful suppression that prevents a proper working through. Paul D, another main character in the novel, is likewise haunted by a past that he endeavors to conceal. He is also marked by his own personal trauma of slavery and shows clear signs of suppression. Just like Sethe, he has decided to "shut down a generous portion of his head" (Morrison 2005: 49), putting each and every one of his painful memories in a tobacco tin in his chest and mustering the strength necessary to keep them there: "It was some time before he could put Alfred, Georgia, Sixo, schoolteacher, Halle, his brothers, Sethe, Mister, the taste of iron, the sight of butter, the smell of hickory, notebook paper, one by one, into the tobacco tin lodged in his chest. By the time he got to 124 nothing in this world could pry it open" (133).

Indeed, Paul D has also suffered a great deal. Patronized by one master and cruelly mistreated by the next, he and the rest of slaves at Sweet Home planned to escape into freedom only to be apprehended, killed, and/or brutally punished. Paul D must learn to live with the uncertain knowledge of his brothers' demise, the horrific memory of one of his friend's torture and bloody death, and the insanity of the other friend. To this he adds his own shame at being put on an iron bit, chain-ganged and sold. Escaped and caught several times, he roamed the country after emancipation in order to avoid feeling too attached to anyplace or anybody. Slavery, he says, has taught him not to love anything too much lest it should be taken away, and that, he believes, was Sethe's main mistake:

> Risky, thought Paul D, very risky. For a used-to-be-slave woman to love anything that much was dangerous, especially if it was her children she had settled on to love. The best thing, he knew, was to love just a little bit; everything, just a little bit, so when they broke its back, or shoved it in a croaker sack, well, maybe you'd have a little love left for the next one. (54)

The inability to love is, according to Judith Herman (2001: 51), one of the possible psychological consequences of unresolved trauma. But this is something else. It is not that Paul D is unable to love; he is *unwilling*, which is a process very similar to voluntary suppression or silence. In both instances, it is the subject who chooses not to love or remember; it is the victim that engages in a willful effort to not feel the future pain that he foresees should any of those two actions take place. Nevertheless, and in spite of Paul D's previous intentions, he unexpectedly finds himself in love with Sethe, willing to form a family with her and share her past.

However, as it turns out, Paul D is not willing to share *all* of her past. When Stamp Paid confronts him with the news of Sethe's crime he shuts off completely and refuses to listen to or believe any of it, again activating suppression or denial:

> Paul D slid the clipping out from under Stamp's palm. The print meant nothing to him so he didn't even glance at it. He simply looked at the face, shaking his head no. No. At the mouth, you see. And no at whatever it was Stamp Paid wanted him to know. Because there was no way in hell a black face could appear in a newspaper if the story was about something anybody wanted to hear. [...]
>
> And he said so. 'This ain't her mouth. I know her mouth and this ain' it.' Before Stamp Paid could speak he said it and even while he spoke Paul D said it again. Oh, he heard all the old man was saying, but the more he heard, the stranger the lips in the drawing became. (183)

Such a refusal to recognize the truth that is staring him right in the face is part of his self-imposed mechanism of defense against trauma, and—interpreting the novel's symbolism in terms of trauma theory—what eventually drives him out of 124. Paul D would claim that the reason he progressively feels compelled to leave the house is because Beloved, the ghost of the murdered infant returned from the afterlife to haunt the living, has 'fixed' him, but if we read—as I propose—in the figure of Beloved a representation of trauma and the return of the repressed,[4] we come up with another explanation. If Beloved stands for the embodiment of the suppressed/repressed memory of 'the unspeakable' event, we could consequently argue that his being able to see and interact with her—something that, until the end of the narrative, no one else outside the family can do—means that he did inadvertently know the truth of Sethe's past all along. That is, he lived with it but did not want to acknowledge it/her,

---

[4] Other authors have ascribed to this character other interpretations—often in conjunction to the one proposed here (Heinze 1993: 179)—such as an embodied return of the figures of both Sethe's mother and her murdered child (Horvitz 1989), a real person traumatized by her experience during the Middle Passage and by the sexual abuse suffered since childhood from a white man (House 1990), Sethe's Doppelganger or "alter ego" (Heinze 1993: 177), or the externalization of the "rememory" of the "Sixty Million and more" dead during the Middle Passage (Flanagan 2002).

despised it/her, and even when he succumbed to its/her charm he despised himself for it. We should note that it is not until Paul D gives in to Beloved's seduction and beds her that his "tobacco tin" is pried open and he feels the full traumatic pain hidden in his bleeding "red heart" (Peach 1995: 96). Bedding Beloved is thus equated to knowing (here both in its common and biblical senses) the truth and is felt by Paul D as a shameful betrayal of Sethe. Not only has he engaged in a relationship with another woman, but he has uncovered her most deeply guarded secret. When all the secrets—both Sethe's and his own—are finally put out in the open, they become too much to bear and drive him away.

Surely the novel goes beyond this simplistic reading of events, and we cannot forget the fact that Beloved becomes pregnant with Paul D's child, nor that Morrison's insinuation that the pregnant, crazy character of Wild in *Jazz*, the novel following *Beloved*, could be Sethe's daughter (Carabi 1993: 96). Can we claim this to mean that working through is never accomplished, even at the end of the novel, and that the force of repression/Beloved is left to repeat and consolidate itself in the future? Moreover, is it safe to say that Beloved does not only embody trauma in this novel but also in other novels, that the symbol of repressed trauma as represented by this female character is a constant throughout Morrison's fiction? This is probably, in the vein of James Phelan's reader-response criticism, up to the reader to decide.

In any case, it is easy to see in the character of Beloved a metaphor for suppression/repression, which affects not only Sethe and Paul D but also Baby Suggs. Compliant with Sethe's attempt at blocking 'the unspeakable,' this is not the only secret that she keeps. Baby Suggs, in turn, is marked by her personal trauma of losing all but one of her eight children at the hands of slave masters only to have her last son, the one who bought her out of slavery, taken from her in unknown circumstances. When she is at last reunited with her grandchildren—though not her son—one of them is also ripped away from her by her deranged daughter-in-law. It is no wonder, after all this, that she decided to give it all up and go think about color. However, this is not the first time that she chose to escape from the shattering force of trauma by refusing to deal with it. Like the rest of the book's characters, she has had her share of repression and denial. " 'My first-born,' " she says. "All I can remember of her is how she loved the burned bottom of bread. Can you beat that? Eight children and that's all I remember.' " To which Sethe knowingly replies: " 'That's all you let yourself remember' " (Morrison 2005: 6). This, of course, is not the only instance in which Baby Suggs has consciously avoided the truth to keep herself from feeling pain. We can see another—more infantile—example when she recalls how news about the death of two of her daughters reached her:

Nancy and Famous died in a ship off the Virginia coast before it set sail for Savannah. That much she knew. The overseer at Whitlow's place brought her the news, more from a wish to have his own way with her than from the kindness of his heart. The captain waited three weeks in port, to get a full cargo before setting off. Of the slaves in the hold that didn't make it, he said, two were Whitlow pickaninnies name of ...

But she knew their names. She knew, and covered her ears with her fists to keep from hearing them come from his mouth. (169)

Baby Suggs refuses to listen to what she knows will hurt her. Just like Paul D and Denver. In an analogous manner to her grandmother and Paul D, Denver shows signs of willful denial by preferring to go deaf rather than listening to the truth about her first few months of life:

'Didn't your mother get locked away for murder? Wasn't you in there with her when she went?'

It was the second question that made it impossible for so long to ask Sethe about the first. The thing that leapt up had been coiled in just a place: a darkness, a stone, and some other thing that moved by itself. She went deaf rather than hear the answer, and like the little four o'clocks that searched openly for sunlight, then closed themselves tightly when it left, Denver kept watch for the baby and withdrew from everything else. (123)

Denver spent two years in her deaf state. Two years keeping watch for the baby, which makes her, probably, the character with the strongest relationship with the ghost and, therefore—if we abide by this interpretation of the figure of Beloved—with the deepest case of suppression. Whereas her mother and grandmother are constantly intent on "keeping the past at bay" (51) yet find themselves repeatedly reminded of it, Denver manages a complete blockage, only shattered by the questions posed by a boy at school. Yet, she realizes, the knowledge had always been there: "But the thing that leapt up in her when he asked it was a thing that had been lying there all along" (121). This knowledge, this 'thing' that leapt up in her had been completely hidden in "a darkness" (123), yet latently present nonetheless and ready to leap at the least provocation.

The reason Denver manages to keep a stronger hold on her traumatic memories is, paradoxically, that she does not actually have those memories of trauma. Born already out of slavery during her mother's flight from it, she—strictly speaking—only knows what little her mother and her grandmother have managed to tell her, which was not much. What is more, she was only a new-born baby when 'the unspeakable' thing happened and was only four months old when she and her mother were released from prison. And yet, the knowledge is still there, "coiled" as she puts it (123). Maybe because of this, maybe because she "took her mother's milk right along with the blood of her sister" (179), she develops an extremely intense relationship with the baby's ghost. It was the first thing that Denver heard after her two years of being deaf, and Denver herself is the first person to recognize Beloved as the incarnation of the baby's ghost.

Such a tight relationship with the ghost/traumatic memory makes her resent the only person that could give her a chance of leading a normal life in a normal family. When Paul D arrives and stomps the ghost out—that is, for a moment triggers the process of working through in the inhabitants of 124—Sethe welcomes him and is willing to share her experiences with him, but Denver refuses to let go of the ghost's company—that is, she refuses to overcome her suppressed memories of trauma—and longs for her return. When the return takes place and the ghost becomes embodied in the person of Beloved, she immediately takes it upon herself to nurse the newcomer back to health and envies the moments of intimacy that Beloved spends with Sethe. Fortunately for Denver, she manages to break free from Beloved's consuming attention when she realizes the harmful potential that she has.

As will be discussed, Denver is the only character in the novel that manages to properly overcome suppression and start the arduous process of working through her traumas. She is also the only character that did not live under slavery and thus does not retain its traumatic memories. Her personal traumas, too, are directly related to the one event that she, in contrast to the rest of characters in the book with the exception of Paul D, could not experience personally or did but could not have recorded given her tender age. Even though she did not go through the traumatic experiences in question, she nonetheless is aware of them, and their significance and—perhaps more importantly—the impact they have had on the lives of the people surrounding her have shaped her personality and attitude to life. She, for instance, exhibits a clear case of hyper vigilance, one of the possible signs of PTSD (Herman 2001: 35). Right after being asked the question that made her 'coiled' memories leap up at her from their dark place, she stops going to school and refuses to leave the yard at all. Convinced—like the inhabitants of Ruby in *Paradise*—that danger came from without, she apprehensively looks out for it at all times:

> All the time I'm afraid the thing that happened that made it all right for my mother to kill my sister could happen again. I need to know what that thing might be, but I don't want to. Whatever it is, it comes from outside

this house, outside the yard, and it can come right on in the yard if it wants to. So I never leave this house and I watch over the yard, so it can't happen again and my mother won't have to kill me too. Not since Miss Lady Jones' house have I left 124 by myself. Never. The only other times—two times in all—I was with my mother. (242–243)

The community also plays a significant role in the story and has its own share of traumas and silencing. Slavery, like the Holocaust, is preeminently a collective trauma. It affected an entire people and its memory is still maintained nowadays by their descendants. And, as has been mentioned, both traumas served to establish the basis for the construction of the collective identities of the communities affected by them. And yet, as mentioned above, a community may implicitly agree to maintain a secret, that is, to suppress certain parts of their past if those are too painful or shameful to be included in the official narrative, yet need nevertheless to remember and acknowledge them if there is to be a reworking of the trauma and some hope of stopping its repetition. The collective silencing of that traumatic memory is what Morrison referred to as "national amnesia" (Angelo 1994: 257) and what she unearths and represents in *Beloved*. Nicola King states this idea when he argues that the term 'rememory' that appears repeatedly throughout the narrative refers both to the effort that Sethe has to make in order to recall the specific—fictive—traumatic events in her past and to the other, more general—sadly real—events in the history of America "whose remembering and representation is a necessary political act" (King 2000: 151). Fei-hsuan Kuo views *Beloved* as a response to a political context—Reaganism—in which the history of slavery had been consistently denied and refused to be acknowledged as having any "lasting traumatic consequences" (Kuo 2009: 83).

Insomuch as this history of slavery was also silenced by African Americans themselves, due to shame (see Bouson 2000), they are the foremost interested party in remembering and acknowledging their painful past in order to put a stop to its haunting and to the perpetuation of the structures that brought slavery into being. This is the type of African American society that Morrison had in mind when she wrote *Beloved*, and this is the collectivity embodied in the community of Cincinnati as portrayed in the book. Most of them ex-slaves, they are all likely to have personal traumas of their own similar to those of Sethe, Baby Suggs or Paul D, and, like these characters, rather than facing those traumas and coming to terms with them, they are likely to suppress them in order to avoid painful memories. The fifth character suffering from the consequences of repression is, therefore, the community. According to David Lawrence,

> The black community of Cincinnati is caught in a cycle of self-denial, a suffocating repression of fundamental bodily needs and wants. The inability to articulate such embodied experience, to find a text for the desiring body within communal codes, obstructs self-knowledge and does violence to the fabric of the community. (1991: 189)

Indeed, the effort to keep so many secrets hidden and buried within the folds of a collective memory can and will do violence to "the fabric of the community," wearing it out until it tears. In the case of *Beloved*, the event that provoked the tearing was Sethe's unspeakable act. From that point on, a community that had been previously united, that, led by Baby Suggs, had even worked together to heal their wounds, to dance, laugh, cry and love their bodies as no one had loved them before, converted all their fear into hatred and turned their backs on the inhabitants of 124. Such a reaction is understandable if we pause to consider its real significance for them: all of them ex-slaves, carrying the weight of their personal traumas, these men and women have arrived in the one place in which they can be free, own a house, be their own masters, and enjoy the company of others in their same situation. Then, somebody who has just arrived from the outside presents them with a scene that could very well have been taken out of the past that each and every one of them had endeavored so hard to suppress. That person, the action itself, and anybody and anything related to her, are to be shunned as a bad influence, as a threat to their hopes of forgetting their own traumas.

It is only when help is asked for, when Denver wakes up and starts fighting to overcome her trauma, that the community decides to follow her example and reunite to help "stomp" the past out (Morrison 2005: 302). Just as they decided to unite against the common threat of further trauma at the hands of Sethe and the memory of her crime, when the ghost of the murdered baby returns from the dead to seek vengeance—thus making the threat bigger and more dangerous—they recognize the necessity of reuniting:

> As long as the ghost showed out from its ghostly place—shaking stuff, crying, smashing and such—Ella respected it. But if it took flesh and came in her world, well the shoe was on the other foot. She didn't mind a little communication between the two worlds, but this was an invasion. (302)

2.2 A Ghost (Hi)story: Beloved as the Return of the Repressed

The invasion that Ella experiences (Morrison 2005: 302) is none other than the return of the repressed that Freud talked about. Whatever the force of the repression, memories are bound to reappear in a variety of forms. From intrusive images to nightmares and dreams, passing through compulsions, ticks and neuroses, among others, there is always a reminder of what the psyche—or the self—has endeavored but failed to hide. Gloria Naylor explains this same idea, albeit in a far more poetic form, in her novel *The Women of Brewster Place*:

> Time's passage through the memory is like molten glass that can be opaque or crystallize at any given moment at will: a thousand days are melted into one conversation, one glance, one hurt, and one hurt can be so shattered and sprinkled over a thousand days. It is silent and elusive, refusing to be dammed and dripped out day by day; it swirls through the mind while an entire lifetime can ride like foam on the deceptive, transparent waves and get sprayed onto the consciousness at ragged, unexpected intervals. (1983: 35)

The memory of the past, as Sethe also realizes, "[c]omes back whether you like it or not" (Morrison 2005: 16), like the memories of Sweet Home that come "rolling, rolling, rolling out before [Sethe's] eyes" (7) despite all her efforts to forget a place in which "there was not a leaf that did not make her want to scream" (7). Even the memories she never knew she had can squeeze their way between one thought and the next and surprise her at the most unexpected moment:

> Sethe walked over to a chair, lifted a sheet and stretched it as wide as her arms would go. Then she folded, refolded and double-folded it. She took another. Neither was completely dry but the folding felt too fine to stop. She had to do something with her hands because she was remembering something she had forgotten she knew. Something privately shameful that had seeped into a slit in her mind right behind the slap on her face and the circled cross. (73)

Keeping oneself active is, indeed, one way of keeping the intrusive force of the past at bay. When the brain is idle, or caught off-guard, as during sleep, recurrent images or dreams are more likely to appear. On the other hand, when in waking life one is intent on 'not thinking' about something, the individual stands a better chance of achieving their purpose. Morrison is aware of this: *Beloved* is not the only novel of hers in which such an overt avoidance of idleness is sought in order to keep the mind active and prevent it from remembering pain. *Jazz* includes a similar passage:

> They are all like that, these women. Waiting for the ease, the space that need not be filled with anything other than the drift of their own thoughts. But they wouldn't like it. They are busy and thinking of ways to be busier because such a space of nothing pressing to do would knock them down. No fields of cowslips will rush into that opening, nor mornings free of flies and heat when the light is shy. No. Not at all. They fill their mind and hands with soap and repair and dicey confrontations because what is waiting for them, in a suddenly idle moment, is the seep of rage. Molten. Thick and slow-moving. Mindful and particular about what in its path it chooses to bury. Or else, into a beat of time, and sideways under their breasts, slips a sorrow they don't know where from. (Morrison 1992: 16)

What Morrison suggests here is that every African American woman—or member of the African American community, one could argue—has suffered the consequences of a perpetuated history of continued oppression and racism, and is used to suppressing those painful traumatic memories. And yet, as Bouson has put it, not only is Morrison intent on portraying the racist and violent treatment of African Americans across centuries and the efforts of the different individuals—and, consequently, the community—of keeping the memories of that past at bay, she also "conveys the haunting and driven quality of traumatic and humiliated memory as she depicts the 'rememories'— that is, spontaneous recurrences of the past—that plague her characters" (Bouson 2000: 3). Perhaps one of the most representative characters in Morrison's fiction, Sethe is, indeed, well accustomed to this type of reawakening, which prevents both individuals and communities from attempting to utilize that past in order to work towards the future. Her brain, after all, "was not interested in the future. Loaded with the past and hungry for more, it left her no room to imagine, let alone plan for, the next day" (Morrison 2005: 83). Stuck in the past as Sethe already is, the events narrated in the narrative's present time only serve to highlight this tendency. Reawakened by the presence of Paul D and of Beloved, representatives of, respectively, her past life as a slave and the murder of her own child, memories keep intruding into Sethe's consciousness. Those passages, narrated as they are remembered, gradually give the reader the whole dramatic picture of Sethe's past, together with that of Baby Suggs and Paul D. The disorderliness of narrative linearity only serves to highlight the disruptive aspect of trauma in the minds of its victims. Sethe is eerily conscious of the disruptive potential that hidden memories have; she even warns her daughter Denver against revisiting the past—both mentally and physically:

> Some things go. Pass on. Some things just stay. I used to think it was my rememory. You know. Some things you forget. Other things you never do. But it's not. Places, places are still there. If a house burns down, it's gone, but the place—the picture of it—stays, and not just in my rememory, but out there, in the world. [...] Someday you be walking down the road and you hear something or see something going on. So clear. And you think it's you thinking it up. A thought picture. But no. It's when you bump into a rememory that belongs to somebody else. Where I was before I came here, that place is real. It's never going away. Even if the whole farm—every tree and grass blade of it dies. The picture is still there and what's more, if you go there—you who never was there—if you go there and stand in the place where it was, it will happen again; it will be there for you, waiting for you. So, Denver, you can't never go there. Never. Because even though it's all over—over and done with—it's going to always be there waiting for you. (43–44)

Through Sethe's voice in the passage above, Morrison seems to intertwine theories of trauma—of the things you forget and those you never do, as well as notions of the transmission of trauma—with a version of Nora's *Lieux de Mémoire*. Of course it is not my purpose to suggest that Morrison necessarily had these two theories in mind when she wrote this passage, but the passage is highly suggestive of a view of trauma and traumatic space as inextricably linked with the notion of memory. Here, Morrison seems to imagine the places in which trauma occurred as impregnated with the memory (or the image/picture) of it, a concept that is decidedly reminiscent of Pierre Nora's, in the purest sense, sites of memory. However—and here fiction beautifully departs from theory[5]—Morrison's narrative presents those spaces as if the memories imbued in them were invisible clouds of gas that can possess anyone who would pass by and breathe them. Even if, Sethe suggests, that person has nothing to do with that memory they are vulnerable to such sites of trauma, even if the person in question never experienced or heard about it (which leads us back to the notion of intergenerational and non-survivor's trauma). In other words, Sethe conceives the notion of 'rememory' in such a way that "trauma on the

---

5 There is actually one instance in which a theoretical trauma critic points to something similar to what Morrison suggests here. In *Writing History, Writing Trauma*, LaCapra references the power of traumatic reminiscence embedded in places by stating that "the ghosts of the past [...] roam the post-traumatic world and are not entirely 'owned' as 'one's own' by any individual or group. If they haunt a house (a nation, a group), they come to disturb all who live—*perhaps even pass through*—that house" (2001: 215. Emphasis added).

mind" becomes "externalized so that those who did not experience it directly can still encounter it" (Flanagan 2002: 395). Obviously, this notion does not entirely correspond to how reality works or how individuals actually feel when approaching a site of memory; it corresponds to a vision of place as expanding, as alive, as never staying put. Otherwise, if the first notion were true, that is, if anyone could 'bump into' anyone else's 'rememory' just by passing through the site in which it took place, we would be constantly experiencing other people's traumas when walking on the street. Certainly there is no proven experience of this ever happening, yet the idea is useful for dramatic purposes, which is how we should take it here.

This notion of 'rememory' is intimately linked with what we referred to previously as 'the phantom,' 'ghostly presences,' or 'the uncanny.' Indeed, Bouson points out, it "recalls descriptions of a visual form of memory that trauma investigators refer to as traumatic memory" (2000: 135). Memories that are ready to 'possess' a person when he/she least expect it, returning thoughts that seem, to the trauma victim, as if they were the ghosts of the original traumatic experience bent on haunting them for the rest of their lives are all highly poetic yet they feel sadly real to those affected by them. In fact, 'haunting' is a term broadly used in psychology to refer to the victim's feeling of the recurrent, unwelcome invasion of memories that often ails them. Suggestive as this idea of the ghost is, how much more so it must be for a writer of fiction like Toni Morrison who, moreover, does seem to believe in the supernatural if we judge by her conviction that her dead father still communicates with her (Heinze 1993: 159–160). Small wonder, therefore, that she chose to represent this recurrent aspect of trauma not only with the notion of 'rememories' you can 'bump into,' or by the presence of an actual ghost at the site of the trauma, but also by giving flesh to the ghost and sending it to personally plague the remainder of the inhabitants of 124 in an expression of "the humiliated fury of the trauma victim and also the despair" (Bouson 2000: 149). These sorts of images, naturally impossible outside the world of metaphor and fiction, are highly reminiscent of the magical realism genre, under which this novel—and Naylor's *Mama Day*—can be classified. This genre employs fantastic elements to highlight the unspeakable aspects of ordinary lives, which includes the appearance of "ghosts, disappearances, miracles, extraordinary talents and strange atmospheres but does not include the magic as it is found in a magic show" (Bowers 2004: 19). Moreover, a ghost like the one found in *Beloved* is one of the most recursive symbols of the grotesque, which "enables the artist to disrupt the familiar world of reality in order to introduce a different, more mysterious reality" (Corey 2000: 31) and to "explore what we do not understand" (Corey 2000: 32). This makes the grotesque, the sublime (Conger 2000a: 67), and magical realism perfect instruments to depict and make sense of the workings of trauma, one of the most disruptive, difficult to process, and therefore defying rationalization, realities in human experience. This is the reason that the ghost is a key presence in those genres and why Morrison uses it in *Beloved* to "maintain a tension between the interior and exterior experiences of slavery and between the historical past and the realm of the uncanny" (Corey 2000: 33).

"Not a house in the country ain't packed to its rafters with some dead Negro's grief" (Morrison 2005: 6), Baby Suggs says. That is, Morrison naturalizes the supernatural, making the ghost of repressed/suppressed trauma a characteristic of daily-life for any African American living at the time. The ghost's activities and the upheaval caused by them at 124 are but reminders of the trauma its inhabitants have been trying to suppress. They have learned to live with the ghost and, except for the two boys who had fled "the moment the house committed what was for [them] the one insult not to be borne or witnessed a second time" (3), its presence becomes bearable at 124. That is, until Paul D arrived, and with him, the opportunity to break the silence and work through the suppressed trauma. He is "the kind of man who can walk into a house and make the women cry" (321), which is precisely the effect he has on Sethe. He, as part of her troubled past, has shared part of her experiences and therefore understands her grief better. Consequently, Sethe can confide in him, telling him what she has not told anyone before and thus starting the process of working through by means of the talking cure. This is how Paul D expels the ghost; how he breaks the power of repression and allows hope for recovery.

But the ghost is too strong; the power of repression too potent, and it will not allow for such an easy escape. She returns in a stronger form, that of Beloved, and works to consistently win back her mother and sister's affections, drive Paul D back out of the house and take revenge on the person that took her life away. She becomes hungry for stories from her mother's past, which, although remembering pains her, Sethe willing to provide, much to her surprise. Beloved makes Sethe remember things she thought she had forgotten and thus becomes the perfect embodiment of the return of the repressed. Even when Sethe recognizes Beloved for what/who she really is and rejoices thinking that she will never have to remember her painful past, memories come rolling back nonetheless:

> I don't have to remember nothing. I don't even have to explain. She understands it all. I can forget how Baby Suggs' heart collapsed; how we agreed it was consumption without a sign of it in the world. Her eyes when she brought my food, I can forget that, and how she told me that Howard and Buglar were all right but wouldn't let go each other's hands.

> Played that way: stayed that way especially in their sleep. She handed me the food from a basket; things wrapped small enough to get through the bars, whispering news: Mr. Bodwin going to see the judge—in chambers, she kept on saying, in chambers, like I knew what it meant or she did. [...] [']They going to let you out for the burial,' she said, 'not the funeral, just the burial,' and they did. The sheriff came with me and looked away when I fed Denver in the wagon. Neither Howard nor Burglar would let me near them, not even to touch their hair. I believe a lot of folks were there, but I just saw the box. Reverend Pike spoke in a real loud voice, but I didn't catch a word—except the first two, and three months later when Denver was ready for solid food and they let me out for good, I went and got you a gravestone, but I didn't have money enough for the carving so I exchanged (bartered, you might say) what I did have and I'm sorry to this day I never thought to ask him for the whole thing: all I heard of what Reverend Pike said. Dearly Beloved, which is what you are to me and I don't have to be sorry about getting only one word, and I don't have to remember the slaughterhouse and the Saturday girls who worked its yard. I can forget that what I did changed Baby Suggs' life. No Clearing, no company. Just laundry and shoes. I can forget it all now (216–217).

This quote shows that Sethe's traumatic memories are not really buried. Far from it, they are ready to arise with the least provocation, which Beloved is happy to provide. Moreover, the action-packed quality of this passage suggests that Sethe is gathering thoughts and actions compulsively, listing the things she can forget while actually engraving them more deeply into her memory. Those actions and memories—her time in prison, her daughter's funeral, her sons' fear and her life after that, how she had to exchange ten minutes of sex with the stone-engraver to have one word put on her baby's headstone, her self-reproach at not asking him to engrave both 'Dearly' *and* 'Beloved' in it instead of just the latter, and her own part in ruining her mother-in-law's life—roll out in this continuous monologue full of regret, shame and guilt linked through an association of ideas suggesting that complete forgetfulness is never achieved.

Regardless of whether she wants it or not, Sethe remembers, and the more she remembers and tells, the stronger Beloved/the hold of trauma becomes, taking thus the role of a parasite that lives off of the life-force of her mother. Almost at the close of the story, before she is exorcised by the women's community of Cincinnati, Beloved is getting bigger and bigger, in contrast to Sethe, who is getting smaller and more worn out by the minute. Once again, the particular nature of fiction allows us to interpret this fact in a variety of ways, without means of discerning which—if any—was originally in the author's mind. We can surmise that Beloved is pregnant with Paul D's child, meaning, as mentioned above, that even if she is expelled from this narrative, it will continue to reproduce itself and plague others. It could just be an indication that suppression is not overcome by the end of the narrative. Or it could mean, as Offut Mathieson argues, that Beloved's fantasy is to make her mother pay by swallowing her and thus being united at last (1990: 13). This last idea is consistent with trauma theory if we understand by it that Sethe is being 'swallowed' by her own trauma. The disruptive force of the return of the repressed is so strong that she finally gives up, leaves her work, the care of her house, her daughter, and herself and gives in completely to her own traumatic guilt. By the end of the novel, she is so consumed by it that she has been literally possessed by her trauma, which uses her as its instrument to repeat itself. In other words: Beloved is the phantom of unresolved trauma; the living reminder of the dead and, at the same time, an undead presence—an embodiment of what Derrida would refer to as 'the specter'—that threatens to overcome the living and bring them to a limbo between life and death, between presence and absence. Sethe stops eating and seems to be in the process of physically disappearing towards the end of the narrative. She is still alive, yet bordering the stillness of the dead because of the weight of her trauma. Louise Erdrich describes this most extreme consequence of unresolved trauma in a similar way in the following passage from *Tracks*:

> We felt the spirits of the dead so near that at length we just stopped talking.
> This made it worse.
> Their names grew within us, swelled to the brink of our lips, forced our eyes open in the middle of the night. We were filled with the water of the drowned, cold and black, airless water that lapped against the seal of our tongues or leaked slowly from the corners of our eyes, within us, like ice shards, their names bobbed and shifted. Then the slivers of ice began to collect and cover us. We became so heavy, weighted down with the lead gray frost, that we could not move. Our hands lay on the table like cloudy blocks. The blood within us grew thick. We needed no food. And little warmth. Days passed, weeks, and we didn't leave the cabin for fear we'd crack our cold and fragile bodies. We had gone half windigo. I learned later that this was common, that there were many of our people who died in this manner, of the invisible sickness. There were those who could not swallow another bite of food because the names of their dead anchored their tongues. There were those who let their blood stop, who took the road west after all. (2006: 6)

As already mentioned, trauma, like violence, has a tendency to fall into patterns of repetition. The recurrence of the intrusive images, as already discussed, is one of the forms in which trauma is repeated, and, in some extreme cases, it can also bring about a repetition and perpetuation of the violence that engendered it. Some of this was mentioned during the analysis of *Paradise*, but it is also present here. Once Sethe is fully under the influence of Beloved—that is, fully overwhelmed by the trauma—as well as apparently giving up on life just like 'those' mentioned in Erdrich's fragment above, she loses the capacity to distinguish past from present. When Mr. Bodwin, the local white abolitionist happens to arrive in her yard to take Denver to work at his place, she completely loses perspective and sees not Mr. Bodwin but schoolteacher. Thinking that she is back then and not here and now, she believes schoolteacher has returned to take her and her children back into slavery. At this moment, violence seizes her again and she is at the point of repeating her past actions, though with one difference: this time her attack is not intended upon her children but upon schoolteacher/Mr. Bodwin. Sethe experiences this as "an unconscious and compulsive repetition" (King 2000: 172), which is made evident by the parallels between her thoughts at these two very different moments:

> [S]he was squatting in the garden and when she saw them coming and recognized schoolteacher's hat, she heard wings. Little hummingbirds stuck their needle beaks right through her headcloth into her hair and beat their wings. And if she thought anything, it was No. No. Nono. Nonono. Simple. She just flew. (Morrison 2005: 192)

> Guiding the mare, slowing down, his black hat wide-brimmed enough to hide his face but not his purpose. He is coming into her yard and he is coming for her best thing. She hears wings. Little hummingbirds stick needle beaks right through her headcloth into her hair and beat their wings. And if she thinks anything, it is no. No no. Nonono. She flies. (308–309)

The similitude in these two excerpts is striking and not at all by chance. The first is part of a longer description of 'the unspeakable' thing as told by Sethe, the second comes from the account of the set of events that took place when Mr. Bodwin came to collect Denver the day the women reunited to expel Beloved from the house. The language used, the image of the hummingbirds and, above all, the 'No. No. Nono. Nonono' that Sethe thinks, mark the second event as an almost exact replica of the first one, thus supporting the idea that traumatic violence tends to repeat itself unless properly addressed and worked through (Bouson 2000: 158).

2.3 *Voicing It out: the Attempt and Failure of the Talking Cure*

One of the ways of attempting to somehow manage grief and move towards a proper working through of trauma is by acknowledging it, breaking the conspiracy of silence and repression and putting it out in the open, making sense of it by means of language, by articulating it into a more comprehensible form through the talking cure. From the beginning, patients of psychoanalysis have been asked to talk—about anything—paying no regard to coherence or even sense, just talk. After several sessions, the treatment would supposedly reveal the origin of the victim's problem; unearth the patient's repressed trauma so that, once out in the open, it can be properly addressed and acknowledged. There were obviously no psychoanalysts in Sethe's Cincinnati, but she is nonetheless offered the possibility of a talking cure at the hands of Paul D. Having gone through most of the same things she underwent, and sharing the same culture and community identification processes, he is the best candidate: she can trust him and share her experiences of racist trauma with him. Together they embark in an attempted talking cure, and they tell each other stories about their painful pasts that they "never told a soul" (85). Sethe believes that, because he has also suffered a good deal of pain, he can understand hers and even envisions the possibility of, in time, telling him her most obscure secret: "Her story was bearable because it was his as well—to tell, to refine and tell again. The things neither knew about the other—the things neither had word-shapes for—well, it would come in time: where they led him off to sucking iron; the perfect death of her crawling already? baby" (116).

And yet, despite this initial trust, and despite the apparent intimation that Sethe and Paul D can move on during their last scene together at the end of the novel, the working through fails and, even though the bodily presence of Beloved is expelled by the community's women, its spiritual presence remains in the house. That is, the force of the trauma remains suppressed both by the community and by the inhabitants of 124. No complete working through has taken place—assuming that is even possible—and, consequently, signs of trauma and suppressed memories keep reappearing after Beloved's disappearance:

> They forgot her like a bad dream. After they made up their tales, shaped and decorated them, those that saw her that day on the porch quickly and deliberately forgot her. It took longer for those who had spoken to her, lived with her, fallen in love with her, to forget, until they realized

they couldn't remember or repeat a single thing she said, and began to believe that, other than what they themselves were thinking, she hadn't said anything at all. So, in the end, they forgot her too. Remembering seemed unwise. [...]

So they forgot her. Like an unpleasant dream during a troubling sleep. Occasionally, however, the rustle of a skirt hushes when they wake, and the knuckles brushing a cheek in sleep seem to belong to the sleeper. Sometimes the photograph of a close friend or relative—looked at too long—shifts, and something more familiar than the dear-face itself moves there. They can touch it if they like, but don't, because they know things will never be the same if they do. (323-324)

This suppression is, as can be seen above, once more completely voluntary and deliberate. Even after the events in the yard, even after the spite of the young Beloved, the inhabitants of 124 and the community surrounding them are back to square one. The presence of repression is again felt in the house in its ghostly form and the trauma retains its destructive potential. The women's exorcism of Beloved has had no long-lasting consequences, for, even though her bodily form has disappeared—not so her ghostly presence—Sethe does not recover from her punishment as should be expected, but "retreats more into her own world and indulges herself in her world with Beloved" (Kuo 2009: 118). The novel's ending is in no way optimistic, for it suggests that "[w]hether the past is crushed or forgotten, [...] it never really goes away because the present does not rule it" (Hefferman 1998: 562). As Barbara Offut Mathieson puts it, at the end of the narrative "Sethe's future remains as ambiguous as the question mark of her last words in the book" (1990: 11). Regardless of the return of Paul D to the house, there is not much hope for her engaging again in the talking cure with him; after all, it was his incapacity to deal with the knowledge of her crime that drove him away, and this, moreover, after having "counted" her feet.

It is in that action, the action of counting her feet, that he inadvertently behaved just like schoolteacher and his two nephews, who listed Sethe's human and animal characteristics using the ink that she herself had prepared. This, as Linden Peach argues, is "emblematic of [...] the discourses around the pseudo-science of hierarchies expounded by scientists such as Herbert Spencer and Francis Galton [who] came to rely upon colonial anthropology and vulgar interpretations of Darwinism to give coherence and respectability to popularly held racist myths" (1995: 106). Those racist myths were used in order to justify the obviously cruel and immoral practice of human slaving. If blacks were seen not as humans, but as animals, their use as brute labor would be justified. Richard Wright describes this in the following terms:

> [T]he white man suffered hang-overs from a feudal morality; he could not enslave others in a confident manner. Having bid for freedom upon the assumption that all men were naturally free, that they possessed in their hearts those impulses that made dignity and nobility a human right, he could not play the role of master with a singleness of heart. So, to keep what he had and to feel safe with it, he had to invent reasons, causes, explanations, rationalizations, all of which amounted to a declaration of the biological inferiority of the enslaved. Paradoxes and contradictions of thought and feeling became commonplace. It was claimed that white men were 'helping' black men by enslaving them; it finally became right to treat black men wrong, and wrong to treat them right. The apex of white racial ideology was reached when it was assumed that white domination was a God-given right. (1993: xxi)

Indeed, blacks were merely animal labor during slavery times; treating them in a humane form was not only viewed unfavorably but considered almost stupid and unnecessary, even counterproductive. There were, for instance, greater punishments for those who killed a neighbor's mule than for those who killed their own slave, for the latter was considered their own loss, while the former was damaging someone else's property. Female slaves, in particular, were seen not only as animal labor—the concept they had of male slaves—but as a valuable property because they had the capacity to breed. They were valued in a similar way to cows or other animals, whose bestial labor could be complemented by their capacity to multiply their owner's property and feed his children. This mentality is represented in *Beloved* through the name that Baby Suggs's former owner gave to her, Jenny, a reference to a sterile crossbreed between a male horse and a female donkey. Moreover, the figures of schoolteacher and his nephews also exemplify this type of reasoning in several instances throughout the narrative. One instance is schoolteacher's resentment of Sethe's mental instability after he witnesses her murderous act not because of the evident tragedy that developed before his own eyes, but because his one property that "made fine ink, damn good soup, pressed his collars the way he liked *besides having at least ten breeding years left*" (Morrison 2005: 176. Emphasis added) is now worthless (Bouson 2000: 145). Another is schoolteacher's attempts to document the, at that time, essentially racist 'scientific' belief of the inferiority of blacks by listing her human and animal-like characteristics in two separate columns and his consequent construction of Sethe as animalistic (Bouson 2000; 140). And finally, schoolteacher's nephews' taking her baby's milk by force, directly from her breasts, is yet another clear identification of Sethe with a farm animal. This last humiliation is—we later know—what breaks her husband and what makes Sethe decide to flee on her own, adding one more trauma to her psychological baggage. When Paul D counts her feet in a manifestation of his "own internalization of schoolteacher's racist thinking" (Bouson 2000: 146), Sethe's trauma is reawakened and, for that reason, she is unable to forgive Paul D and trust him again. She no longer feels he understands her, and thus she can no longer trust him enough to tell him about her traumas: "Sethe knew that the circle she was making around the room, him, the subject, would remain one. That she could never close in, pin it down for anybody who had to ask. If they didn't get it right off—she could never explain" (Morrison 2005: 192). Even before their breakup, however, trust was never complete. Because her memories were so painful, Sethe felt that "[e]ven with Paul D, who had shared some of it and to whom she could talk with at least a measure of calm, the hurt was always there—like a tender place in the corner of her mouth that the bit left" (69). It is also for this reason, to protect herself from pain, that, even though she tells Paul D that she is willing to listen to his traumas (85), when the telling gets too tough she stops him:

> Paul D had only begun, what he was telling her was only the beginning when her fingers on his knee, soft and reassuring, stopped him. Just as well. Just as well. Saying more might push them both to a place they couldn't get back from. He would keep the rest where it belonged: in that tobacco tin buried in his chest where a red heart would be. Its lid rusted shut. He would not pry it loose now in front of this sweet sturdy woman, for if she got a whiff of the contents it would shame him. And it would hurt her to know that there was no red heart bright as mister's comb beating in it. (86)

Paul D is willing to stop his telling because it will shame and hurt him, but also because it will hurt her. Thinking of both, he is glad to stop his own process of recovery, allowing suppression to keep trauma's hold on him. At the end of the novel, he finds himself back in 124 trying to help Sethe, and wanting "to put his story next to hers" (322), though it is uncertain whether he will ultimately achieve the release he needs.

2.4 The Light at the End of the Tunnel: Denver and Recovery from Trauma

The only character in the novel that clearly holds some hope of recovery is Denver. Realizing the harmful potential that the presence of Beloved has for her mother allows Denver "the necessary confrontation with, and working through of the past" (King 2000: 166–167). In fact, it is thanks to her willingness to move on and leave her past fears behind that the women of the community learn about the existence of Beloved and agree to help expel her. Denver, at the sight of the danger her mother is in, "replaces the solitary maternal bond with a larger community of adults and opens herself to an empathetic network of fellows" (Offutt Mathieson 1990: 16). But, in order to do this and raise the alarm, she must leave the yard to which she has been confined since childhood. At first, as during infancy, the grip that trauma and terror have on her prevent her from doing so, but with the spiritual help of Baby Suggs, she manages to acknowledge the memories of trauma passed on to her and move on:

> Remembering those conversations and her grandmother's last and final words, Denver stood on the porch in the sun and couldn't leave it. Her throat itched; her heart kicked—and then Baby Suggs laughed, clear as anything. 'You mean I never told you nothing about Carolina? About your daddy? You don't remember nothing about how come I walk the way I do and about your mother's feet, not to speak of her back? I never told you all that? Is that why you can't walk down the steps? My Jesus my.'
> But you said there was no defense.
> 'There ain't.'
> Then what do I do?
> 'Know it, and go on out the yard. Go on.' (Morrison 2005: 287–288)

It is knowing the past, acknowledging it despite the hurt it entails that helps Denver move forward both literally and figuratively. Years later, Morrison would depict a similar process in *Home*. A young and easily deceived African American girl is tricked by her boss, a doctor, into allowing him to use her as a guinea pig for his eugenics experiments. When she is finally rescued by her brother, and after a long a painful recovery process, she learns that she will never be a mother. Although she admits being shocked by the news at first, she is able to process it, together with the grief it causes her: "I can be miserable if I want to. You don't need to try and make it go away. It shouldn't go away. It's just as sad as it ought to be and I'm not going to hide from what's true because it hurts" (Morrison 2013: 131). This healthy acknowledgment of pain and trauma helps her brother to start moving forward in his own traumatic process. This brother carries his own personal history of trauma that starts from the moment in which he—allegedly—forgets having witnessed the hurried and clandestine burial of a murdered black man and continues with his experiences during the Korean war that include the death of his two best friends and his guilt over having killed a small Korean girl. Because of all this, he suffers from various trauma symptoms consisting of repeated flashbacks, nightmares, hallucinations, spells of color blindness and violent outbursts, among others. Having refused to go back home out of guilt over having survived his friends but, most especially, over his murder of the Korean girl, he learns a valuable lesson in his sister's behavior: "His sister was gutted, infertile, but not beaten. She could know the truth, accept it, and keep on quilting. Frank tried to sort out what else was troubling him and what to do about it" (Morrison 2013: 132).

It is a similar voluntary act that motivates Denver to leave her past behind and to start working through her trauma. She decides to leave the yard, walk down the road, meet the gaze of her neighbors and receive the help and kindness of her old teacher, which "inaugurate[s] her life in the world as a woman" (292). After this, the novel subtly suggests, she even finds love and the possibility of starting a new family of her own with, ironically, the very boy that provoked her two years' of deafness. All this is thanks to her willingness to overcome silence and remember the past as it was in order to move forward into the future. This can be interpreted as one of the morals of the novel: suppression and silence about the traumas of the past can be extremely dangerous for the individual and collective unconscious. Therefore, the silence must be broken and the past acknowledged in order to lay the ghosts of the past to rest and proceed into the future. Nicholas T. Rand, in his introduction to Abraham and Torok's volume points to this necessity in psychoanalytical terms when he says that "[w]hether with our own strength, with the help of loved ones, or with an analyst if need be, we must be able to remember the past, recall what was taken from us, understand and grieve over what we have lost to trauma, and so find and renew ourselves" (1994a: 13).

"This is not a story to pass on" (Morrison 2005: 324), the novel repeatedly intones towards its close. There have been several interpretations of this phrase, including the already mentioned idea of the 'unspeakability' of such horrors that would prevent its bearers from telling others. For the present purposes, however, two other rather similar readings of the phrase must be mentioned here because of their emphasis on the necessity of remembering rather than on perpetuating silence; namely, Nicola King's and David Lawrence's. The former suggests that the term 'pass on' is synonymous with 'ignore' or, as I have argued, 'deny' or 'suppress.' "This is not a story to pass on," therefore, literally means that this story, or any other story like this, should never be ignored, for "it is ignorance, or inadequate recognition of the claims of the past, which, Morrison suggests, leads to the danger of repetition" (King 2000: 173). Similarly, David Lawrence provides another meaning of 'to pass on' and plays with the idea of 'passing' as in 'dying' to argue the following: "While the painful heritage of slavery cannot simply 'pass on,' cannot die away [...], enslavement to that heritage, Morrison implies, must 'pass on,' must die away, in order to undertake the task of re-membering and re-articulating the individual and the communal body" (Lawrence 1991: 200. See also Matus 1998: 120 and Bouson 2000: 161). In other words, it is time for the period of 'national amnesia' to end and to begin acknowledging the inheritance of slavery both in the lives and minds of the individuals affected by it and of American society in general. Just as Morrison herself put it, African Americans "in rushing away from slavery, which was important to do—it meant rushing out of bondage into freedom—also rushed away from the slaves because it was painful to dwell there, and they may have abandoned some responsibilities in so doing" (Darling 1994: 247). That is, the silenced and suppressed stories of past traumas must be recognized and reworked now into a constructive narrative in an attempt to engage in an "ongoing process of generating narrative meaning out of an irretrievable past" (Tal 2003: n.p.) out of responsibility to those who succumbed to that traumatic past.

Paule Marshall seems to be of the same opinion when in her novel *The Chosen Place, the Timeless People*, Saul, an American, reflecting on Merle's willful attempt to recover the traumatic memories of her childhood, utters the following:

> I know what you're trying to do. This with your mother is all part of an attempt to come to terms with the things that have happened in your life. To go back and understand. And it's a good thing you're doing. More of us should try it. It's usually so painful though: looking back and into yourself; most people run from it. I know I did for a long time. But sometimes it's necessary to go back before you can go forward, really forward.
>
> And that's not only true for people—individuals—but nations as well [...]. Sometimes they need to stop and take a long hard look back. My country, for example. It's never honestly faced up to its past, never told the story straight, and I don't know as it ever will. (Marshall 1969: 359)

Unlikely as it may seem to Saul in the quote above, this remembering is all the more imperative if we take into account the fact that the history in question is a history that has been previously dis-remembered, erased and unaccounted for. For example, as Teressa Heffernan points out, there is a vast lack of documentation about the histories of Africans transported in slave ships (1998: 560). If to this we add the fact that, upon arrival, whole families were dismembered and forever separated, that slaves were sundered from all their past roots and their histories replaced with memories of trauma upon trauma that they later endeavored to forget, we come up with an immense gap in the history of the African American community that novels like *Beloved* try to bridge. The figure of Beloved, according to Barbara Offut Mathieson, is the embodiment of these lost memories that, "like the beloved dead child, must be recognized, embraced and openly mourned but finally laid to rest before the living can understand the present or proceed with the future" (1990: 5–6).

"[W]e got more yesterday than anybody," Paul D tells Sethe. "We need some kind of tomorrow" (Morrison 2005: 322). Even for those who did not directly experience the 'yesterday' that Paul D refers to here; even for the descendants of those who did, the process of remembering is of great significance. The loss has to be acknowledged not only to put the past to rest and proceed into 'tomorrow,' but also because of a moral obligation to all those who were lost during that traumatic past; the sixty million and more. This necessity of recovering history leads us to the next chapter, in which we will see how, in some instances, the recovery of the past must be done not just as a social practice, but as a personal search for identity and sense of self.

CHAPTER 4

The Recovery of History: Toni Morrison's *Song of Solomon* and David Bradley's *The Chaneysville Incident*

> So we beat on, boats against the current, borne back ceaselessly into the past.
> F. SCOTT FITZGERALD, *The Great Gatsby*

> This is how the angel of history must look. His face is turned toward the past. [...] But a storm is blowing from Paradise and has got caught in his wings; it is so strong that the angel can no longer close them. This storm drives him irresistibly into the future, to which his back is turned, while the pile of debris before him grows toward the sky.
> WALTER BENJAMIN, "On the Concept of History"

∴

How do we approach the matter of history? Or rather, how does history affect us? Are we, as Fitzgerald argues, "borne back ceaselessly into the past," or are we driven "irresistibly into the future," with our sight turned to the past as Benjamin and the traditional African symbol of the Sankofa suggest? I argue that both stances are equally valid and, in fact, interrelated. With its characteristic pendulous movement, history tends to repeat itself—especially, as we have seen, if that history is of a traumatic origin or if the structures that put the original violent events into motion are still in operation—to the point that Benjamin saw in it not a chain of events but "one single catastrophe, which keeps piling wreckage upon wreckage" (2003: 392). From that point of view, it would seem that our progress towards the future is but a procession leading to one repetition or another of something that has already occurred, thus being essentially borne back to the past again and again. On the other hand, and despite the ineffability of history, it is part of our human nature to look back to the past in order to learn from it and apply that knowledge to the present and future, thus moving forwards with our sight in what we leave behind.

Be that as it may, my contention is that history and our relationship to it are instrumental in shaping our personal and collective identities, in the sense that people in the past and—most importantly—the consequences of their actions have repercussions for the present that fashion our lives and allow both the world and us to become what we are. Consequently, a certain knowledge of the events in our past is important to better understand ourselves and the society we live in. History, as Michaels suggests, "can give us memories not only of [...] our 'own' lives but of 'other lives lived long ago.' And it is in giving us these memories that history gives us our 'identity' " (1996: 3).

Thus, we observe a bi-directional motion: history and the events that occurred in the past shape our present lives and identities while our active revisiting of history from our own present vantage point helps us work towards the future. However, there is a vital distinction between these two movements: although the influence of the past on the present is something in which we—as present individuals with no power to interfere with historical events—take no active part, we are solely responsible for the second part of the equation. We have a moral responsibility to future generations to embark on a recovery of the past in order to extract from it the necessary knowledge to make a better world in the years to come, which becomes especially significant whenever that past has been previously silenced, as in the case of the traumatic history of slavery, racism and the oppression of the African American community, or when the system that allowed for those past traumatic events to occur is still in operation. It is for this reason that the recovery of hidden and suppressed histories has, of late, acquired such relevance in contemporary sociological and political discourses. In those cases in which collectivities—like the African American community—have "possessed reserves of memory but little or no historical capital" (Nora 1989: 7), there exists a self-imposed need to reclaim what was once lost or silenced. The African American community has recently endeavored to pursue this route both in its literary works and in its socio-political struggle. As Melvin Dixon argues, African Americans have operated with an "urgency of [...] recovery of cultural memory" (1994: 20), which is reflected, for instance, in the names of the streets of Harlem that were changed to names such as Frederick Douglass Boulevard, Johnny Hartman Plaza, Marcus Garvey Park and Adam Clayton Powell Boulevard not only to "celebrate and commemorate great figures in black culture," but also "to provoke our active participation in that history" to the point that "[w]hat was important yesterday becomes a landmark today" (Dixon 1994: 20). This is a highly significant process, since "[b]y calling themselves to remember Africa and/or the racial past, black Americans are actually re-membering, as in repopulating broad continuities within the African diaspora" (Dixon 1994: 21). Moreover, not only the physical spaces—like the aforementioned streets—work as *lieux de mémoire*, literary works can also undertake the mission to actively unearth the hidden past. For instance, several of Du Bois's works, but more specifically *Black Reconstruction in America* (1935), have contested the white man's history and offered an African American view of events, and, at the same time recovered some of the community's long silenced past. Such an effort has transformed DuBois into a "self-conscious creator of black counter-memory" (Blight 1994: 46).

However, if the recovery and knowledge of history is significant in the development of individual and collective identities, the unearthing of past traumas may become paramount. In the recovery of traumas, a community not only achieves the contestation of the master-narrative version of history, but it can also put an end to cycles of repetition and re-enacting that are consequence of an ongoing process of oppression. This chapter will explore the literary recreation of the effort that individuals and communities alike sometimes need to make in order to unearth the hidden key events in their pasts, recover their roots and come to terms with their history.

1 A Quest for One's Past: Individuals, Collectivities, and Recovered Memory

Traumatic memory, as already mentioned, tends to manifest itself through ragged, unexpected and often incomplete reminiscences, usually in the form of flashbacks or intrusive memories. A patient suffering from these types of recursive symptoms and reminiscences may find him/herself in a state of acute psychological fragmentation, confused between the memories of the past, the present recollections of those past memories and his/her experience of the present time. Often, the unexpected return of past painful experiences leaves the patient depressed and without hope for the future, making "the relationship between the self 'before' and the self 'after' " highly problematic (King 2000: 3). This disruption of the patient's sense of self and linear time can be repaired when the victim recognizes what is past as passed, different from the present time and independent from the future. In order to do this, a proper acknowledgment of past traumas is necessary and, when hidden, an effort must be made towards recovery.

This quest for the hidden past through the recovery of clues seems almost like detective work, for—to quote Paul Ricoeur—it was processes like these that were "the joy of Sherlock Holmes" (2006: 173). They also resemble the work of an archeologist, in that the subject needs to dig and shift through the different layers in the (quick)sand of his memory. As Walter Benjamin puts it, "[h]e who seeks to approach his own buried past must conduct himself like a man digging.

Above all, he must not be afraid to return again and again to the same matter; to scatter it as one scatters earth, to turn it over as one turns over soil" (1999: 576). In fact, there are many contemporary trauma theorists who utilize this metaphor to describe the arduous process of recovering hidden traumatic memory. Cathy Caruth[1] capitalized on several images and extracts from works such as Willhelm Jensen's *Gradiva: A Pompeiian Fantasy* and Sigmund Freud's take on the same text to foreground the importance of traces as the hypothetical route that the archaeologist/historiographer/psychoanalyst/trauma victim must follow in order to get to the hidden core of the historical event(s) in question (Caruth, 31st March 2011). Specifically, she used the image of footprints left in the ashes of Pompeii, as well as the gaps left by the decomposed buried bodies found by the archeologists when digging up the ill-fated city, to explain how traces become a remainder of history available to anyone that wishes to revisit and make sense of that history. Similarly, Paul Ricoeur dwells on the notion of traces and its origin in hunting—as in following the traces/tracks left by an animal upon the ground—and links them to the actual idea of an imprint, or the marks left on paper when writing as studied graphologically. All those traces, marks and tracks are used, he argues, as "clues" in order to interpret something that happened in the past and, when coupled with testimony, form what we understand as a "document" (2006: 175). This idea of history seen as a series of traces goes back to the notion of place as a palimpsest showing the imbrication between space and (traumatic) memory and will be referenced below in the analyses of both *Song of Solomon* and *The Chaneysville Incident*, particularly with regard to the passages in which the protagonists of both novels embark on an archeological/hunting quest synonymous with their respective searches for the past.

Insomuch as a trace is "a pure referral of the past" (Ricoeur 2006: 381), it becomes a tie to it, a link between the past and the present that resides in memory; and it is through memory that a person's "temporal continuity" is preserved (Ricoeur 2006: 96), making the exercise of it the perfect recourse against the fragmentariness of trauma. The act of recovering one's past, therefore, is not only the first step towards the overcoming of trauma, but also an avenue towards the building of a person's identity and sense of self. Sometimes, as we will see in the analysis of the novels presented here, individuals may need to recover their families' or their communities' hidden past in order to reconnect with their roots and better understand their origins and therefore their own selves. Identity is thus shaped—or re-shaped—by the

---

1 In her opening address at a trauma conference held in Zaragoza, Spain: "After the End: Psychoanalysis in the Ashes of History." University of Zaragoza, Spain, 31st March 2011.

new information and the implications that it has for the subject's present and past life. A new process of identity formation then takes place, and the individual has to re-learn, to see the world according to the events unveiled. Both Milkman in *Song of Solomon* and John Washington in *The Chaneysville Incident*, after their quest for truth in their family's past, must forcibly undergo a rearrangement of their own conceptions as individuals as well as of their convictions concerning the society they live in and the lives of their ancestors. Those individuals who, like Milkman and John Washington have remained apart from their families' and communities' history have been prevented from forming a fully informed choice of identity and now need to reevaluate the way in which they see themselves and others. Such a process of identity re-formation mirrors the process that formerly oppressed and silenced communities must undergo when the truth about their past and the suffering of their ancestors finally come to light.

Individual and collective memory are therefore intimately related. According to Ricoeur, "it is on the basis of a subtle analysis of the individual experience of belonging to a group, and through the instruction received from others, that individual memory takes possession of itself" (2006: 120). This is also perfectly applicable to identity formation, since so much of it depends on the exercise of memory in a socially-defined environment. In fact, as Ricoeur points out, the discovery of historical memory—highly influential in the formation of a culturally-dependent individual identity—is done through an "acculturation to externality" consisting of a "familiarization with the unfamiliar" by means of "moving through the concentric circles formed by the family nucleus, school chums, friendships, familial and social relationships, and, above all, the discovery of the historical past by means of the memory of ancestors" (2006: 394). However, at some point during the perusal of the information kept within those concentric circles, the individual may encounter a (sometimes hidden) traumatic memory that affects not only the individual exploring the memory, but also all those located within the same circle in which the trauma happened downwards toward its center. Depending on the circle in which trauma occurs, and also on the attention previously paid to it, the trauma could range from what Kaplan calls "family trauma"—also called "quiet trauma" or "common trauma" by other scholars—(2005: 19), to cultural or founding ones. In either case, whichever trauma the individual encounters will force the self to regard the society one lives in and the collective affected by it through the lens of one's changed perception, having a similarly significant effect on the individual's identity and self-conception.

Similarly, collectives occasionally feel the need to discover their hidden past—especially in cases in which it has been forcibly silenced—and, upon the discovery of trauma, they may sublimate it into the center of their shared identity. This, of course may also serve a parallel and often necessary retaliatory agenda in which nationalistic and vindicatory purposes are never far off. Nicola King, for instance, finds this kind of effort towards the "recovery of the 'pure' past" at the center of nationalist movements as varied as Nazi Germany and the Serbian memory of Kosovo (the difference between the two being the type of past that is recovered: an "idealized organic past" for the former, the memory of traumatic events for the latter) (2000: 5). Disempowered communities occasionally resort to the glorification of a traumatic past—in order to achieve some public voice and a sense of belonging—into a narrative from which they had been previously excluded, as in the case of the African American community. The re-appropriation of the past in such terms is often seen as a self-defining act in which identity becomes "a question of empowerment" (Friedman 1992: 837), usually "experienced as a threat" and therefore criminalized and punished by the dominant identity which it menaces (Friedman 1992: 854). The recovered traumatic past, once unearthed, and despite the resistance of the silencing community, can be turned into "something monumental" that can be "memorialized in a narrative of pain" (Hacking 1995: 214) and thus elevated "to the level of an object of study" (Ricoeur 2004: 388).

This is precisely what is happening to the African American community, where a previously silenced history—that of slavery and, later on, segregation and continued oppression and racism—is being publicly enunciated not only through the publication of literary works like those discussed here, but also through actual archaeological work, especially after the Civil Rights Movement, as Paul A. Shackel points out (2003: 7). Indeed, "the actual act of performing an archaeology of a subordinate group and trying to make its history part of the official history is another level of remembering" (Shackel 2003: 9), one that can co-exist with the literary re-enactment of past traumas. But of course, within these broader traumatic experiences, there are a myriad of smaller, more private events, similarly traumatic yet less publicized. Those are the specific experiences of particular persons that, while encompassed under the terms slavery, racism or segregation, may have been doubly muted, both by the dominant narrative that silenced the general African American experience, and by the very persons that endured them. Both *Song of Solomon* and *The Chaneysville Incident*—as well as the rest of the novels analyzed here—reference not only the broader scope of the African American traumatic experience, but also the family histories interwoven through it. Those family histories are the germ of the master narrative around which the identity of the family affected by it evolves (just as the overall ordeal in which they took place is for the African American community broadly). In cases in which that master narrative has failed to be preserved for the family's future generations, the family's history needs to be rediscovered and acknowledged so that future descendants can reconnect with their original roots and work towards a better understanding of themselves and their ancestors. As we will see, Milkman—like John Washington—embarks on a quest for his origins "that traces the journey of the subject towards a fuller understanding of the interplay of forces which have produced him" (King 2000: 50). In other words, the knowledge they come across in their willful return to the past is of such personal and collective transcendence that it shifts the way in which they see and think about themselves as well as their place in the world.

2   The Truth Shall Make You Fly: Unearthing the Past in *Song of Solomon*

> [I]f you want to be a whole man, you have to deal with the whole truth.
>
> TONI MORRISON, *Song of Solomon*

2.1   *Trauma in* Song of Solomon

There are many ways to classify *Song of Solomon*; it is a *bildungsroman* in which the protagonist, Milkman Dead, goes on a trip to find himself and mature ethically and psychologically. It is also a Rite of Passage Novel in that Milkman's trip takes the form almost of a ceremony (there is even a hunting trip) in which he sheds his old self and acquires his new understanding and personality. And it is, of course, a trauma novel.

In *Song of Solomon* Morrison once again offers a portrayal of the African American plea and of the racial inequalities extant within American society. Covering a time span of just over thirty years—from 1931 to 1963—the novel addresses not only contemporaneous events like the fight for civil rights, the lynching of Emmet Till in Mississippi in 1955 or the 1963 Sunday School Bombing in Birmingham, but also, by extending the narrative to episodes taking place prior to the time of the novel, issues like emancipation, segregation or racial inequalities. However, as is often the case in Morrison's works, this general view of the African American traumatic past is merely the background against which the characters' personal traumas are set.

From the insurance collector who jumps off a roof at the beginning of the novel, to the last member of the Dead family, most of the characters in *Song of Solomon* seem to be affected by one traumatic event or another. Milkman, the main protagonist, is paralyzed into inaction and utter apathy by having been brought up in a rigidly governed house. Moreover, he was nursed by an extremely possessive mother until a ridiculously late age, a fact that gave him his nickname and that he endeavored to suppress in his unconscious until some unexpected knowledge about his past brings it back to his mind with "[c]old sweat [breaking] out on his neck" (Morrison 2006: 77). Likewise, his mother's behavior can be explained by her having been subjected to the wills of the two most powerful males in town who were, in turn, directly opposed to each other and who disregarded her almost to insanity. Guitar, Milkman's most intimate friend, in turn, is deeply traumatized by the death of his own father who was literally cut in two at the sawmill where he worked, and his mother's subsequent abandonment. Guitar was only a child when this happened, and is therefore fixated on the memory of the candy he was given by his father's boss the day of his demise, and by that of the other candy he was given by his mother on the day of the funeral—the latter bought out of the meager compensation his father's boss gave Guitar's mother in order to cheat her out of the insurance money that was rightfully hers. Since then, the mere thought of sweetness made him "think of dead people. And white people. And [...] start to puke" (61). The memory of the injustice committed against his family "traumatized him and fired him up with hatred and retaliation" (Kuo 2009: 154) eventually leading to his allegiance to an anti-white terrorist group.

However, the trauma central to the narrative is that which lies at the heart of the Dead family. This trauma has been transmitted across generations and has affected subsequent family members to different degrees. It is the one trauma that Milkman needs to extricate from within his family's suppressed memory and come to terms with in order to achieve full knowledge of his past and his cultural inheritance, and to obtain a long awaited freedom from it. This family trauma is "rooted in the legacy of slavery which entails a family line of blacks sharing a profound discontinuity with the past and wandering homelessly and living distortedly in an unwelcoming nation" (Kuo 2009: 152). The intergenerational trauma begins with Solomon, an African slave in America who, hampered by the psychological constraints that the institution of slavery imposed upon him, together with the longing for his native home in Africa, decided to 'fly' back to his homeland leaving behind his wife and twenty-one children. Motivated by the trauma of separation from his roots and family, Solomon inaugurated with this act the Dead family's generationally transmitted trauma of abandonment and rootlessness which is suffered by Jake (later known as the first Macon Dead, and the last son of Solomon), his son Macon Dead II, and the latter's son Milkman. This trauma is manifested in Jake's lament "[y]ou just can't fly on off and leave a body" (Morrison 2006: 147) transmitted posthumously to his daughter Pilate. She, together with her brother Macon, will in turn suffer the childhood trauma of losing their father when Jake was "[b]lown off a fence five feet into the air" (140). This other—shorter lived and more fatal—flight has the same consequences as Solomon's: leaving Jake's children, like Jake, destitute and forever longing for a father that they can no longer reach, trying to make up for the loss the best way they can. Jake dealt with the loss of his father by building a paradise—Lincoln's Heaven—"the only farm in the county that grew peaches, real peaches like they had in Georgia" (234) in which his descendants could grow in a clear reconstruction of the life he would have wanted to have with his own father. However, he was tricked out of his farm, and then "white men [...] strutted through the orchards and ate the Georgia peaches after they shot his [...] head off" (250), forcing Macon and Pilate to leave and cope with their own loss. Pilate will, in several instances, see and talk with her father's ghost, proving, Bouson argues, that she is not only a conjure woman, but that she is trauma-haunted (2000: 94). Macon, on the other hand, will somehow mimic his father's coping mechanism by "loving extremely what he loved and seeking exceedingly what he was deprived of" (Kuo 2009: 148), that is, respectively, Lincoln's Heaven and property. To his son he would describe his father's farm in the following, unmistakably idealized terms:

> I worked right alongside my father. Right alongside him. From the time I was four or five we worked together. Just the two of us. [...] He called our farm Lincoln's Heaven. It was a little bit of a place. But it looked big to me then. I know now it must a been a little bit a place, maybe a hundred and fifty acres. We tilled fifty. About eighty of it was woods. Must have been a fortune in oak and pine; maybe that's what they wanted—the lumber, the oak and the pine. We had a pond that was four acres. And a stream, full of fish. Right down in the heart of a valley. Prettiest mountain you ever saw, Montour Ridge. We lived in Montour County. Just north of the Susquehanna. We had a four-stall hog pen. The big barn was forty feet by a hundred and forty—hip-roofed too. And all around in the mountains was deer and wild turkey. You ain't tasted nothing till you taste wild turkey the way Papa cooked it. He'd burn it real fast in the fire. Burn it black all over. That sealed it. Sealed the juices in. Then he'd let it roast on a spit for twenty-four hours. When you cut the black burnt part off, the meat underneath was tender, sweet, juicy. And we had fruit trees. Apple, cherry. Pilate tried to make me a cherry pie once. (Morrison 2006: 51)

Macon Dead II's words evince the veneration he felt both for his father and for their former lifestyle, but the degree of idealization of the latter is also evident, very much so if we take into account that he was a little child when he was forcibly separated from it all, and that his memory could not have retained such minute detail and information. The fact that "[h]is father had sat for five nights on a split-rail fence cradling a shotgun and in the end died protecting his property" (51), motivates Macon to make his motto "[o]wn things. And let the things you own own other things. Then you'll own yourself and other people too" (55). This derives from the first Macon Dead's intention to make the land his father was brought to his own, and to pass it onto his children, as reflected in the admonition that his neighbors sensed coming from the farm itself before it was taken from the Dead family: "Grab it. Grab this land! Take it, hold it, my brothers, make it, my brothers, shake it, squeeze it, turn it, twist it, beat it, kick it, kiss it, whip it, stomp it, dig it, plow it, seed it, reap it, rent it, buy it, sell it, own it, build it, multiply it, and pass it on—can you hear me? Pass it on!" (235). However, the second Macon, unlike his father, does not want to own the land for its own sake, or for the sake of the future generations, but in order "to own other people;" (55) that is, in order to gain power. Blinded by the remnants of the rage he must have felt after witnessing his father's murder, he refocuses his retaliatory impulses in an attempt to gain control over other people; the kind of control that white men had over his father when they took his farm. Macon realizes from a very early age that the power to own things and to subjugate those who don't own things themselves, lies in the hands of the white men and the only way he sees of escaping from that system is not to reverse it, but to imitate it. His resolve and self-assurance are directly linked to the increasing number of keys in his pocket (22), whose magic is none other than the fact that they give him power over the tenants living in the properties associated with those keys. Similarly, Jerome Johnson in Paule Marshall's *Praisesong for the Widow*, chooses not to become involved in the social plight of his fellow African American citizens, but to focus instead on owning: "Instead of marching and protesting and running around burning down everything in the hope of a handout, we need to work and build our own, to have our own. Our own! Our own!" (Marshall 1983a: 135).

Just as Jerome Johnson takes pride in the fact that he has managed to—supposedly—improve himself by getting hold of some of the white men's power and learns to despise "these Negroes out here" (134) that did not follow his example, Macon does not feel any sympathy for his tenants and thrives in his position of power believing it is only the inevitable consequence of economic and personal progress. He has suffered a "slippage from ownership as resistance to slavery to ownership as slavery's repetition in the 'free market' of capitalism" (Rothberg 2003: 510). Macon Dead despises his father-in-law for behaving like a white man, but he is no better than him, for, as Mrs. Bains once says after he threatens to evict her, "[a] nigger in business is a terrible thing to see. A terrible, terrible thing to see" (Morrison 2006: 22). Contrary to his father's method of achieving success "at the expense of the white folks; [...] a source of community pride for blacks" (Blake 1980: 81–82), he gains his power by subjugating his own people, thus testifying "to his alienation from the black community" (Blake 1980: 82). In other words, immersed in the business of owning things, Macon Dead II has become a replica of the people he hates.

2.2   That's Not My Thing: Milkman's Initial Disinterest in the Past

Despite Macon Dead II's insistence on forming his son as his successor in the family business, Milkman does not seem to be very interested in his father's plans. He does not seem, in fact, to be very interested in anything at all. Comfortable in his comparably easy, middle-class life, he has never had to worry about his future, his past or his present, nor that of his fellow beings. He is oblivious to the problems of the society surrounding him, and to the fight for civil rights for that matter, since "[p]olitics—at least barbershop politics and Guitar's brand—put him to sleep. He was bored. Everybody bored him. The city was boring. The racial problems that consumed Guitar were the most boring of all" (Morrison 2006: 107). This leads him into several arguments with his friend Guitar, which would gradually drive a wedge between them that would ultimately make them enemies. And yet, he could not be less concerned. Similarly, his and his family's past do not interest him. Even when he was a little boy, he did not like to sit in the family's car facing backwards, for it "made him uneasy. It was like flying blind, and not knowing where he was going—just where he had been—troubled him. He did not want to see trees that he had passed, or houses and children slipping into the space the automobile had left behind" (32). This uneasiness about what is behind him accompanies him into adulthood, and when his father—and later his mother—insist on telling him about their history, he finds himself wanting to

> escape what he knew, escape the implications of what he had been told. And all he knew in the world about the world was what other people had told him. He felt like a garbage pail for the actions and hatreds of other people. He himself did nothing. Except for the one time he had hit his father, he had never acted independently, and that act, his only one, had brought unwanted knowledge too, as well as some responsibility for that knowledge. When his father told him about Ruth, he joined him in despising her, but he felt put upon; felt as though some burden had been given to him and that he didn't deserve it. None of that was his fault, and he didn't want to have to think or be or do something about any of it. (120)

THE RECOVERY OF HISTORY 153

This unwillingness to deal with the events of the past—a past that affects him too—makes him want to "beat a path away from his parents' past, which was also their present and was threatening to become his present as well" (180), which he does when he embarks on a quest to find the gold that his aunt Pilate had supposedly hid near her father's farm. However, as Morrison explained in an interview with Nellie McKay, it is not until he begins this chase that he "found out that there was something valuable to chase" (1994: 145), although the value of what he finds is not at all material. As Linden Peach puts it, "his quest for the lost family gold eventually becomes a search for spiritual values and the black ancestry in which he had previously shown no interest" (1995: 55).

2.3 *Of Roots and Ancestors: the Recovery of History as a Treasure Hunt*
Kill your ancestors, you kill all. There's no future, there's no past, there's just an intolerable present. And it is intolerable under the circumstances, it's not even life.

TONI MORRISON, Interviewed by Anne Koenen

Persuaded by his father to steal Pilate's "inheritance" (Morrison 2006: 97), which he believes is a bag full of gold, Milkman eventually ends up going on a quest for a much more profound legacy, one that happens to be not so much materially as existentially significant. Retracing what he thought was his aunt's journey to hide the gold, Milkman gets in touch with his roots as he unravels the story of his ancestors and the trauma hidden in it that has affected his family generation after generation. For Milkman, finding his roots means getting to know his family's past and getting in touch with his forefathers through a healthy and restorative process, a first step towards the prevention of a repetition of trauma. Formerly prevented from knowing the truth about his own family's history and traumas, he has likewise never had access to his roots and has always felt isolated from everyone else, which led him to an apparent lack of concern. However, once he reaches the lands of his ancestors, once he realizes he is among his people, Milkman feels something change in him: "He was curious about these people. He didn't feel close to them, but he did feel connected, as though there was some cord or pulse or information they shared. Back home he had never felt that way, as though he belonged to anyplace or anybody" (Morrison 2006: 293). This feeling of connectedness is something everyone is supposed to feel in regard to one's kin, to one's community. It consists of a series of shared memories, set of views and culturally modified behaviors that serve as emotional and identificatory bonds that link each one of us to those we consider 'our folks,' that is, the group of people we feel ourselves to be part of. Paule Marshall vividly describes this feeling in her novel *Praisesong for the Widow*:

> Sometimes, standing with her family amid the growing crowd on the pier, waiting for the *Robert Fulton* to heave into sight, she would have the same strange sensation as when she stood beside her great-aunt outside the church in Tatem, watching the elderly folk inside perform the Ring Shout. As more people arrived to throng the area beside the river and the cool morning air warmed to the greetings and talk, she would feel what seemed to be hundreds of slender threads streaming out from her navel and from the place where her heart was to enter those around her. And the threads went out not only to people she recognized from the neighborhood but to those she didn't know as well, such as the roomers just up from the South and the small group of West Indians whose odd accent called to mind Gullah talk and who it was said were as passionate about their rice as her father.
>
> [...]
>
> Then it would seem to her that she had it all wrong and the threads didn't come from her, but from them, from everyone on the pier, including the rowdies, issuing out of their navels and hearts to steam into her as she stood there holding the bag containing the paper plates and cups, napkins and tablecloth which she was in charge of. She visualized the threads as being silken, like those used in the embroidery on a summer dress, and of a hundred different colors. And although they were thin to the point of invisibility, they felt as strong entering her as the lifelines of woven hemp that trailed out into the water at Coney Island. [...]
>
> While the impression lasted she would cease being herself, a mere girl in a playsuit made out of the same material as her mother's dress, someone small, insignificant, outnumbered, the object of her youngest brother's endless teasing; instead, for those moments, she became part of, indeed the center of, a huge wide confraternity. (1983a: 190–191)

The links that the young Avey Johnson perceives in this passage are indeed unaccountably strong, connecting people and their descendants to their communities for generations. Moreover, when those links are forcibly broken, there often ensues great personal and collective trauma. Much of African American literature revolves around the trauma of rootlessness and bonds-severing that took place in that community on multiple occasions, from the dislocation from Africa to the division of entire families during slavery as their members were usually sold separately. Toni Morrison is no stranger to this theme, and as a consequence, many of her novels "favour community, the moral responsibility of individuals to each other, the reclamation of traditional moral values and the importance of the ancestor" (Peach 1995: 17). In the case of Milkman in *Song of Solomon*, however, the loss of roots and links to ancestry is due to a mere lack of knowledge maintained through generations. His own father knows little about his parents' origins, he even ignores their real names. Likewise, the first Macon Dead was merely a baby when his father disappeared and consequently ignores—or has forgotten/suppressed—the circumstances of his departure. All this has lead Milkman to a state of disconnection that can only be broken—that is, repaired—when he begins the work of putting his ancestors' story together. Once the process is started, he is able to feel emotions that he never knew he could feel, including anger for his grandfather's murder, an event that had never succeeded in provoking any emotion in him before (Morrison 2006: 232). Once he begins to learn what having an ancestry means, he can feel pride and understanding at other people's manifestations of it: "It was a good feeling to come into a strange town and find a stranger who knew your people. All his life he'd heard the tremor in the word: 'I live here, but my *people* ...' or: 'She acts like she ain't got no *people*,' or: 'Do any of your *people* live here?' But he hadn't known what it meant: links" (229. Italics in the original).

This discovery of the meaning of links and family ties is presented in the novel as a sort of rite of passage, for the gaining of knowledge is not something that comes easily to Milkman. He, who was once described by the inhabitants of Shalimar as having the heart of a white man (266), must first endure a series of both literal and allegorical phases in which he must strip himself of his previous lack of concern and assimilated white values in order to gain access to the ancestry and the Africanness that he has lost. According to Marc C. Conner, the ancestor for Morrison is "the 'matrix' of yearning and source of healing for the African-American" (2000b: xxv), and therefore something that the disconnected Milkman must become reacquainted with at the expense of his previous set of alliances (i.e.: middle class commodities and white western capitalist ideals inherited from his father). On his way to meet Circe, an almost phantasmagorical, atemporal creature—not unlike her mythological namesake—that stands as the physical link between himself and his grandfather, he must physically traverse a river that, like the mythical Lethe, erases his past in order to prepare him for his future. According to Peach, "[t]he journey to Circe's home [...] is made difficult as much by his city clothes as by his ineptitude. Gradually, he loses his clothes, watch, suitcase and shoes, symbolizing the white cultural values he has absorbed and assimilated at the expense of black values" (1995: 59–60). Similarly, in his grandfather's original hometown, Shalimar, he must face first a fight and then take part in a hunting trip in order to gain the clarity necessary for his final epiphanic knowledge. Both ordeals, traditional components of rites of passage into manhood, are part of Milkman's "own harrowing—in the older sense of being torn, lacerated, cut through—in order to find who he is and where he has come from" (Conner 2000a: 60).

However, Milkman's historical education does not begin in Shalimar, nor even with Circe, but at the hands of Pilate, the only member in his family that seems to have a certain—though by no means concrete—knowledge of the family's past. Also severed from her roots at an early age, she nevertheless maintained some degree of connection to her ancestral past. Due perhaps to the fact that she has unwittingly carried for years her father's bones with her, she has kept a firm grip on her memories of the past to the point that she has been repeatedly visited by her father's ghost. A reflection of her inner trauma of parental loss, her father's ghost stands as a reminiscence and as a continual link between Pilate and her as yet unknown past, as a way for her unconscious to make her aware of the importance of recovering her lost legacy. Indeed, even though Pilate does not physically undertake Milkman's journey into the past, she stands as a guide and a beacon of light to show him the way—we must not forget that the trip that takes Milkman to Shalimar, his ancestors' hometown, is a retracing of Pilate's own youthful steps. This is reflected in her very name; Pilate, homophonous with the English word 'pilot,' serves both to highlight the idea of Pilate as leader and the trope of flight present throughout the novel.

2.4 It Is All in There: Myth, Tales and Folk Culture as a Repository of Memory

From the very beginning of the narrative, Pilate seems to be the key to linking Milkman to his past; she is the sole repository of ancestral knowledge and traditions. The folk song—"one of the basic repositories of collective memory" (Benito 1998: 64)—she sings right at the beginning of the novel—"*O Sugarman done fly away / Sugarman done gone / Sugarman cut across the sky / Sugarman gone home ...*" (Morrison 2006: 6. Italics in the original)—"binds her to her community," for it turns out to be a fragmented and altered version of her grandfather Jake's story as well as the myth of the Africans who could fly (Atkinson 2000: 21). This myth, collected in several folk tales like "People who Could Fly" or "All God's Chillen Had Wings" draws on the traditional African American belief that the original African people where somehow special thanks to their most intimate knowledge of their roots and traditions, of which they themselves were brutally stripped. In the traditional folk tale about the Africans who could fly, the magical power bestowed upon the original people is that of being able to fly away, leaving the misery of slavery behind. However, other writers have modified this myth by ascribing other magical abilities to the Africans. Paule Marshal, for example, includes a similar myth in her novel *Praisesong for the Widow*:

> It was here that they brought 'em. They taken 'em out of the boats right here where we's standing. Nobody remembers how many of 'em was, but they was a good few 'cording to my gran' who was a little girl no bigger than you when it happened. The small boats was drawed up here and the ship they had just come from was out in the deep water. Great big ol' ship with sails. And the minute those Ibos was brought on shore they just stopped, my gran' said, and taken a look around. A good long look. Not saying a word. Just studying the place real good. Just taking their time and studying it.
>
> And they seen things that day you and me don't have the power to see. 'Cause those pure-born Africans was peoples my gran' said could see in more ways than one. The kind can tell you 'bout things happened long before they was born and things to come long after they's dead. Well, they seen everything that was to happen 'round here that day. The slavery time and the war time my gran' always talked about, the 'mancipation and everything after that right on up to the hard times today. Those Ibos didn't miss a thing. [...] And when they got through sizing up the place real good and seen what was to come, they turned, my gran' said, and looked at the white folks what brought 'em here. Took their time again and gived them the same hard look. [...] And when they got through studying 'em, when they *knew* just from looking at 'em how those folks was gonna do, do you know what the Ibos did? Do you ...?
>
> [...]
>
> ... They just turned, my gran' said, all of 'em [...] and walked on back down to the edge of the river here. Every las' man, woman and chile. And they wasn't taking they time no more. They had seen what they had seen and those Ibos was stepping! And they didn't bother getting back into the small boats drawed up here—boats take too much time. They just kept walking right on out over the river. Now you wouldna thought they'd of got very far seeing as it was water they was walking on. Besides they had all that iron on 'em. Iron on they ankles and they wrists and fastened 'round they necks like a dog collar. 'Nuff iron to sink an army. And chains hooking up the iron. But chains didn't stop those Ibos none. Neither iron. The way my gran' tol' it [...] 'cording to her they just kept on walking like the water was solid ground. Left the white folks standin' back here with they mouth hung open and they taken off down the river on foot.

Stepping. And when they got to where the ship was they didn't so much as give it a look. Just walked on past it. Didn't want nothing to do with that ol' ship. They feets was gonna take 'em wherever they was going that day. And they was singing by then, so my gran' said. When they realized there wasn't nothing between them and home but some water and that wasn't giving 'em no trouble they got so tickled they started in to singing. (1983a: 37–39. Italics in the original)

This passage, told by Avey Johnson's great-aunt bears a striking resemblance to the myth of the Africans who could fly as adapted by Julius Lester in "People Who Could Fly," (1969) in which most of its fantastic elements—people walking on or under the water, magical properties—together with the less magical ones—the ships of the middle passage, the cruelty of the institution of slavery and the wish to escape—also appear:

It happened long, long ago, when black people were taken from their homes in Africa and forced to come here to work as slaves. They were put onto ships, and many died during the long voyage across the Atlantic Ocean. Those that survived stepped off the boats into a land they had never seen, a land they never knew existed, and they were put into the fields to work.

[...] Some would run away and try to go back home, back to Africa where there were no white people, where they worked their own land for the good of each other, not for the good of white men. Some of those who tried to go back to Africa would walk until they came to the ocean, and then they would walk into the water, and no one knows if they did walk to Africa, through the water of if they drowned. It didn't matter. At least they were no longer slaves.

Now when the white man forced Africans onto the slave-ships, he did not know, nor did he care, if he took the village musicians, artists, or witch doctors. [...] If he had known, and had also known that the witch doctor was the medium of the gods, he would have thought twice. But he did not care. [...]

It was to a plantation in South Carolina that one boatload of Africans was brought. Among them was the son of a witch doctor who had not completed by many months studying the secrets of the gods from his father. This young man carried with him the secrets and powers of the generations of Africa.

One day, one hot day when the sun singed the very hair on the head, they were working in the fields. They had been in the fields since before the sun rose, and as it made its journey to the highest part of the sky, the very air seemed to be on fire. A young woman, her body curved with the child that grew deep inside her, fainted.

[...] The young witch doctor worked his way to her side and whispered something in her ear. She, in turn, whispered to the person beside her. He told the next person, and on around the field it went. They did it so quickly that the white man with the whip noticed nothing.

A few moments later, someone else in the field fainted, and as the white man with the whip rode toward him, the young witch doctor shouted, 'Now!' He uttered a strange word, and the person who had fainted rose from the ground, and moving his arms like wings, he flew into the sky and out of sight.

[...]

Not too many minutes had passed before the young woman fainted once again. The man was almost upon her when the young witch doctor shouted, 'Now!' and uttered a strange word. She, too, rose from the ground and, waving her arms like wings, she flew into the distance and out of sight.

[...] 'Now! Now Everyone!' He uttered the strange word and all of the Africans dropped their hoes, stretched out their arms, and flew away, back to their home, back to Africa. (1969b: 147–152)

This folk tale is the backbone of *Song of Solomon* and the legend that Milkman must learn in order to be reacquainted not only with his ancestral African roots, but with his own family history and identity. In the words of Fei-hsuan Kuo, "folklore is by definition the expression of a community—of the common beliefs, values and experiences comprising the traditions and identity of a group" (2009: 135). "It is in stories like these," says Julius Lester in the foreword to his *Black Folktales*, "that a child learns who his parents are and who he will become" (1969a: vii), which is precisely what Morrison had in mind when using this folk tale in *Song of Solomon*. The myth establishes an "equivalence between Milkman's discovery of community and his achievement of identity" (Blake 1980: 77) and underlines the significance of African heritage in the African American community. In the words of Toni Morrison: "I also wanted to use black folklore, the magic and superstitious part of it. Black people believe in magic. [...] It's part of our heritage." (Watkins 1994: 46). In order to be able to fly like his great-grandfather and the other original Africans of the myth, Milkman must forget about his western ideals and move towards the original Africans' primal understanding of men and nature. It is an understanding that Pilate already has in some way, for she, unlike the rest of the characters in the novel, is acquainted with some version of the flying African myth.

And yet, this is not the only connection to her African heritage that Pilate displays, for even her physical appearance evinces her deeper linkage, as Macon Dead once points out: "If you ever have a doubt we from Africa, look at Pilate. She look just like Papa and he looked like all them pictures you ever see of Africans. A Pennsylvania African. Acted like one too. Close his face up like a door" (Morrison 2006: 54). Further reference to Pilate's dark complexion and non-western attire and posture is made when Milkman first lays eyes on her:

> They found her on the front steps sitting wide-legged in a long-sleeved, long-skirted black dress. Her hair was wrapped in black too, and from a distance, all they could really see beneath her face was the bright orange she was peeling. She was all angles, he remembered later, knees, mostly, and elbows. One foot pointed east and one pointed west.
>
> [...] The whites of her fingernails were like ivory. [...] Of course she was anything but pretty, yet he knew he could have watched her all day: the fingers pulling thread veins from the orange sections, the berry-black lips that made her look as though she wore make-up, the earring ... And when she stood up, he all but gasped. She was as tall as his father, head and shoulders taller than himself. Her dress wasn't as long as he had thought; it came to just below the calf and now he could see her unlaced men's shoes and the silvery-brown skin of her ankles. (36–38)

Part of Milkman's fascination with Pilate is the very surprising fact that she was born without a navel, that "she gave birth to herself," as Morrison puts it (McKay 1994: 146). This unprecedented detail further characterizes her as the ultimate ancestor, a kind of Eve that not only has direct access to the original people, but is part of them; a "source of innocence and, paradoxically, of primal knowledge" (Peach 1995: 68). Pilate becomes a woman that "[w]ithout ever leaving the ground, she could fly" (Morrison 2006: 336), just like her ancestors did and Milkman will ultimately do as well. Her unsuspected knowledge and direct link to her roots qualifies her as "the novel's clearest representative of personal and racial heritage and continuity with the past" (Harris 1980: 75); one of the original magical people who could soar.

2.5   Lieux de Mémoire: *Places of History and the History in Places*

Much of the importance of the African ancestors lies in the fact that they were originally from Africa, that is, that they had direct contact with their roots by way of the land itself. Although the loss of that homeland is at the root of *Song of Solomon,* Africa is not the only land that becomes central for the Dead family. Abandoned by his father in his flight home, the first Macon Dead loses the opportunity to return to his father's homeland, so he decides to establish his own home in America. Although he later moves away from his original town and severs his own future family from their true origins, his legend and that of his predecessor are forever linked to Shalimar, the town named after his own father, Solomon. Those are the roots that Milkman must reacquaint himself with, and he can only do that by actually visiting them and physically standing in the places imbued with his family's trauma. The Dead family—except for, again, Pilate, whose house is "filled with the smell of nature with which she is associated, of the forest and of blackberries" (Peach 1995: 69), and who has read only one book in her life and that, significantly, a geography book—is not only estranged from their historical connections, but also from nature (Heinze 1993: 84), and therefore land and the Africans' intimate communion with it. The original space, that is the place where someone or someone's ancestors were born, is highly valued in the African American community, for, according to Barbara Christian,

> [i]n the ancestral African tradition, place is as important as the human actors. For the land is a participant in the maintenance of folk tradition it is one of the necessary constants through which the folk dramatize the meaning of life, as it is passed on from one generation to the next. Setting then is organic to the characters' view of themselves. And a change in place drastically alters the traditional values that give their life coherence. (qtd. in Heinze 1993: 131)

This is the reason behind the African Americans' trauma of estrangement from Africa as well as the Dead's family sense of uprootedness. The family is left without history thanks to their forefathers' refusal to communicate it, but they are also rendered ignorant of their communal ties to their native land because their predecessors moved away from it. This is a common theme in Morrison's novels, as Denise Heinze points out, where those families or communities that have forgotten their past and traditions in favor of the dominant white ideology have "clustered in the industrial Midwest: Lorain, Ohio; Southside, Michigan; Medallion, Ohio; Cincinnati, Ohio and the City" (1993: 108). Consequently, "[t]hose communities that have more successfully retained their ethnicity and a measure of independence are located in the South: Shalimar, Virginia; Pilate's Virginian Island Colony; Eloe, Florida; and, one might add, the Isle of the Chevaliers" (Heinze 1993: 108). As a result of this, she continues, "the further south blacks travel, the closer they are likely to come to cultural and spiritual fulfillment, to *communitas*" (Heinze 1993: 108. Italics in the original). This is what happens to Milkman, who needs to actually make the trip down south to his family's ancestral land to recover what was lost to him. From the moment that Milkman starts his trip south, the presence of nature is shown in the narrative through "a heightening of natural perception, a richness of symbolism, and the supernatural presence of natural and ancestral spirits" (Krumholtz 1993: 568), although it is not until Milkman reaches Shalimar, "the community furthest removed geographically and ideologically from white society" (Heinze 1993: 140), that "the cathartic moment for Milkman's transformation from disconnection to connection" (Heinze 1993: 140) takes place. Moreover, as if to further highlight the significance of the land, the earth itself, it is only when he is left alone at night in a dark forest during a hunting expedition that he begins to feel that long lost symbiosis with nature: "Down either side of his thighs he felt the sweet gum's surface roots cradling him like the rough but maternal hands of a grandfather" (Morrison 2006: 279). Such a communion with nature actually saves his life because it is nature itself that warns him about an impending attack from his friend Guitar:

> Feeling both tense and relaxed, he sank his fingers into the grass. He tried to listen with his fingertips, to hear what, if anything, the earth had to say, and it told him quickly that someone was standing behind him and he had just enough time to raise one hand to his neck and catch the wire that fastened around his throat. (279)

This experience leaves him "exhilarated by simply walking the earth. Walking it like he belonged on it; like his legs were stalks, tree trunks, a part of his body that extended down down down into the rock and soil, and were comfortable there—on the earth and on the place where he walked. And he did not limp" (280–281). His intimate knowledge of his ancestral land has not only cured him of his limp—a birth defect (he has an undersized leg) and a clear metaphor for his previous lack of wholeness—but has made him finally aware of where his roots lay; where he belonged. As a consequence, he begins to understand the traumatic impact of his family's past and to show some feeling in reaction to it: "Maybe it was the whiskey, which always made other people gracious when he drank it, but Milkman felt a glow listening to a story come from this man that he'd heard many times before but only half listened to. Or maybe it was being there in the place where it happened that made it seem so real" (231). Consistent with *Beloved*'s notion of rememories hanging in the place where a trauma occurred, waiting for someone to pass by to possess him/her, Milkman feels the full impact of the past trauma at the site where it occurred, where its memory is maintained with a fuller force. Nevertheless, there is a significant difference; whereas Sethe warns Denver against revisiting her ancestors' places of trauma lest she should become enslaved to the suffering embedded in them, Milkman's return is a freeing one in that it enables him to understand his family's hidden past.

2.6 Hallowed Be Thy Name: Naming and the Power of Designation

Sitting in the woods, Milkman gains the knowledge that enables him to properly feel and understand the trauma of his forefathers. Standing on the site of the trauma, he is able to recover the memory of the past and to make sense of its traces in the present. One of those traces is in the very naming of the town in which Milkman comes to this realization. In Shalimar, Benito and Manzanas argue, names have been kept intact without the white man's intervention, as can be seen in the fact that they do not have Coke but Cherry Smash (1994: 200). Indeed, the town is named after his ancestor Solomon and is actually full of people and places with the same name, a fact that particularly pleases Macon Dead when he learns about it, although "[h]e wasn't a bit interested in the flying part" (Morrison 2006: 334). Naming is a very important part of the novel from its very epigraph: "The fathers may soar / And the children may know their names," where the central themes of naming and flying are conflated. A person's name is intimately related to his identity and his cultural heritage. In the words of Paul Ricoeur, "[e]ach of us bears a name that we have not given to ourselves, but we have received from another: in our culture, this is a patronym that situates me along a line of filiation, and a given name that distinguishes me from my siblings" (2006: 129). Names are therefore part of our identity, and individuals often resist any outside attempt to change them, as is the case with Indigo, the little protagonist of Ntozake Shange's *Sassafras, Cypress & Indigo*:

> Indigo had always liked her name. There was nothing wrong with her name. She was particularly herself. She changed the nature of things. She colored & made richer what was blank & plain. The slaves who were ourselves knew all about indigo & Indigo herself. Besides there was great danger in callin' out their name. Spirits get confused, bring you something meant for someone else. Folks get upset, mere with wrath instead of grace, when callt by a name not blessed & known on earth. (2010: 35)

However, this relationship between names and identity is problematic in the case of the African American community, whose members lost their original African names when they were renamed by their masters during slavery. Just as

Indigo worries in the excerpt from *Sassafrass, Cypress & Indigo*, Africans had a very tight relationship with their names, a relationship based on ancestors, on land and on spiritualism, and believed in the 'great danger' of changing someone's name. Toni Morrison herself has reflected on this predicament: "If you come from Africa, your name is gone. It is particularly problematic because it is not just *your* name but your family, your tribe. When you die, how can you connect with your ancestors if you have lost your name?" (LeClair 1994: 126. Italics in the original). This "huge psychological scar" (LeClair 1994: 126) is part of the loss of connections with the original land and cultural heritage that the African slaves suffered after being transplanted to America, and part of their collective traumatic history. Slave owners could not be bothered to learn the strange sounding, original names of their slaves and therefore changed them in yet another example of the complete control they exerted over their property. Usually, slaves received some name taken from the Bible or based on their external characteristics followed by their master's surname to mark them as his property. This ideology is what, Benito and Manzanas argue, makes Baby Suggs reject her 'official' name of Jenny Whitlow—given to her by her master—and adopt the name her husband used to call her—Baby—together with his surname—Suggs—which she in turn gives to her son Halle instead of their master's surname Whitlow (1994: 273). Such a rejection of the characteristics of owned property which with the slave's name was imbued also took place in later years, when some African Americans began rejecting those names indicative of white supremacy, and many changed their surnames to X as a symbol of their lost heritage. The X was the signature of the illiterate and it therefore also 'marks the spot' of the slaves' exclusion from written culture and history. The African American practice of changing one's surname to X was highly common during the civil rights era among the Nation of Islam followers, led by Malcolm X, and is reflected in *Song of Solomon* in the following conversation among Guitar and Milkman:

> You sound like that red-headed Negro named X. Why don't you join him and call yourself Guitar X?
> X, Bains—what difference does it make? I don't give a damn about names.
> You miss his point. His point is to let white people know you don't accept your slave name.
> I don't give a shit what white people know or even think. Besides, I do accept it. It's part of who I am. Guitar is *my* name. Bains is the slave master's name. And I'm all of that. Slave names don't bother me; but slave status does. (Morrison 2006: 160. Italics in the original)

Guitar's argument here hinges on the aforementioned impact that names have on identity, as well as on W. E. B. DuBois's idea of double consciousness. He argues here that the slave name—and therefore the former status thereof—is part of the African American's identity together with the African heritage which was lost together with the cultural knowledge and ancestry it entailed. However, slave-owners were not the only way in which African Americans lost their identificatory names, and a certain amount of renaming also took place during the reconstruction. Gloria Naylor, for example, reflects on how, at that time, the ineptitude of a particular white man could also change the name and thus the identity—with all the traumatic consequences that that entails—of a black man without paying the least attention to the deeper repercussions that such an apparently simple act can have for the person affected as well as for his descendants:

> Papa said that when the emancipation came, his daddy was just a little boy, and he had been hard of hearing so his master and everyone on the plantation had to call him twice to get his attention. So his name being Michael, they always called him Michael-Michael. And when the union census taker came and was registering black folks, they asked what my granddaddy's name was, and they said Michael-Michael was all they knew. So the dumb Yankee put that down and we been Michael ever since. (1983: 17)

Likewise, in his autobiographical work *Black Boy*, Richard Wright recounts how his grandfather was cheated out of a military pension after having his surname changed by a white officer while being discharged from action during the Civil War:

> In the process of being discharged from the Union Army, he had gone to a white officer to seek help in filling out his papers. In filling out the papers, the white officer misspelled Grandpa's name, making him Richard Vinson instead of Richard Wilson. It was possible that Grandpa's southern accent and his illiteracy made him mispronounce his own name. It was rumored that the white officer had been a Swede and had had a poor knowledge of English. Another rumor had it that the white officer had been a Southerner and had deliberately falsified Grandpapa's papers. Anyway, Grandpapa did not discover that he had been discharged in the name of Richard Vinson until years later; and when he applied to the War Department for a pension, no trace could be found of his ever having served in the Union Army under the name of Richard Wilson. (1945: 153)

Similarly, in *Song of Solomon*, this is how the Dead family got their surname:

> When freedom came. All the colored people in the state had to register with the Freedmen's Bureau. [...] They all had to register. Free and not free. Free and used-to-be-slaves. Papa was in his teens and went to sign up, but the man behind the desk was drunk. He asked Papa where he was born. Papa said Macon. Then he asked him who his father was. Papa said, 'He's dead.' Asked him who owned him, Papa said, 'I'm free.' Well, the Yankee wrote it all down, but in the wrong spaces. Had him born in Dunfrie, wherever the hell that is, and in the space for his name the fool wrote, 'Dead' comma 'Macon.' (Morrison 2006: 53)

This is how the family loses the memory of their original name—which becomes, in a way, 'dead' to the future—and the reason that the name of Solomon does not mean anything to them. The family then loses its "heritage, history and identity and constitutes a family line of cultural orphanage" (Kuo 2009: 156). With the mistake of a single man, the family's tradition "becomes 'dead,' as the new family name suggests" (Kuo 2009: 156), and Milkman's trip south becomes necessary to recover this tradition. Macon Dead (Milkman's father, and the speaker in the previous quote) is aware of the significance that their family name has, and what was lost to their previous one:

> Surely, he thought, he and his sister had some ancestor, some lithe young man with onyx skin and legs as straight as cane stalks, who had a name that was real. A name given to him at birth with love and seriousness. A name that was not a joke, nor a disguise, nor a brand name. But who this lithe young man was, and where his cane-stalk legs carried him from or to, could never be known. No. Nor his name. His own parents, in some mood of perverseness or resignation, had agreed to abide by a naming done to them by somebody who couldn't have cared less. Agreed to take and pass on to all their issue this heavy name scrawled in perfect thoughtlessness by a drunken Yankee in the Union Army. (Morrison 2006: 17–18)

And yet, even though Macon complains here about his parents' recklessness in maintaining a joke of a name, born out of the carelessness of a drunken white man, he seems to gloss over the rather peculiar way in which the members of his family get their names. In what also are exertions of power upon the babies, all family members (except for the first-born son, who is invariably named Macon Dead) are to be named by randomly picking names from a Bible—which is also how Toni Morrison's mother was named. This results in quite absurd female names like First Corinthians or Pilate. As a child, however, Pilate was fully aware of the significance that names have on the individuals that bear them, for even though "[y]ou can't get much worse than that for a name" (19), she took the piece of paper where her name was written—the only word her father ever wrote—and hung it from her ear in an earring devised out of a golden brooch and a little brass box. Pilate was therefore conscious that, as Guitar puts it, "[n]iggers get their names the way they get everything else—the best way they can" (88), and therefore must deal with them and with what the names indicate about them and their history.

Sometimes, however, names can be changed, and the act of changing a name has a strong significance in itself. In the same way that African Americans started changing their surnames to X to signify that they rejected the name their predecessors were given as slaves, the first Macon Dead decides to keep his new name instead of sticking to his rightful Jake for "it was new and would wipe out the past. Wipe it all out" (54). At other times, however, individuals might prefer not to hide (from) the past but exhibit it proudly in their names as an external marker of the internal changes that that past had made in them. An example of this can be seen in the story of a fugitive slave named Henry Brown, who after spending "27 grim hours entombed in a tight-fitting box that was tossed and turned repeatedly during the 350-mile journey" (Cowan 2010: n.p.) on his way to freedom, adopted the word "Box" as his middle name to signify his ordeal.

Naming, therefore, is an expression of the power and dominion of someone over something.[2] Consequently, ex-slaves' renaming of themselves is a way of expressing their recovered dominion over their own selves and destinies, as well as dominion over their past traumas. In the words of Rafael Pérez-Torres, "[t]he power to rename represents a reclamation of agency when many other venues are closed that would help the characters establish a sense of subjectivity" (1993: 697), which is reflected in the "common practice, among the community, to give a name to someone according to their characteristics: it's life that gives you a name, in a way" (Morrison qtd. in Pérez-Torres 1993: 697). Thus, it is the community, or blacks themselves, that construct "through a communal act of rechristening a self meant to counteract the disempowerment of a slave past" (Pérez-Torres 1993: 697). According to Linden Peach, it is Morrison's "conviction that black people, at the level of the personal self, have the capacity to 'invent themselves'" (1995: 8), which is exemplified not only throughout

---

2 For further information about the theory of naming, see Saul A. Kripke, *Naming and Necessity* (1980).

her novels, but in the very fact that she published her first book *The Bluest Eye* under a pseudonym in order to prevent her employer from knowing she had published it with a competing press (Peach 1995: 7–8). In light of all this, Macon Dead's acquiescence to his new name, although born out of an act of white dominion, should be read not as mere complacency with white men's ways, as his son does, but as a reaffirmation of his own free will to leave his traumatic past behind[3] and start again in a new place with his new wife. Likewise, his later choice of names for his farm animals—President Lincoln for the horse and General Lee for a pig—and actual farm—Lincoln Heaven—is a way not only of reaffirming his power to possess and name what's possessed but also of subverting the white man's power to do the same (Benito and Manzanas 1994: 191). A similar subversion is at stake in the naming of several streets and locations in Milkman's native town:

> Not Doctor Street, a name the post office did not recognize. Town maps registered the street as Mains Avenue, but the only colored doctor in the city had lived and died on that street, and when he moved there in 1896 his patients took to calling the street, which none of them lived in or near, Doctor Street. Later, when other Negroes moved there, and when the postal service became a popular means of transferring messages among them, envelopes from Louisiana, Virginia, Alabama and Georgia began to arrive addressed to people at house numbers on Doctor Street. The post office workers returned these envelopes or passed them on to the Dead Letter Office. […] Some of the city legislators, whose concern for appropriate names and the maintenance of the city's landmarks was the principal part of their political life, saw to it that 'Doctor Street' was never used in any official capacity. And since they knew that only Southside residents kept it up, they had notices posted in the stores, barbershops, and restaurants in that part of the city saying that the avenue running northerly and southerly from Shore Road fronting the lake to the junction of routes 6 and 2 leading to Pennsylvania, and also running parallel to and between Rutherford Avenue and Broadway, had always been and would always be known as Mains Avenue and not Doctor Street.

> It was a genuinely clarifying public notice because it gave Southside residents a way to keep their memories alive and please the city legislators as well. They called it Not Doctor Street, and were inclined to call the

---

3 This is not the only instance in which Macon Dead decides to forget a name (in this case his own) in order to escape from trauma. When his wife died, he would not let anybody pronounce her name, which is the reason his two children do not know it (Morrison 2006: 43).

charity hospital at its northern end No Mercy Hospital since it was 1931 [...] before the first colored expectant mother was allowed to give birth inside its wards and not on its steps. (Morrison 2006: 4–5)

This tension between the Southside residents and the city legislators resides once again in a conflict of power between those allowed to officially name people and places and "the indigenous authority and the oral tradition of the people who actually live in the community" (Middleton 1993: 67). Just like the naming of people, naming places asserts the namer's ownership and control over those places. In conflict zones like those areas forcibly governed by colonizers, it has always been the rulers' place to give names to the places they controlled. It is a way of mapping, even if it meant changing the names originally given to them by the colonized. In Ireland, for instance, during the English occupation new names were given to the towns, villages, cities and landmarks that already bore a name in Gaelic. That process was done in several different ways: by literally translating from Irish into English (an Abhainn Dubh/Blackwater), by inventing some altogether new names (Baile Átha Cliath/Dublin),[4] or by Anglicizing the Gaelic name into English phonology and spelling (Ciarrai/Kerry). As a manifestation of these national troubles, Irish literature has portrayed the obvious political import of such practices in several works, such as the play *Translations* (1980) by Brian Friel. By means of this type of name-adscription, the English managed to establish their dominion over a subjugated people, who lost their language, their independence, their religion and even their capacity to name their own territory. It should come as no surprise, then, that some of these changes were reverted after the country's independence in 1922 in a clear attempt to regain the Irish's long-lost autonomy and dominion over their landscape. In *Song of Solomon*, a similar subversion of roles takes place with the renaming of Mains Avenue and the Hospital as Not Doctor Street and No Mercy Hospital, respectively.

Language, in sum, "can be and has been manipulated by those in authority to maintain their advantage and protect their positions" (Peach 1995: 40). This is the reason why the white city legislators in *Song of Solomon* try so actively to prevent the renaming of Mains Avenue as Doctor Street; they fear that, if they allow such a change to take place, their position as the "authority" might shift. A further example of this is the way in which the white farmer at the beginning

---

4 The name Dublin actually comes from an Anglicization of the Viking name Dubh Linn, meaning black pool, which was another name used for the place prior to the English conquest.

of *Sula* uses language to manipulate a black slave and trick him into accepting a bad piece of land:

> A good white farmer promised freedom and a piece of bottom land to his slave if he would perform some very difficult chores. When the slave completed the work, he asked the farmer to keep his end of the bargain. Freedom was easy—the farmer had no objection to that. But he didn't want to give up any land. So he told the slave that he was very sorry that he had to give him valley land. He had hoped to give him a piece of the Bottom. The slave blinked and said he thought valley land was bottom land. The master said, 'Oh, no! See those hills? That's bottom land, rich and fertile.'
> 'But it's high up in the hills,' said the slave.
> 'High up from us,' said the master, 'but when God looks down, it's the bottom. That's why we call it so. It's the bottom of heaven—best land there is.'
> So the slave pressed his master to try to get him some. He preferred it to the valley. And it was done. The nigger got the hilly land, where planting was backbreaking, where the soil slid down and washed away the seeds, and where the wind lingered all through the winter. (Morrison 1982: 5)

Since the white master was the one in possession of the authority to name, the slave had no reason to doubt him, and therefore, language was manipulated once more to gain advantage over the powerless. As a marker of historical memory, the name stuck, and the hilly part of Medalion in *Sula* kept on being known as the Bottom, even though it was "a nigger joke" (4). Names, therefore, do not only carry the ideology of the namer and the identity of (or forced upon) the named, but they also carry down in history the—sometimes traumatic—memory of the events related and leading to the naming itself. This is why Milkman, after realizing the importance of historical knowledge and discovering the true past and names of his predecessors,

> read the road signs with interest now, wondering what lay beneath the names. The Algonquins had named the territory he lived in Great Water, *mich gami*. How many dead lives and fading memories were buried in and beneath the names of the places in this country. Under the recorded names were other names, just as 'Macon Dead,' recorded for all time in some dusty file, hid from view the real names of people, places and things. Names that had meaning. No wonder Pilate put hers in her ear. When you know your name, you should hang on to it, for unless it is noted down and remembered, it will die when you do. Like the street he

lived on, recorded as Mains Avenue, but called Not Doctor Street by the Negroes in memory of his grandfather, who was the first colored man of consequence in that city. (Morrison 2006: 329)

It is Pilate, precisely, who starts opening Milkman's eyes to the significance of language and naming. When he first knew her, she lost no time in lecturing him about the necessity of expressing oneself properly: "You all must be the dumbest unhung Negroes on earth. What they telling you in them schools? You say 'Hi' to pigs and sheep when you want 'em to move. When you tell a human being 'Hi,' he ought to get up and knock you down" (37). In this exchange, Pilate is not only criticizing Milkman's language, she is criticizing the kind of white-dominated education that taught it to him. Just as James Baldwin argues, "the whole process of education occurs within a social framework and is designed to perpetuate the aims of society" (1985a: 326). Therefore, 'them schools' preserve and instill "hegemonic ideologies of oppression" (Krumholz 1993: 552) through what they teach as well as through the language in which they teach it. A similar lecture on the proper use of language and communication skills is again repeated when Circe chides Milkman saying: "You don't listen to people. Your ear is on your head, but it's not connected to your brain" (Morrison 2006: 247), implying that he suffers from a disconnection between his senses and his historical memory (Benito and Manzanas 1994: 199) but also that he is not able to communicate properly. Insomuch as the receiver is just as important as the speaker in the communicative process, and that a shared understanding of the code—the language in which the communication takes place—is paramount, the fact that Milkman is unable to listen highlights his deficient use of language. It is not only that Milkman does not listen to Circe or anyone else, he does not *understand* her; they do not share the same language. Much older than Pilate, Circe stands in the novel as an even closer link to African heritage and therefore to the African language. This is reflected in her way of speaking, similar to what we now call Black English. According to Geneva Smitherman, Black English is "an Africanized form of English reflecting Black America's linguistic-cultural African heritage and the conditions of servitude, oppression, and life in America. Black language is Euro-American speech with an Afro-American meaning, nuance, tone, and gesture" (1977: 2). Language is therefore historically and ideologically marked, and the kind of language a person uses marks him/her with the ideology and historical conscience embedded in it. This is one of the reasons that Milkman does not understand Circe. He has lost all connection to his original language and knowledge and uses the language of white supremacy instead. Circe, however, is still in touch with her African roots and her speech reflects her historical knowledge. This is the source of Milkman's mistake with the name of his grandfather's hometown Shalimar. All its inhabitants pronounce it *"Shalleemone"* (Morrison 2006: 261), which is almost homophonous with Solomon, after whom the town was named, and after Milkman asks her where his parents were from, this is presumably what Circe says. Milkman, however, trapped within his white supremacist language, "leaps from this phonemic configuration to the name of a medieval European emperor with its exotic French spelling" (Middleton 1993: 68), Charlemagne, and it is not until he gets to a local AAA office that he recognizes his error. Estranged from his roots, he does not share the same linguistic knowledge as those who have remained in the south—and are therefore closer to the original site of memory. This linguistic knowledge comes to him during his hunting trip in Shalimar, when he is lost in the woods. Once in communion with the very patch of earth that his great-grandfather once walked, he is able to gain the historical knowledge that he lacked in an epiphany that he experiences in linguistic terms: "It was all language. An extension of the click people made in their cheeks back home when they called a dog to follow them. No, it was not language: it was what there was before language. Before things were written down. Language in the time when men and animals did talk to one another" (Morrison 2006: 278). It is only after he comes to understand the language of his predecessors that Milkman is able to make the connection between Charlemagne, Shalimar, Solomon and the Sugarman of Pilate's song and acquire the full historical knowledge that he had so long lacked.

2.7 *Learning (in Order) to Fly: the Acquisition of Historical Knowledge as a Liberating Process*

> Truth and Freedom; two great things for a poor man, a son of slaves and ex-slaves.
>
> WALTER MOSLEY, *Black Betty*

Knowledge—not only linguistic knowledge, but knowledge about the hidden past—is the key to freeing Milkman from his bonds to the white dominant ideology and allowing him to fly—both in a literal and in a figurative way. The motif of flying is highly recurrent in African American literature and is often equated with freedom as "a way of escaping, of elevating oneself away from the oppressive land with its imposed machineries of control" (San José 2009: 68). This is especially evident in the myth of the flying African, in which the African slaves still in contact with their heritage[5] are able to elevate themselves above

---

5 Precisely this (not being in contact with one's heritage), Peach argues, is the reason that Robert Smith fails to fly at the beginning of *Song of Solomon* (1995: 66).

the white man's oppressive force and escape to freedom. It is also doubly present in Ralph Ellison's short story "Flying Home." In it, we first find the story of a young black pilot who, ever since he saw a little white boy's toy plane, had dreamed of being able to fly one of those machines. His yearning is clearly that of equality, of being able to do what white men do, and of being respected for it. But this dream of freedom and equality is suddenly brought to an end when the plane he is flying hits a buzzard—a metaphor for the vulture-like white society that preyed on the lives and work of African Americans—and crashes. Just as in the myth of Icarus, his flight towards freedom ends in tragedy. In his semi-conscious state he encounters another black man that comes to his rescue and tells him the second story about flying present in the narrative. In the old black man's tale, flying is once again equated with the idea of freedom and escaping from the white man's control. The story is about a black man who dies, goes to heaven and becomes an angel. However, even in death, he cannot achieve total equality, for the white angels are set on literally harnessing him so that he can only fly with one wing. When he repeatedly disobeys and begins "throwin' feathers in everybody's face" (Ellison 1967: 159), he is ultimately expelled from heaven, thus putting an end to his being "free at last" (159).

This idea of flight as a means of escaping inequality and becoming free from oppression is also present in many slave spirituals, as Benito and Manzanas argue, which were in turn based mostly on passages of the Bible in which deliverance for the Israelites or for the perseverant is announced as coming on eagles' wings (1994: 184–186). Similarly, in *Song of Solomon*, Milkman offers the possibility of "[b]uy[ing] a plane ticket" (Morrison 2006: 104) as a trivial solution for his problems. However, the motif of flight in the novel detaches itself from the previous examples of flight as a mere metaphor for liberation from oppression and racism since, at a later stage in the narrative, "the liberation signified by flight becomes an act of self-creation rather than simply escape—one can fly without leaving the ground" (Krumholz 1993: 556). Flight, therefore, signifies much more than that and is equated with knowledge and connectedness with one's history, something that Milkman eventually learns to yearn for.

Still, even without that incentive, Milkman has always been obsessed with the idea of flying, probably unaware of its most profound significance for African Americans. Marked from his birth on the day after Robert Smith jumps from the roof of Mercy—or No Mercy—Hospital with a pair of blue silk wings attached to his person in an attempt to "fly from Mercy to the other side of Lake Superior" (Morrison 2006: 3), when Milkman "discovered, at four, the same thing Mr. Smith had learned earlier—that only birds and airplanes could fly—he lost all interest in himself. To have to live without that single gift saddened him and left his imagination so bereft that he appeared dull even to the women who did not hate his mother" (9). Such disconsolation can be understood in the terms that Benito proposes: "To his materialistic mind, the world of memory, of the metaphysical, of mythical men who can fly, the world of his own ancestors is a world apart, not to be resuscitated or retrieved" (1998: 63). Therefore, even though Milkman has always felt an "unrestrained joy at anything that could fly" (Morrison 2006: 178), he can only contemplate the possibility of a human achieving such a feat after he reconnects with the mythical world of his ancestors, and the idea that his very own great-grandfather was one of those mythical men fills him again with that "unrestrained joy" he has been feeling since he was a child:

> He could fly! You hear me? My great-granddaddy could fly! Goddam! [...] The son of a bitch could fly! [...] That motherfucker could fly! Could fly! He didn't need no airplane. Didn't need no fucking tee double you ay. He could fly his own self! [...] Oh, man! He didn't need no airplane. He just took off; got fed up. *All the way up!* No more cotton! No more bales! No more orders! No more shit! He flew, baby. Lifted his beautiful black ass up in the sky and flew on home. Can you dig it? Jesus God, that must have been something to see. (328. Italics in the original)

Such an achievement is also reserved for Milkman, though he will not accomplish it until he learns to rid himself of his detached manner of living, of his false sense of superiority acquired through a lifetime of living easily, without racial or social preoccupations and without any connection to his cultural heritage. Just as Guitar realizes when pondering the inability to fly of a long-tailed peacock, "[c]an't nobody fly with all that shit. Wanna fly, you got to give up the shit that weighs you down" (179), meaning that Milkman must free himself from his socio-psychological baggage and open his eyes to the long-lost past in order to fly like Solomon. Knowledge about his family's past frees Milkman from the constraints of white society and its set of rules. It also frees him from his previously dissolute life and from the traumatic repression/suppression of the past. As Denise Heinze claims, "[t]he myth of flying that distinguishes Shalimar served as the antistructure to slavery, but for Milkman, it becomes the vehicle for escape from the distorted values that have corrupted his own home and community" (1993: 140). Having the knowledge to openly face the hidden past not only renders Milkman finally capable of understanding the language of his ancestors and the plight of his friends and family, it also renders him able to love. And this knowledge together with this capacity to love allow him to elevate himself over the previous difficulties and hindrances and "ride" the air (Morrison 2006: 337). Despite some pessimistic readings of the novel's ending (Bouson 2000: 100), I argue that the knowledge that Milkman has achieved does make him free to love and to give himself to the community, in a leap of faith that makes him fly, if not (perhaps) literally, most surely in a transcendent way. In the words of A. Leslie Harris, it does not really matter if Milkman lives or dies after his leap over a cliff and into the arms of his friend Guitar, intent on killing him; for her, Milkman's "joyful acceptance of the burden of his past transforms his leap toward Guitar into a triumphant flight" (1980: 76). Likewise, Benito argues that in the last scene of the novel, Guitar is aware that "death does not equal finality" in the sense that, thanks to the knowledge of the past gained through his reconnection with his roots, he has "transcended Western rationalism and has learned to fill the gap between past and present, life and death" (1995b: 37). Insomuch as, according to Bouson, "[t]hrough its insistent mythologizing of African-American roots, *Song of Solomon* effectively transforms the disgrace, degradation and stigma of slavery and racist oppression into racial pride and the transcendence of suffering [...] represented in the originary figure of Solomon, the flying African" (2000: 78), Milkman's final flight should therefore be read in the same terms.

2.8 Turning the Tables: Reversal of Stigmas and Our Debt to the Future

According to Bouson, one of the merits of *Song of Solomon* is that, through an emphasis on the importance of the recovery of historically lost roots and legacies, Morrison is also exercising a reversal of the stigmas traditionally associated with African Americans and African heritage (2000: 78). The narrative consistently works to overturn negative associations such as the common argument among white slaveholders that black men were mentally inferior and incapable of producing art or devoid of an aesthetically rich cultural tradition. Through the use of the myth of the flying African, for instance, Morrison draws attention to the value of African folk heritage. Likewise, she again picks up the issue of skin color and of color prejudice among African Americans when she explicitly compares dark, unkempt Pilate with Milkman's mother and praises the former in the result:

> They were so different, these two women. One black, the other lemony. One corseted, the other buck naked under her dress. One well read but ill traveled. The other had read only a geography book, but had been from one end of the country to another. One wholly dependent on money for life, the other indifferent to it. (Morrison 2006: 139)

According to Denise Heinze, "Pilate revivifies black American womanhood because she is so tied to her African heritage, unlike the impure Mrs. Dead who epitomizes the extent of western influence" (1993: 136). The narrative, thus, "works to undermine the color-caste hierarchy, which values light-skinned, middle class women and devalues those who are dark skinned and lower class" (Bouson 2000: 85), valuing instead a closer connection to the original African roots and traditions. As a result of this, "Ruth may appear, to those unaware of African American culture, to be correct and beautiful while Pilate is strange and even ugly. But when viewed through the lens of their culture, Ruth is strange and Pilate is beautiful" (Atkinson 2000: 24).

This reversal of stigmas is more clearly represented in the motives and ideology behind the Seven Days, a violent organization intent on avenging any act of white violence by reproducing it on white instead of black victims. However, despite the patent injustice that such conduct entails, there is a clear narrative intention at play here, for, as Bouson puts it, "[i]f *Song of Solomon* at first glance appears to reinforce the stereotype of the pathological, violent black man in its description of the Seven Days, the narrative also actively reprojects the shame associated with this derogatory stereotype onto whites" (2000: 93). Guitar cannot see the cruelty and the unjust repetition of violence that killing innocent people—no matter their skin color—entails because, "[u]sing the white racist discourse of difference and pathology to define whiteness" (Bouson 2000: 92), he ascribes to them all the derogative epithets of violent, brutish and unnatural that they—the white people—had traditionally ascribed to blacks:

> Every time somebody does a thing like that to one of us, they say the people who did it were crazy or ignorant. That's like saying they were drunk. Or constipated. Why isn't cutting a man's eyes out, cutting his nuts off, the kind of thing you never get too drunk or ignorant to do? Too crazy to do? Too constipated to do? And more to the point, how come Negroes, the craziest, most ignorant people in America, don't get that crazy and that ignorant? No. White people are unnatural. As a race they are unnatural. (Morrison 2006: 155–156)

What transpires from this—according to Guitar—is that blacks actually need to defend themselves by treating whites as whites had treated them and rid the world of a race that is naturally evil and therefore has no innocent members:

> There are no innocent white people, because every one of them is a potential nigger-killer, if not an actual one. You think Hitler surprised them? You think just because they went to war they thought he was a freak? Hitler's the most natural white man in the world. He killed Jews and Gypsies because he didn't have us. Can you see those Klansmen shocked by him? No, you can't. (155)

Hence, according to Guitar, the difference between blacks and whites; the latter's 'unnaturalness' makes them kill and harm people for fun, which they have been doing for centuries now:

> Milkman, if Kennedy got drunk and was sitting around a potbellied stove in Mississippi, he might join a lynching party just for the hell of it. Under those circumstances his unnaturalness would surface. But I know I wouldn't join one no matter how drunk I was or how bored, and I know you wouldn't either, nor any black man I know or even heard tell of. Ever. In any world, at any time, just get up and go find somebody white to slice up. But they *can* do it. And they don't even do it for profit, which is why they do most things. They do it for fun. Unnatural.
> [...]
> I don't know about the women. I can't say what their women would do, but I do remember that picture of those white mothers holding up their babies so they could get a good look at some black men burning on a tree. So I have my suspicions about Eleanor Roosevelt. But *none* about Mr. Roosevelt. You could've taken him and his wheelchair and put him in a small dusty town in Alabama and given him some tobacco, a checkerboard, some whiskey, and a rope and he'd have done it too. What I'm saying is, under certain conditions they would *all* do it. And under the same circumstances we would not. So it doesn't matter that some of them *haven't* done it. I listen. I read. And now I know that they know it too. They know they are unnatural. Their writers and artists have been saying it for years. Telling them they are unnatural, telling them they are depraved. They call it tragedy. In the movies they call it adventure. It's just depravity that they try to make glorious, natural. But it ain't. The disease they have is in their blood, in the structure of their chromosomes. (156–157. Italics in the original)

What is ironic here is that Guitar turns out to be only too capable of doing those things he argues only white men can do. He kills, he presumably tortures, and he even hunts down his best friend, blinded by hatred and greed. His story, like that of the citizens of Ruby in *Paradise*, is one of repressed past traumas, traumas that, not properly faced and verbalized, are bound to repeat themselves in an endless cycle of self-perpetuating violence that can only end in destruction and more trauma. Guitar, also stranded from his own past by the blinding force of unmanaged trauma, does not understand, as Pilate does, that "the dead you kill is yours. They stay with you anyway, in your mind" (208).

What Pilate is referring to here is the necessity of taking responsibility for your own actions. Believing Macon killed a man after they both escaped from their father's farm, she goes back years later to the exact spot where it happened and collects what she believes are the bones of the dead man (but which are actually the bones of her father). She calls them 'her inheritance' and carries them, together with stones from all the places she lived as "a symbol of an obligation to a past event" (Peach 1995: 74). Indeed, we carry not only our past actions with us, but also our ancestors', and when that psychological baggage is lost, steps towards its recovery must be taken in order to come to terms with it and prevent unwanted repetitions. Likewise, when an individual is left stranded from his/her cultural heritage and roots, he/she must endeavor to reacquaint him/herself with them if he/she wants to be whole and free again. Pilate is aware of this, and it is for this reason that she is the most genuinely connected character in the book. Her link to the past is embodied in her literal attachment to it through her—unknowing—guardianship over her father's bones as well as the importance she gives to her name and its origin. All this attention to her roots translates into her acquisition of a knowledge that makes her fly without leaving the ground. In order to obtain that type of knowledge and connection with his roots, Milkman must also 'find the bodies' of his ancestors, their history and their names. Once he manages this, he is able to make sense of his family's traumatic past and therefore free himself to face his future in the novels' closing scene.

3 Digging up History: *the Chaneysville Incident* and the Ethnic Historian

> And now I was coming back, passing little towns knowing their improbable names [...]. The bus was an express, nonstop between Philly and Pittsburg, but I was making local stops.
> DAVID BRADLEY, *The Chaneysville iIcident*

Both *Song of Solomon* and *The Chaneysville Incident* emphasize the relevance of discovering one's and one's family's past in coming to terms with oneself, one's history and family. Through reconnection with the ancestral roots, the subject can better identify with his/her forebears and understand the trials and traumas unearthed in his/her lineage's history. And yet, although both novels are similar in many ways, they differ in the approach that their respective protagonists have towards that unearthing of the past. Whereas in *Song of Solomon* Milkman embarks on a trip of discovery of his ancestral land (a land he had never visited or even knew existed), *The Chaneysville Incident*'s protagonist John Washington carries out a *return* to his hometown, a place he fled and a set of memories he endeavored to actively suppress. While Milkman was quite ignorant of the ancestral import that the place to which he is headed has, John Washington knows that the town he left years ago is his home, and the site where his family's history took place—even though he is not completely aware of what that history actually is. As a good historian, he reflects on this as he approaches his hometown:

> And so I settled myself in my seat [...] and thought about how strange home is: a place to which you belong and which belongs to you even if you do not particularly like it or want it, a place you cannot escape, no matter how far you go or how furiously you run; about how strange if feels to be going back to that place and, even if you do not like it, even if you hate it, to get a tiny flush of excitement when you reach the point where you can look out the window and know, without thinking, where you are; when the bends in the road have meaning and every hill a name. (Bradley 1990: 13–14)

In knowing where he is going to—in knowing the names of the hills and the meaning behind every road's bend—John Washington holds a certain advantage over Milkman, and even though he hates his ancestral place, he recognizes it as such. Contrary to Milkman, John Washington knows he is moving toward a recovery of his family history because, unlike Milkman, he has been concerned with history for some time.

3.1 Historians vs. Archeologists: Study or Action?

Obsessed with history ever since he learned "how much fun it can be to shock with the truth" (144–145), John endeavors to become a historian in order to "find out where the lies are" (186) and discover the "things that still mean something [...] trying to understand what it is that they mean, so that you can hate the right things for the right reasons" (274). Therefore, he is not only well aware of the history of African Americans and the slave trade—and he demonstrates it throughout the novel in a series of "little lectures" (241) concerning his race's past and their traumatic history—but, as a historian, he has devoted himself to the "study of atrocities" (186) or what can otherwise be expressed as the study of trauma and history. In the words of Matthew Wilson, John Washington "conceives of his task as an historian as bringing to light, excavating, what's been buried—forgotten on purpose" (1995: 98) and therefore his historiographical search for his ancestors' past takes the form—both literally and figuratively—of archaeological work. In John's own words, "[t]he best way to find out what they did is to find out where they hid the bodies" (Bradley 1990: 186), which is literally what he will end up doing.

And yet, John's historico-archeological work does not deal with "regional history" (186). This is an expression of his initial resolve not to dwell on the story that most concerns him and his family, which is significant because in turn this points to the extent to which John is in the grip of a trauma that thrives on his not knowing—and not caring about—his own family's trauma. Clearly a sign of suppression and denial, he chooses to identify himself with the *history* of his people but not with the *story* of his ancestors, even though the traumatic consequences of the latter are far more liable to affect him personally than that of African Americans in general. Traumatized by his atypical relationship with his father as well as his father's sudden death and his younger brother's early demise, he places the blame of his personal unresolved trauma on white society in general and their inhuman treatment of blacks throughout history. This results in a certain feeling of hatred towards whites which materializes in his troubled relationship with his white girlfriend, whom he likes to mortify with long digressions about the whites' history of violence against blacks and his frequent hints at her being a descendant of slaveholders. That hatred, however, does not derive—although he believes it does—from his knowledge about the African Americans' past, but from his own unresolved traumas. The solution, therefore, does not lie in the study of the country's history, but in that 'regional history' he despises. The latter is far more personal and therefore potentially more destructive, which is the reason why John chooses to avoid it.

Facing one's personal traumas is the first and most important step towards overcoming them, which makes John's reconnection with his past of paramount importance. Such a reconnection is finally achieved when he unwillingly returns home to care for his father's old friend Jack. After Jack dies, John unexpectedly comes across an inheritance from his father that, as in the case of Milkman, does not turn out to be money and wealth—although there is also some of that in this case—but knowledge. Moses Washington had bequeathed his son a number of documents that would eventually lead John to discover the forgotten history of his forefathers which is also the story behind Moses's suicide when John was only a child. This legacy will lead John to the actual discovery of the truth beneath a local legend concerning a group of runaway slaves. Following his father's clues, he ultimately discovers the very bodies of the runaway slaves in a group of unmarked graves, thus literally finding where they hid the bodies.

This discovery, however, entails much more than the mere location of a bunch of bodies. It marks the site of his own personal and family's traumas and presents John with the lost history of his ancestors. The actual discovery of the graves provides tangible proof of the existence of the group of runaway slaves involved in the local legend while at the same time links it to the story of John's great-grandfather, C.K. Similar to *Song of Solomon*, the story in *The Chaneysville Incident* revolves around a myth of liberation whose origin happens to directly involve the character's lineage. Instead of the myth of the flying African, in *Chaneysville* we find a story about thirteen African slaves that, about to be captured, preferred to die rather than return to slavery. John, unlike Milkman, does know the legend, but ignores the fact that his own great-grandfather was leading them and consequently died with them. This knowledge is lost in the family until John's father, Moses, decided to investigate and learns the truth. However, again, his findings were not immediately passed on to his descendants, and it was only after some time that John—with his father's documents in hand—re-discovers it and learns about the hidden past.

The reason Moses did not pass on this story is that its discovery left him so incredibly traumatized that he chose to commit suicide at the very place of the burials. And yet, as Ensslen argues, Moses's

> final act of self-immolation is not to be taken as the logical result of self-destructive tendencies [...] but rather as a meaningful symbolic gesture by which Moses intentionally joins his ancestors, collapsing his life story with that of C.K. and other exemplary black men, while at the same time providing a self-willed closure to the arcane text of his life which his son John will have to decipher. (1988: 290)

Thus, the site of the trauma—the death of the thirteen runaway slaves—becomes the site of connection with ancestors, which is the reason Moses chose it as the place to kill himself, in the hopes of joining them in the afterlife: "You don't throw your whole life away if you're not sure that the dead really are there, waiting for you" (Bradley 1990: 389). In this sense, "[d]eath assumes a particularly African dimension as the slaves intuitively see themselves as going to join ancestors. Death is not to be feared but embraced as a simple change in forms of being, and the spiritual, which they become, is as real as the material" (Harris 1981: 204). Just like flying in *Song of Solomon* or walking upon water in *Praisesong for the Widow*, here, death is the means of returning home for an oppressed people who, in their traditional belief, see death not as an end, but simply as a change of state. Just as John informs the reader in one of his historical digressions, for the African peoples, a dead person would not die, "he simply took up residence in an afterworld that was in many ways indistinguishable from his former state" (Bradley 1990: 208). This is illustrated, John argues, by the way the living continue to interact with them, leaving out food offerings for the deceased, having their children no matter how long ago they passed away, building houses for them, etc. From this John surmises that,

> if, following his 'death,' a man [...] hangs about in the corner, talking to his friends, if he has an apartment, eats hoagies or hero sandwiches, drinks Pabst or Budweiser, goes on hunting or fishing trips as a means of relaxing from his job as a policeman or a judge, is vulnerable to price gouging, and can be slapped with a paternity suit, he cannot really be said to be, in the Christian sense of the term, dead. (209)

If archaeology is present in the novel as the—sometimes literal—unearthing of the past and the truth behind the African beliefs and myths that permeate local legend, this task is also consistently seen as a hunting expedition. The truth must be unearthed, but prior to that, it must be *found* by following the clues left in the present as if they were the tracks an animal left in the snow. Therefore, hunting and tracking are not seen in this novel as merely a rite of passage as in *Song of Solomon*, but as the arduous process of getting to the truth behind the hidden traumatic past. Hunting is, from the beginning of the novel, equated with the search for the past. Moses's official cause of death, for instance, is a hunting accident, although his friend Jack is not quite sure: "Seems to me if a man was gonna get killt out huntin', the least thing he could do was to be hunting somethin' worth huntin'. I recall a time when Moses Washington woulda rather drunk warm water than be huntin' a groundhog. Matter a fact, I don't recall him ever huntin' a groundhog" (36). As it turns out, he was not hunting a groundhog, but following the clues that led him to the site of his grandfather's suicidal act. Something that is indeed "worth huntin'." This metaphor of hunting as pursuing historical truth is repeated when Moses asks Jack to teach his son how to track (36) should anything happen to him. Moses wanted his son John to do the same historical inquiry that led him to the discovery of his family past, which is the reason he bequeathed him his grandfather's journals and documents, but he is aware that, in order to get to the truth, John would need to set aside his scholarly knowledge and western assumptions in order to make room for ancestral knowledge, imagination and intuition. Those are the tools with which John will be able to excavate his family's past and make sense of himself, his father's death and his legacy. In the words of Klaus Ensslen, hunting is a "ritualized reenactment of Jack's and Moses' 'natural' way of life, implying a rejection of John's role as historian and researcher" (1988: 285).

3.2 Scholarly Knowledge vs. Ancestral Wisdom

In order to reconnect with his roots and make sense of the mythic central nature of his own personal history, John—like Milkman—needs to embrace nature and the traditional way of living and tracking. This is exemplified in the passage about the voices in the wind. Different characters in the novel interpret a particular sound of wind on the hill where the central event—the collective suicide of the runaway slaves—took place as either singing, the souls of Indians living there before the white man expelled them or as the running and panting of the runaway slaves before they died. This is consistent with the notion that the dead—or their memories—remain in the place where they died, making it a site of memory. However, John's access to western education has made him adopt a white man's frame of mind and he therefore begins to despise his ancestral mythical beliefs as those belonging to ignorant and savage men:

> I had gone to the far side to sit with Old Jack and drink toddies and listen to the sound the wind made as to glory in the power of *knowing* what it was. I had told him what I had learned and he had looked at me blankly, and shaken his head and said he didn't give a damn about what the book said; it was the souls of Indians. And I had realized for the first time that even though I loved him, he was an ignorant old man, no better than the savages who thought that thunder was the sound of some god's anger, and for the first time, I had argued with him about it. But then it had started, and I had left off arguing to listen. And what I had heard had filled me with cold fear. For I had not heard a sound like a car honking; I had not heard vibrations of a frequency that varied directly or inversely with anything at all; I had heard singing. I had sat there, clutching my toddy, trying to perceive that sound as I had known I should, trying not to hear voices in it, trying not to hear words. But I had heard them anyway. (Bradley 1990: 383. Italics in the original)

This passage comes just before John makes the final discovery that leads him to the location of the hidden graves, and it is notable that he remembers this moment of his past at that precise instant. By placing the memory of the one time in which he had to set his western knowledge aside to embrace his own ancestral intuitive notions right before the moment in which he makes his final, crucial discovery of the past, the narrative highlights the re-connection process that John had to undergo. In the words of Klaus Ensslen,

> It is a motif which transcends rational analysis and historical quest and thereby helps to lift John's cognitive endeavor to a more imaginative and

magical level where story opens into myth and assumes instinctual and somatic overtones that point away from the criteria generally accepted in western culture, seeking connection with other cultural norms. [...] In Bradley's text the voices in the wind are [...] a central part of the imaginative dialogical structure of the novel, an indispensable thread in the warp and woof of the narrative texture in which history, landscape, and personal voices become blended as a quasi-elemental force appealing to John's emotional and imaginative faculties. (1988: 288)

The type of collective, traditional wisdom in which the voices in the wind are much more than simply 'vibrations,' is embodied in the text in the figure of Old Jack. The old man doesn't "give a damn" about what the book says (Bradley 1990: 383) and maintains the ancestral knowledge, unpolluted by foreign influences. He does not trust what the white man's school has to teach John and once tells him: "God*damn*it, Johnny, you may have been to college, but you don't know nothin'; you don't know where you growed up at" (67). As a consequence, he endeavors to teach John that, in order to track, he must learn to trust his instincts and stop trusting too much to his intellect, which translates—for his historical quest—into less focus on facts and more on imagination. In doing so, Jack becomes "the mediator of folk norms and of a lifestyle bound to the local community and the landscape" (Ensslen 1988: 283) and, as such, almost a mythical figure himself. When, at the start of the novel, John tells his girlfriend he must go back home because Jack is sick, the following dialogue ensues:

'Jack?' she said. 'The old man with the stories?'
'The old man with the stories.'
'So he's really there.'
I looked at her. 'Of course he's there. Where did you think he was—in Florida for the winter?'
'I thought he was somebody you made up.'
'I don't make things up,' I said.
'Relax, John,' she said. 'It's just that the way you talked about him, he was sort of a legend. I would have thought he was indestructible. Or a lie.'
(Bradley 1990: 3)

It is to Jack that Moses leaves his son's 'traditional' education; it is Jack that he trusts with John's upbringing in the secular hunting techniques that will prove to be priceless in his later quest for historical truth. However, it is Moses himself that tries to instill in John the thirst for historical knowledge as a way of reaching the hidden truth in the traumatic past of African Americans in general and of his own family in particular. The grandchild—as it later transpires—of a slave who taught himself to read and write, Moses attempts, in his own rough, cryptic way, to inculcate in John the necessity of acquiring knowledge, while he leaves Jack to take care of the more ancestral type of wisdom. It is after a serious talk with his father—and a bit of a fight with a schoolmate—that John learns that "knowing nothing can get you humiliated and knowing a little bit can get you killed, but knowing all of it will bring you power" (284). However, Moses's emphasis on reading and learning does not stop there:

> Another time, shortly before he died, he had come down slowly and had stood above me as I sat reading a book. I had tried to look up at him then, but he had put his hand on my head and forced me to look at my book, and we stayed like that, a tableau in tension, until, for reasons known only to him, he had let me go. I had turned to look at him then, and had found that I could not look away; his eyes met mine and held my gaze more firmly than his hands had held my head. We had stayed that way for a while, and then he had turned and gone back upstairs. (138)

What Moses tries wordlessly to make John understand is that he has something prepared for him, and that he wants him to pay close attention to the written word, for it is only in and through written records that he will later be able to recover his predecessors' past. He wants John to reach the same conclusions that he has, and by the same means. He refuses to actually tell him about his findings but rather leaves his research intact so that he can discover the truth himself. When, after Moses dies, John goes up to the attic where Moses kept all of his records, he somehow senses his father's intention:

> I was almost going back in time, and when I thumbed the switch on the flashlight and sent a cone of weak light on a handmade chair and a large, roughly carpentered table on which sat an open book and a kerosene lamp, I was looking at a perfect memory; dusty, but perfect. It was almost as if the chair, the table, the book, the lamp, the empty fireplace, were items under glass; they were the keys to a man's mind, laid bare to me, clues to a mystery, the answer to every question there. All I had to do was interpret them. It was the greatest thrill I had ever known. (140)

Of course, John does try to uncover the mystery, but he does not yet have the sufficient maturity or knowledge; the former comes with age, the latter, he only achieves when he receives his father's legacy several years later. This is the final encouragement that he needed to pursue the uncovering of the mysterious circumstances behind his father's death and unveil his family's past. In Moses's will, John sees—quite accurately—his father's design for him:

> [N]ow I knew that Moses Washington had had plans for me. More than plans; a will. I did not know yet what he had wanted me to do. I did not know if I could do it the way he would have wanted it done—I could not imagine how he would want it done. But this I did know: I was going to understand. He had left me the means for that. [...] Because he had left me more than books and papers; he had left me power. (161–162)

Moses leaves John the means to acquire a certain knowledge that is not incompatible with the sort of knowledge that he has asked Jack to pass on to him, even though at times may seem so. Jack does not wholly approve of John going away to study, and his reproach evinces his fear that John will lose his identity. He regards college as one more mechanism for the white man to perpetuate its ruling ideology and therefore extrapolates its capacity to brainwash black men and turn them white to education in general and reading in particular:

> You know somethin', Johnny—'scuse me, I mean Mistuh Washington, suh—these white folks, ones wouldn't give you the time a day last year? Now they think you're somethin'. Course, they ain't 'xactly sure *what*, an' I 'spect as how they're jest as pleased you ain't gonna be around here makin' 'em try an' figger out what, but they sure do think you're somethin'. Why, you know, the mayor hisself set up here an' tole me you was a credit to your race. Yes indeedy, that's jest 'xactly what he said. Course, I didn't correct him, an' tell him that you wasn't colored no more, on accounta you read enough a them damn books to turn your head clear white ... (135. Italics in the original)

There is, indeed, a danger that John might become imbued with white ideology while reading, but it is not on account of the reading itself, but on the books. If he reads books that are complacent with the dominant ideology and are consistent with the master narrative instead of contesting it and offering the silenced history of the minorities, he could be led to comply with it and forget the primal teachings of Jack. Or, as trauma studies have themselves been accused of, he might begin to apply typically western analytical tools to the analysis of specific non-western narratives. This, the novel tells us, is in fact what ultimately happens. Even though John is conscious that the official history of his country hides many secrets and has, in fact, made it his business to make them known, his education as a historian has made him too heavily reliant on facts and, accordingly, he has lost the instinctual feeling necessary to actually uncover them. The narrative is indeed full of historical facts concerning the hidden history of the African American people, but those are facts and events that he has not discovered himself, he has merely learned about them. His task now is to leave his western education behind and recover his native one, to reconnect with the ancestral knowledge that will allow him to take an active role, to become less of a historian and more of an archeologist.

Moses Washington realized his son would need this type of primal wisdom, and trusted Jack with the task of transmitting it to him, but the passage in which Moses holds his son's head, quoted above, shows that he is also concerned with literacy. Being able to read helps John learn about the events in the past, while the type of ancestral and experiential knowledge that Jack has to offer gives him the wisdom necessary to question those narratives and form an opinion of his own. The mixture of both is what allows John to finally succeed in his endeavor. Literacy is a two-part ability in which the capacity of writing complements the ability to read. Reading—and learning—about the past is significant, but writing about it is also very important. In writing, the aforementioned process of learning and contesting history can be transmitted to the following generations, for putting the silenced subtexts of history down in words gives them substance and permanency. This is, in fact, how the silenced history of the Washingtons is passed on. It is notable that there is little to no oral communication among the members of the Washington family and yet they manage to pass on their story through documents. This is the reason that the story of how C.K. Washington learned to write acquires great relevance within the narrative.

Born into slavery under the name of Brobdingnang Washington, John's great-grandfather shows from a very early age an intense inclination towards the written word. However, fearful of the power that that sort of knowledge could give to slaves, masters did not permit slaves to read and write, and therefore Brobdingnang was severely punished several times for his literary interests. At age twelve, he was chastised for merely looking at a book, and three years later he was heavily flogged and branded for drawing letters in the dust. This, however, did not stop him in his endeavors. Most probably, it made him grasp the importance of reading and writing. In a clear act of rebellion against the cruel and unjust institution of slavery, as well as its specific emphasis on barring all slaves from any access to literacy, Brobdingnang, at age sixteen, learns by heart every letter and mark on the document that his master had drawn concerning his, that is Brobdingnang's, father's manumission plans, even though he could not understand them. Years later, he taught himself to read and write, and he used that knowledge to do what the slave masters feared most: spread the word about the injustices of the institution beyond his immediate circle. The only way he could do this was by retelling the atrocities committed by the slave owners in a process that both denounces injustice and helps give voice to the trauma and promote empathy and understanding. His style, John says, was apparently not perfect, but he nevertheless fully enjoyed it, together with the actual capacity to write. John provides the reason for this in the following passage:

> It's obvious that he loved writing, and he loved his own style, which is understandable; when you've been flogged trying to read your own name and branded for trying to write your father's name, it's probably quite a thrill to not only read books but quote from them in your own hand, even if nobody else is going to read it. (337–338)

John pinpoints here two incidents in the life of his great-grandfather that proved to be fundamental to the formation of his identity as well as his literary style, and as mentioned before, both incidents are related to names. They are his first two punishments at the hands of his master, and they both revolve around the same issue. While the first involves his given name—the book he was found with was a copy of *Gulliver's Travels*, from which his master had taken his name—the second had to do with his father's name, and resulted in the changing of his own. Given the two letters that he did not manage to scrub out when he was caught—C and K—it seems that he had been writing his father's name: Jack. When he was caught and punished for writing, his master branded him with those two letters, which he later took as his own appellation. He kept this name even after every slave catcher in the County was looking for a black man called C.K. Washington. Even though John "can't imagine why" (340) he didn't change it in the hopes of escaping detection, it is clear that C.K. felt attached to the significance of the letters with which he had been branded. He took them as his name in order to be reminded of all the willpower he had needed to teach himself to read and write despite the great danger that it put him in. This reminds us of the relationship between a person's name and identity. Moreover, it underscores the importance of naming as an assertion of (self-)dominance and power as reflected in my analysis of *Song of Solomon*.

The Chaneysville Incident shows a similar concern with this theme, as Ensslen (1988: 282) and Wilson (1995: 100) point out, which is clear not only in the fragment about Brobdingnang changing his name to C.K. or, as Ensslen argues, in Bradley's using the surname Washington for his three main protagonists (1988: 282). It is also apparent in John's preoccupation with the origin of the names of the places and towns around the Chaneysville area. As part of his frequent historical asides, he repeatedly goes on lengthy digressions detailing how each little town and landmark was named, after whom and, when possible, the story of the people for whom they were named. Furthermore, there is one reference to an old man whose "master had called him Jacob, but, that, he said, was not his name; his name was Azaca, he had been given it by his father, who had come from Haiti" (Bradley 1990: 415). It is clear that, when talking about the African American experience, names take a central role, as both *Song of Solomon* and *The Chaneysville Incident* clearly illustrate.

3.3   *The Contesting and Therapeutic Value of Recovering the Past*
Song of Solomon and *The Chaneysville Incident* share much more than an interest in the significance of names in the African American experience. Although a relevant issue, it is not central in either narrative for, as mentioned above, the primary focus of these novels is the importance of the recovery of silenced or forgotten memory. In the words of David Bradley,

> you can do three things with a novel: you can talk about the past, you can talk about the present, and you can talk about the future. To talk about the future is science-fiction, so you're going to have to talk to Chip Delaney about that. Talking about the present is—I think—pretty boring because nobody knows what's happening. And, in fact, by the time you're finished talking about it, it's past anyway. So, that's what you're left with. (Blake and Miller 1984: 36)

This novel concerns itself with a historically informed past that contests and rewrites the official master narrative of history. Just as Matthew Wilson puts it, "Bradley's historian, John Washington, goes outside the Western tradition and taps into the residue of African beliefs in African American culture [...] to create an alternative and heroic history" (1995: 97). This type of 'alternative and heroic history' needs to be created in novels like these in order to give voice to the long silenced history of trauma, racism and oppression that the African American community has suffered for centuries. However, this is not something new, and, indeed, we find it in most novels by African American writers. According to Ensslen,

> [f]or black Americans the countermanding of official versions of their history through authentic self-representation is as old as the story-telling impulse itself: masked in the multiple coding of the oral tradition, this revisionist narrative informs master-and-slave as well as animal stories, work and church songs, ritualized speech acts belonging exclusively to

the black group (like signifying, rapping and jiving, the dozens) as well as speech acts adapted and skillfully recoded from the dominant culture (such as minstrelsy and vaudeville). (1988: 281)

Such a rewriting is also primordial in the African American process of regaining control and power over themselves, a power that was long denied to them by slave holders first and by white society later. As part of the de-humanizing process that the institution of slavery carried out over Africans, they were denied any possibility of decision-making, self-agency or self-definition. They, ultimately, had no control over their own lives, which is the utmost dehumanizing measure, as Jack argues: "If [a man] don't have no say over the things he needs to live, he ain't got no say over whether he lives at all, an' if he ain't got no say over that, he ain't no man. A man has to have say" (Bradley 1990: 41). Having been stripped of any type of self-agency for such a long period of time, the recovery of the past helps the African American community not only to give testimony to the hidden truths of its history, but also to own it, accept it, and act accordingly. Thus, such a recovery empowers individuals with authority over themselves and over their own future. In other words, it allows "African Americans to write themselves rather than being written" (Wilson 1995: 106).

This empowering process is manifest in the novel through the acquisition of knowledge. As previously discussed, literacy is in itself a powerful tool because it allows its user to give voice to his and his people's trauma, thus contesting the official version of history and subverting the dominant community's hold on power. This is what Moses does when he lets everybody think that he has been keeping a written record of all the white customers of his moonshine business. By apparently creating "a small historical text to subdue his symbolical white masters" (Benito 1995b: 38), he has re-invested himself with the power of literacy and history-making previously denied to his race. This is what leads John Washington to affirm that his father had not left him "merely books and papers; he had left [him] power" (Bradley 1990: 162). That is, the power to know, manage and speak out the historical truth. In Ensslen's words, at the end of the narrative "John [...] has shifted his ancestors' bid for power to the intellectual or cognitive sphere, with power becoming the control over and mediation of knowledge" (1988: 286).

This re-assertive process also has a very clear therapeutic side to it, for re-asserting one's identity and exerting power over oneself again is one of the most important steps towards recovery from trauma. However, in order for this to happen, a process of giving voice to the trauma must take place first. It is certainly no coincidence that John's girlfriend is a psychoanalyst;

it is only after he decides to open up to her and verbally tell her what he knows of his forefathers' story that he is able to reach its end and figure out all the blind spots he had been finding during his research. Nevertheless, this is not a process that came easily to him: he initially had great trouble talking to her due, in part, to his lack of trust in her—the main reason for his distrust being her white race—but, more importantly, because of his own unwillingness to verbalize his trauma. As a psychoanalyst, Judith is aware of these two problems and is willing to prompt John to talk while, at the same time, allowing him his own space and time in which to do so. There are several instances throughout the narrative in which John actually refuses to speak to Judith about his past, which is indicative of the amount of suppressive force that he must exercise to forget—or rather, following McNally, to not think about—the place and the experiences he left behind. We can see this suppressive process at play in one of their many discussions of the matter of his significant silences, when John exclaims: "[W]ell, let me tell you something: the things I don't talk about I don't talk about because I don't like to talk about them, I don't like to *think* about them. And I'll be damned if I'm going to wring my guts out to get some blood on the floor so you can feel loved" (Bradley 1990: 71. Emphasis added). Despite feeling hurt by this, Judith does not press John to talk, even though she knows the good it would do him. However, she does let him know at every available opportunity that she is a willing listener: "Someday, [...] you're going to talk to me. And when you do I'm going to listen to you. I'm going to listen to you so Goddamn hard it's going to hurt" (4). Judith understands John's troubles and thinks of them in psychoanalytic terms, aware that his refusal to speak is not because of her personally—and her skin color—but basically because of an unconscious process of repression:

> I realized that you hide things. Not just some things; everything. You don't even think; you just hide them. You've got a big lead vault in your head and you put things in it. If there's anything you haven't figured down to the last quarter inch, anything you're not absolutely sure about, anything you haven't torn to pieces a hundred times, you keep it in there. And if there's something you never understand in there, it will stay; nobody else will ever see it. (260)

This applies to his pains in trying to make sense of his forefather's history, and his repeated failures to do so. Without the help of his lost ancestral instincts, John is unable to understand the raw historical facts and fails to find closure for his family's traumatic past. When he voices his frustrations to Judith, she tells him that he might have been unconsciously leaving something out, to which he responds: "This is history, [...] not psychoanalysis" (268). However, this is where he is wrong. When history is so intertwined with pain that it becomes traumatic, it needs to be made sense of in much in the same way as trauma. Since John has been personally involved in his family's past, he has appropriated not only his predecessors' story but their trauma. When trauma is vicariously passed on like this, it must be resolved in psychoanalytical terms, and this is where Judith plays her role.

When Judith finally realizes that giving John space to voice his trauma in his own time is not going to work, she takes action and travels to John's native town to join him and force him to open up. This is ultimately what helps him put into words the story that has been troubling him and draw it to a close. In acting as a listener and prompting John to actually voice the story, she is the vehicle through which John finally expresses himself. An empathetic listener is absolutely necessary in the therapeutic process of giving voice to trauma; without it, complete closure cannot be achieved. This is what happened to C.K. and to Moses, who, for lack of a proper, physical listener were overwhelmed by the force of the trauma and had no other choice but to escape from it by choosing to die. By the end of the narrative, we can see that Judith's help and empathy has been highly beneficial to John and there is hope that he will finally overcome his personal and family traumas: "From being a puzzled archivist reacting to the material pushed on him by others, John achieves the role of active interpreter of discrete signs and actions leading themselves to the assumption of the meaningful shape of story as history, while at the same time warding off the threat of becoming victimized" (Ensslen 1988: 294).

This is reflected in the final conversation scene in which John undergoes a physical as well as an emotional thawing. After repeatedly complaining of feeling cold—a symbol of his emotional numbness and symptom of trauma victims—throughout the narrative, he finally feels some warmth spread through him and unequivocally puts it down to Judith's presence in the room:

> I closed my eyes then and waited, waited for the question. But she did not ask a question. When I opened my eyes I saw her sitting, not moving, just sitting, and I realized that there would be no questions. And then I realized that something strange was happening. Because I was no longer cold. At first I thought it was because the wind had died, but when I listened I still heard it singing to the hills. And then I saw that the candle no longer flickered, that she had moved a little, just a little, but enough to block a draft, or perhaps create a new draft that balanced out the old one. (Bradley 1990: 413)

In her role as therapist, Judith keeps asking questions, prompting John's narrative up until the point at which he starts expecting the questions but realizes there will be none because he is speaking on his own accord now. It is then that his thawing begins and he is finally able to open himself emotionally and allow Judith's empathy to warm him. After he realizes this, he resumes C.K.'s story and links his own emotional melting with his ancestor's, now fully understanding where the warmth came from. At this point, C.K.'s story merges with his own, and the cold metaphor can be read as applying to both men:

> He was warm now [...]. He was warm, and the feeling was strange. Because he had not realized how cold he had been. He had known that his hands and feet and face were cold, even though they were so numb he had lost feeling in them—he had known that because anyone who knew the weather and who knew how long he had been exposed would have known—and so he had not been surprised when the heat from the fire had caused the feeling to come pounding back to them. But he had not known about the other cold, the cold inside, the glacier in his guts that had been growing and moving, inch by inch, year by year, grinding at him, freezing him. He had not known that. But he knew it now. Because he could feel it melting. The heat that melted it did not come from the fire; it came from her, from the warmth of her body that pressed against his back, the warmth of her arms around him, the warmth of her hands that cupped the base of his belly. He lay there, feeling the warmth filling him, feeling the fatigue draining from him, feeling the aching in his ribs easing, becoming almost pleasant, and wishing that he would never have to move. (413)

Such a profuse and detailed account of his great-grandfather's feelings is not something that John would normally provide. On the previous pages of the novel, every time John embarked on an account of past events, his narrative centered on facts, dates and events, stripping the feelings away from them. He had always endeavored to be a detached researcher, and has always believed feelings and emotions were not advisable in a good historian. "You think there's something good about getting the feelings out of things. Don't you?" Judith asks him once, to which he responds: "Yes [...]. Not ordinary feelings; a historian has to have ordinary feelings—a little sympathy, a little anger. That's what makes him human. But if the feelings are so strong they get in the way of the facts—" (344–345). However, such an approach had not proved to be very useful in his search for his family's truth. In order to fully engage in the story of his forefathers, he must forget his western conception of history and tap into his native tradition, allowing for his intuition to open the way to imagination and, with it, to empathy and understanding of the motives behind his predecessors' actions, rather than the actions themselves. In the previous quote about C.K.'s physical and emotional melting, John is able to finally *imagine* what his great-grandfather must have felt, rather than merely provide a raw account of the facts. He finally becomes "free to reject the restraints of an ending forged and manipulated by white historical discourse and to rewrite his own version [...] which falls within the realm of heritage" (Benito 1995a: 188–189). This is the only way in which he can provide closure to his and his family's trauma.

3.4   *The Coalescence of Fact and Fiction: Bridging Genres and Cultures*

Once John Washington learns, with Judith's help, to put himself in the place of his forefathers, he begins to understand their experiences, using empathy and imagination instead of facts and logic. At this point of the narrative, fiction and history coalesce and become supportive of each other, for, as Ensslen puts it, "history can only become meaningful through active imaginative appropriation of its raw material, which is to say by an act of imaginative completion, by the fictional reconstruction of the unfinished story-line of history" (1988: 286). Imagination is therefore a necessary part of a fully informed historical research project, and the lack thereof is the cause of John's previous failures, as he eventually realizes:

> I had sat there at that table, with the flame from the lamp flickering over the pages of notes that I had made, and had known that I had failed. Not just taken a wrong path, or run into a dead end in research. Failed. Completely. I had put the facts together, all of them, everything I could cull from books and his notebooks and my notebooks: everything. I had put it together and had studied it until I could command every fact, and then I had stepped back and looked at the whole and seen ... nothing. Not a thing. Oh, I had seen the facts, there was no shortage of facts; but I could not discern the shape that they filled in. There were, it seemed, too many gaps. But what I had feared was that there were not too many gaps; only too many for me, my mind. For I could simply not imagine what I should see. Could not imagine what it was I was looking at part of. I had everything I needed, knowledge and time and even, by then, a measure of skill—I could follow a fact through shifts and twists of history, do it and love it. But I could not imagine. And if you cannot imagine, you can discover only cold facts, and more cold facts; you will never know the truth. I had seen the future stretching out before me, my life an endless round of fact-gathering and reference-searching, my only discoveries silly little

deductions, full of cold, incontrovertible logic, never any of the burning inductive leaps that take you from here to there and let you really *understand* anything. I had known that was how it would be, had known that if I could not look at the things Moses Washington was looking at and, at least, discover what it was he had been working on, then I could not do anything important at all. (Bradley 1990: 146–147. Italics in the original)

According to Matthew Wilson, "[i]n his meditations on his failings as an historian [...] Washington has almost obsessively linked the word *imagine* with the word *understand*" (1995: 102. Italics in the original), as reflected in the previous passage. "[A]s if in acknowledgment of the limitations of the methods of history when it comes to the experience of African-Americans" (Wilson 1995: 103), John finally understands "the necessity of developing an intelligence embedded in a kind of wisdom which intuitively knows when to act and when to think" (Harris 1981: 205). In other words, he embraces an imaginative intuition based on the primal teachings of Jack and his ancestors and uses it to complement his formation as a western historian, thus mixing the two traditions in a more complete and faithful version of the history of African Americans. Once he has finally completed his great-grandfather's history by imaginatively filling in the gaps of the facts he had, he burns all of his files in a final break with his former way of understanding history. Those files and cards are now "dead material" in the face of the "vivid story" that John has made of his formerly dry historical research (Ensslen 1988: 293).

This necessary vision of fact and fiction is what Bradley himself seems to favor in his understanding of history. In an interview he once declared that "History to [him] is raw material, the past is raw material. We can't be governed by it" (Blake and Miller 1984: 33), which seems to be the reason that he mixes historical facts with fiction in his novel. Much of the plot of *The Chaneysville Incident* is based on actual historical research, mainly that of his own parents. The central event in the narrative—that of the mass suicide of thirteen runaway slaves led by C.K. Washington and the later finding of their graves—was actually taken from his own mother's research, which she undertook in order to write a history of the county for its bicentennial (Blake and Miller 1984: 26). She summarizes the event in a couple of lines—"On the Lester Imes farm below Chaneysville one can still find the markers for twelve or thirteen graves of runaway slaves. Mr. Imes relates that when the slaves realized their pursuers were closing in on them, they begged to be killed rather than go back to the Southland and more servitude. Someone obliged" (qtd. in Wilson 1995: 100). Her son David, however, expands it into a complete narrative. It is notable that, in his fictionalization of the story, he did not change either the name of the town or the number of unmarked graves and he only slightly altered the name of the white farmer—from Imes to Iiames—whom he also turned into a miller in the novel. Apart from that, the factual story is left almost intact.

Surely, as I argued in the first chapter of this volume, fact can easily coalesce with fiction, especially when dealing with traumatic history. Such a coalescence can even be beneficial for the sharing and unearthing of past traumatic memories, for their testimony, as well as for their transcendence into a valuable tool for future action. The 'real' history, as in Harriet Bradley's discovery, must be acknowledged, remembered and transmitted, but any attempt to doing so, insomuch as the actual victims of the trauma—like Margaret Garner or the thirteen runaway slaves—are dead, must unavoidably be fictionalized. Just as John Washington must do in *The Chaneysville Incident*, authors have no recourse but to fill in the gaps of history with fiction in order to make sense of the past and help raise awareness of the injustices of history.

In doing so, Bradley succeeds in bridging not only fact and fiction, imagination and scholarly knowledge, but also, through his protagonist's experience, different attitudes towards history itself. It is only by coalescing his former approach—Western-mediated—and his new—more ancestral and myth-based—approach to history, that John Washington is able to fully understand the events in his family's past, and their bearing on its members' dispositions and experiences. Therefore, unlike in *Paradise* or *Mama Day*, different accounts of history are interconnected and finally allowed to coexist and merge, transforming each other in order to provide a multifaceted view of the past that allows for understanding and agency in the present. This is what Bradley achieves in this text: an alignment of "his novel with modern revisions of history as he deconstructs the traditional privileges of history over story, and exposes different histories, created by different discourses" (Benito 1995a: 190).

However, the most important bridge that Bradley draws in this novel is the one embodied in the relationship between John and his girlfriend Judith and their hopeful evolution as a couple. As pointed out before, one of the main reasons that John refused to speak to Judith about his personal traumas—besides suppression, that is—was the fact that Judith is white. John incessantly accused her of not understanding what he, his family or his people had to go through, and he even hints at the possibility of her being the descendant of slaveholders. Although he loves her, he strongly believes that they have no future as a couple because there is too much trauma and antagonism in their cultures' histories. Nevertheless, the end of the narrative seems to offer a more optimistic prospect for both, since it is thanks to Judith's help that John has finally managed to work through his and his family's traumas. As a counterpoint, at the end of John's narrative Judith has achieved a higher level of empathy and understanding of his problems, which is a necessary step towards a full sharing of experiences. According to Ensslen, the former antagonism between the races represented in the lack of trust between the two lovers changes towards the end of the narrative "into the shape of a true promise for the marriage of two minds: for an active collaboration in giving history (through fiction or imaginative reconstruction) a new shape capable of mutual endorsement" (1988: 290–291). Thus, if we see in Judith, as Wilson does, a sort of "stand-in for the white reader" (1995: 104), the optimistic ending expands towards the hope of a mutual understanding not only between the lovers, but between cultures achieved through the sharing of previously silenced histories.

Both *Song of Solomon* and *The Chaneysville Incident* present the reader with similar processes of unearthing traumas in which the hidden past is recovered and re-acknowledged in order to promote a better understanding of the self, the other and the community. In order to do that, both authors resort to myth and folk tradition and interweave them with their storylines thereby creating sophisticated narratives that discuss links, roots and the significance of one's past for the construction of the future. Through these processes, both Morrison and Bradley successfully appeal to the reader—black or otherwise—in moving and eloquent ways. Though fictional, both novels rely on the historical truth within the African American experience—and argue for its recovery—in order to come to terms with the traumas buried within it and start the necessary process of individual working through and collective moving forward.

Epilogue: Is Closure Possible? the Use of Trauma in Art as a Vehicle for Political Struggle

> I don't want to give my readers something to swallow. I want to give them something to feel and think about, and I hope that I set it up in such a way that it is a legitimate thing, and a valuable thing.
> TONI MORRISON, Interviewed by Nelly McKay

∴

When Paul D urges Sethe to go as far inside as she needs to because he will hold her ankles and make sure she gets back out (Morrison 2005: 55), Toni Morrison is also encouraging her readers to take a similar journey back. It is not a pleasure trip, for the reader, like Sethe, is invited to face the traumas buried in the past and *work through them*. It is the first stage of a long and torturous process of acknowledging the past and giving it presence, a process that is unavoidably painful, as Amy once warns Sethe: "It's gonna hurt, [...] [a]nything dead coming back to life hurts" (Morrison 2005: 42). The hurt, as the novels analyzed here demonstrate, has many sides, nuances, and layers, and neither stagnation nor forgetting will help overcome it. The hurt, as the tree-shaped scar that was left in Sethe's back after a particularly severe lashing illustrates, is not static, but changes with time, and can be a lifeless scar, almost forgotten except when caressed, but sometimes takes the shape of the ravishing blooms of a chokecherry tree. It can be activated as if on cue, but can also lay dormant under the mantle of ignorance or indifference. The novels seen here revisit these stages and manifestations of a painful past; they plunge into the pool of history and resurface with the knowledge necessary to prevent a repetition of the past and work toward a better future.

1   "National Amnesia": Searching for Its Cure

> The future is when people talk about the past.
> JANE YOLEN, *Briar Rose*

It was not until the 60s that the African American story of trauma and oppression was told in novels such as the ones analyzed here. The reasons for that silence have already been explored, and they range from shame to institutionalized silencing, passing through repression, guilt, or lack of a suitable listener. However, many contemporary authors have begun to understand that silence had to be broken, and have endeavored to do so in compelling and highly imaginative narratives. These five novels are, each in its own way, a telling example of this process of voicing the past. But what past? The widespread "white lie" that "black people did not have a memory" (Peach 1995: 101). This alleged absence was used as part of a dominant narrative that erased and silenced atrocities. Once erased, the only way for African Americans to go back to that past was to "literally acquire for themselves the texts of which they had been deprived" (Peach 1995: 102), thus creating a narrative that stands as a counterpart to national amnesia. And yet, as LaCapra argues, absence should not be equated with loss, since "one cannot lose what one never had" (2001: 50). Consequently, the African American past is not absent in the sense that it never existed and that black people did not have a memory. Rather, that past—the traces of it—has been traditionally silenced and, as such, apparently lost. The writers that started publishing novels dealing with slavery and other stages of the African American past and present experience of racism and oppression went back to this alleged absence to certify that the absence was not such; it was brimming with narratives, songs, oral stories, and newspaper clippings. These are some of the ingredients of a revisionist writing that does not merely serve the purpose of recovering a silenced past; the narratives resulting from this type of writing also "finger [the] jagged grain" (Ellison 1972a: 78) of racist subjugation, as they reveal the interior life of the characters, those feelings that remained behind the veil in previous writings and in white writing. In the process, these narratives promote and create understanding in the readership. It is my understanding that the role of witness does not comfort the reader: since it situates him/her in the midst of a troubling journey that never ends, the reader cannot help relating past to present traumas and therefore the past, he/she learns, is never passed. However, the type of active witnessing that the reader performs is key in the process of acknowledging the perpetuation of structures that account for the apparent repetition of traumatic violence, which is, in turn, central to the hope of halting that perpetuation.

"For memory to be effective on a collective level," LaCapra argues, "it must reach large numbers of people. Hence the acts or works that convey it must be accessible" (1998: 139). These five narratives prove to be especially suited for this task. As if following Louis Montrose's discussion of the fictionalization of history, their writers historicize fiction and incorporate into their works a vast array of historical repositories, including songs, oral narratives, and anecdotes like the traditional folk tale of the Africans who could fly in *Song of Solomon*, the real-life case of Margaret Garner in *Beloved*, or the unmarked tombs of the runaway slaves that David Bradley's mother discovered prior to his writing *The Chaneysville Incident*. Moreover, this historical corpus goes beyond the traditional repositories of history as the novels flesh out the alleged absence of historical records. They recover and re-appropriate the black cultural tradition that had been neutralized by the white cultural tradition, thus turning the objects of culture into the agents of that culture. There is agency in this process, as well as a degree of reconciliation with the traumas of the past. The journey of recovery and re-appropriation opens the possibility of finding some meaning amidst the painful memories of the past, and it also offers a way to contest the master narrative of history.

2 Fighting Our Own Battles: the Use of Trauma in Political Struggle

> They burned all the documents, Ursa, but they didn't burn what they put in their minds. We got to burn out what they put in our minds, like you burn out a wound. Except we got to keep what we need to bear witness. That scar that's left to bear witness. We got to keep it as visible as our blood.
> GAYL JONES, *Corregidora*.

Whenever history needs to be recovered, there is a possibility that all the documents are gone, as Gayl Jones writes in *Corregidora*. One may find that only the scars of history, like the chaotic writing of slavery on Sethe's back in Toni Morrison's *Beloved*, remains. That scar needs to be as visible as blood in the process of bearing witness. It needs to be at the center of the willful effort to recover the past and start the process of working through, helping promote social understanding and political agency. Consequently, the visibility of the scar becomes paramount in the process of making the past visible. This is, Kuo argues, the reason behind the publication of Morrison's *Beloved*, for its appearance coincided with Ronald Reagan's presidency, a period during which the president repeatedly tried to deny "the scars of slavery and also the injustice of slavery that were felt by African Americans as if wounds had not any lasting traumatic consequences" (2009: 83), in what David W. Blight has called "ahistorical chauvinism" (1994: 60). In this way, *Beloved*—with its recreation of Margaret Garner's case and the evils of suppression—serves as a warning against forgetting—or against an imposed erasure of the past. Like *Beloved*, the rest of the novels analyzed here respond to the Postmodernist crisis of historical representation, in which history is seen as merely a text. Published from the early 1980s onwards, they all constitute an attempt to revert postmodernism's lack of trust in historicism and history's claims of truth, showing that, not only does history shape our lives in irreversible ways, but that, behind the text, we can find the scars and the bodies—literally so, in the cases of *Beloved* and *The Chaneysville Incident*—that are the actual traces of history. Shaping up this elusive historical evidence into narratives raises awareness about the consequences of history, the traumas within it and the suffering of the communities affected by it.

Trauma is thus inevitably linked with politics, for, as Judith Herman points out, "[t]hree times over the past century, a particular form of psychological trauma has surfaced into public consciousness. Each time, the investigation of that trauma has flourished in affiliation with a political movement" (2001: 9). Just as the study of female hysteria erupted in support of the feminist movement at the hands of several female psychologists like Judith Herman, the recovery of the African American traumatic past of slavery and segregation was instrumental in the context of the Civil Rights Movement. In bringing this previously silenced past into the public eye, novels such as these promote the artistic recovery of the past at the same time that they suggest a different version of history. Thus, these novels stem from a double commitment to art and to politics. Ellison, Conner argues, saw novels as fulfilling both notions (2000b: ix) as did DuBois and Hughes (Conner 2000b: xiv). Even though some authors do not believe in this conflation of politics and art (Bradley once claimed that he wrote novels merely for the fun—and the money—they provided him, not for political reasons (Blake and Miller 1984: 35)), some others do, and have admitted it openly. Toni Morrison, for instance, once claimed that for her, "the best art is political and you ought to be able to make it unquestionably political and irrevocably beautiful at the same time" (1984: 345), and she endeavored to follow this ideal even in her literature for children (see López Ropero 2008).

For a novel to be socially responsible and politically meaningful, it must, inevitably, engage the reader by means of appealing to his/her empathy, but without leaving out the aesthetic pleasure that the reader expects to extract from it. This type of balancing is what Morrison refers to and what she strives to achieve with her poetic prose and her style infused with the echoes and cadences of African American music and folklore. The reader, while enjoying the reading, must become a witness to the related atrocity thus achieving "a broader understanding of the meaning of what has been done to victims, of the politics of trauma" (Kaplan 2005: 123). If witnessing, as Kaplan argues, "involves wanting to change the kind of world where injustice, of whatever kind, is common" (2005: 122), then novels like the five analyzed here are relevant in the process of recovering and giving voice to the African American past.

3 Trauma as Art or the Art of Trauma?

> I've always felt that creative artists and historians are somewhat in the same business, the task of capturing life.
> GLORIA NAYLOR, *Linden Hills*

If the experience of trauma is not registered at the moment of its occurrence but after a period of latency, how can we represent it? If, moreover, trauma resists verbalization to the point of becoming almost unutterable, how can we ever attempt to represent it in written form? And, to go one step further, if trauma is a horrific and horrifying experience how can it be represented aesthetically? These are questions that I have endeavored to tackle in this volume. Trauma can be translated into writing, and represented faithfully enough to arouse the empathy of the reader and even guide him/her through a rediscovery and recreation of past silenced memories. As the five novels analyzed in this volume amply prove, the representation of the painful past can be done with a high degree of mastery and artistic talent. Thus, novels like *Beloved* or *Mama Day* can move readers not only empathically because of the trauma represented, but also aesthetically given their unparalleled lyricism and compelling narratives. Furthermore, Kathleen McHugh argues, trauma can be aesthetically conveyed given its very inaccessibility: "[I]f aesthetics is the affect that thought cannot represent and trauma is the experience that affect cannot contain, then the aesthetics of wounding testify to the experiences which we can neither represent nor contain within ourselves but which happen nonetheless" (2002: 251). Similarly, in the words of Lisa Garbus, "Literature is about what it means to be a speaking being faced with things that are unspeakable. […] [It] uses language as the vehicle to arrive at the very place where language breaks down" (1999: 53). Consequently, literature—and art—is not only capable of, but a very able means to convey and make sense of the disruptive aspect of trauma.

Whenever the trauma represented is of a historical nature, we must concern ourselves not with the possibility of its representation—since that has already been established—but with the manner of it. In other words, how can we faithfully represent historical events? Is historical discourse really that different from historical fiction? This has been an ongoing debate for the better part of the twentieth century, of which Hayden White with his *Metahistory: The*

Historical Imagination in Nineteenth-Century Europe (1973) is probably the most representative exponent. Paul Ricoeur also dealt with this issue in his volume *Memory, History, Forgetting*, and although most of his affirmations refer to the work of historians, they are applicable to literature in general and fiction in particular. He argues that, if there is a suspicion of a betrayal of the truth by the historian/writer, it should be answered in the way the actual written text articulates "the two prior moments of explanation/understanding and of documentation, and, if we move back even further, in the articulation of history on the basis of memory" (Ricoeur 2006: 275). In other words, and as has been argued here, any written text is historically coherent as long as it is backed by properly carried out research and a process of historical explanation. Therefore, novels, as long as they adhere to these two conditions, can be considered historically faithful even if they are fictional, the only difference with history books being the "expectations on the side of the reader" and the "promises on the side of the author" that each establishes (Ricoeur 2006: 261). A novel, even a historical novel, does not promise to offer verifiable, fully historically accurate events, characters and situations—which a history book does—but a series of fictional episodes that may not actually have occurred, but that are feasible and coherent within the historical context.

Furthermore, the fact that something did not happen does not mean that it *could* not have happened. This is what Michael Wood means when he states that the fact that "fiction is something that happens to us, if not (fortunately) as finally as history happens to us, is one of Morrison's most demanding and enabling convictions" (2000: 119), which applies also to authors like Bradley, Gaynor, Hurston, Walker, and Marshall among many others. And because fiction portrays events that could very well happen to us—and in a way do happen to us even if only while we are reading about them—when it portrays trauma, we can feel its impact as if we were being told about a true occurrence. Trauma, I argue, can therefore be represented artistically, as these five novels amply prove, and provide a more than valid ground for addressing past wrongs.

4 Is Closure Possible?

> Under history, memory and forgetting.
> Under memory and forgetting, life.
> But writing a life is another story.
> Incompletion.
> PAUL RICOEUR, *Memory, History, Forgetting*

Sethe's doubts at the end of *Beloved*, after Paul D tells her that they have "more yesterday than anybody" and that they need "some kind of tomorrow" (Morrison 2005: 322), ask whether coming to terms with the atrocities of the past can achieve some kind of closure, as Paul D desires in *Beloved*. Dominick LaCapra argues that "certain wounds from the past—both personal and historical—cannot simply heal without leaving scars and residues—in a sense archives—in the present" (2004: 104). LaCapra seems to use Gayl Jones's imagery of scars and blood when he claims that those scars "may even have to remain open wounds, even if one strives to counteract their tendency to swallow all of existence and incapacitate one as an agent in the present" (LaCapra 2004: 104). It could be argued that novels like the five analyzed in this volume strive to counteract the effects of trauma while keeping the wound always open. This is Roger Luckhurst's argument when he says that "*Beloved* is at once an act of recovery and memorialization, but also a testament to the immemorial, the ethical impossibility of bringing to any close the mourning for 'sixty million and more' for subsequent generations" (2008: 95). My argument here is that trauma narratives provide the means to deal with painful yet significant past events in a way that does not erase that pain—but also does not trivialize it by creating false exits or closures—and instead open the door to a degree of agency through recognition in the present and towards the future. This is best exemplified in Sethe's scar: while very clearly a reminder of the traumatic events that originated it, the narrative transforms it from a bleeding wound into a tree of life, soothing the memory yet at the same time maintaining its presence and meaning.

If we assume the premise that narratives can at least help overcome the shattering effects of trauma, the next premise is that a full recovery can only be achieved by means of forgiving. However, when dealing with such atrocities, the question is whether forgiving is possible or even advisable. Paul Ricoeur devotes the epilogue of his large volume on memory, history and forgetting to the difficult process of forgiveness and, while he states that "[f]ault in its essence is unforgivable not only in fact but by right" (2006: 466), he also asserts that "forgiveness is directed to the unforgivable or it does not exist at all" (2006: 468). This sentence dismantles the very process it suggests, just like, as Luckhurst argued, *Beloved* can be an act of both recovery and memorialization. Forgiving is further complicated in the case of slavery, for the original atrocities were committed more than a hundred years ago. What happens when there is no one to punish? Ricoeur offers a plausible solution when he argues that "more important than punishment—and even reparation—remains the word of justice that establishes the public responsibilities of each of the protagonists and designates the respective places of aggressor and victim in a relation of appropriate distance" (2006: 475). It is my contention that acknowledging past wrongs in the name of those who committed them and publicly conceding the victims their rightful status as such provides the crucial first step towards a necessary moving on from the past or at least an attempt to prevent a repetition of similar events in the future. In the words of LaCapra, "the maxim is not 'forgive and forget' but rather: remember in a certain way so that forgiveness becomes possible and letting-bygones-be-bygones constitutes a hope for the future" (1998: 197).

We should then ask ourselves whether full closure is even advisable. When atrocities are enacted against a whole people, why should they be left behind and forgotten? Why should the events of the past be laid to rest? Of course trauma at a personal level must be overcome for the well-being of the affected individual, but when we are talking about a cultural, historical trauma, maybe closure is neither the best nor the most ethical path. Acceptance may be a better option, for it is only through acceptance that change—although perhaps not closure—can be enacted. Narratives like those this volume analyzes point precisely to this dichotomy, this ambivalence between the desirability of working through at a personal level and the necessity of recovering the memory of past traumas for the future. The very fact that narratives such as these are still being written today testifies to the fact that these authors are not attempting to provide a final, closed version of the traumas of the past in their works—for such desire for closure could be counterproductive and play to the advantage of the oppressors. Instead, these authors seem to be attempting a reenacting, a re-memorialization. In a world in which proposals of building walls-to-separate instead of bridges-to-join are still being publicly broadcasted and popularly backed, or in which unarmed black men are shot to death in front of their girlfriends just because their skin color is automatically registered as a menace in the mind of a white police officer, the traumas of the past need to be heard and voiced not to point fingers or to find or punish the long-gone perpetrators, but in order to acknowledge them. This necessary acknowledgment involves recognizing the role of the victims as such as well as the mechanisms and ideological structures that made those traumas possible in the first place, together with admitting the possibility of the persistence of those mechanisms and structures in today's world. We need, in sum, to look back and accept the terrors we may find there in order to face the path that still needs to be walked.

Works Cited

Abraham, Nicholas and Maria Torok 1994. *The Shell and the Kernel*. Volume I. Chicago: The University of Chicago Press.

Alexander, Jeffrey C. et. al. 2004. *Cultural Trauma and Collective Identity*. Berkeley: University of California Press.

Alexander, Jeffrey C. 2004a. "Toward a Theory of Cultural Trauma." In Jeffrey C. Alexander et. al. 1–30.

Amengual, Marian, Maria Juan and Joana Salazar (eds.) 2009. *New Perspectives on English Studies*. Palma: Edicions UIB.

Angelo Bonnie 1994. "The Pain of Being Black: An Interview with Toni Morrison." In Danille Taylor-Guthrie ed. 255–261.

Assmann, Jan 1995. "Collective Memory and Cultural Identity." *New German Critique* 65: 125–133.

Atkinson, Yvonne 2000. "Language that Bears Witness: The Black English Oral Tradition in the Works of Toni Morrison." In Marc C. Conner ed. 12–30.

Baker, William 1970. "William Wilberforce on the Idea of Negro Inferiority." *Journal of the History of Ideas* 31.3: 433–440.

Baldwin, James 1985. *The Price of the Ticket: Collected Nonfiction 1984–1985*. New York: St. Martin's / Marek.

Baldwin, James 1985a. "A Talk to Teachers." In James Baldwin. 325–332.

Baldwin, James 1985b. "Nothing Personal." In James Baldwin. 381–393.

Baldwin, James 1985c. "Many Thousands Gone." In James Baldwin. 65–78.

Baldwin, James 1985d. "On Catfish Row." In James Baldwin. 177–181.

Baldwin, James 1985e. "The Fire Next Time." 333–379.

Baldwin, James 1985f. "White Man's Guilt." In James Baldwin. 409–414.

Benito, Jesús 1995a. "David Bradley's *The Chaneysville Incident*: The Narrator as Historian." In Susana Onega ed. 181–191.

Benito, Jesús 1995b. "Novels of Memory: The Subversion of History in Ethnic Literature." In Aitor Ibarrola ed. 29–43.

Benito, Jesús 1998. " 'History is Always Written Wrong': *Song of Solomon* and 'The Memories Within.'" In Michel Fabre and Claude Julien eds. 59–67.

Benito, Jesús y, Ana María Manzanas Calvo 1994. *La Estética del Recuerdo: La Narrativa de James Baldwin y Toni Morrison*. Cuenca: Servicio de Publicaciones de la Universidad de Castilla la Mancha.

Benjamin, Walter 1999. "Excavation and Memory." In Michael W. Jennings, Howard Eiland and Gary Smith eds. 576.

Benjamin, Walter 2003. "On the Concept of History." In Howard Eiland and Michael W. Jennings eds. 389–400.

Blake, Susan L. 1980. "Folklore and Community in *Song of Solomon*." *MELUS* 7.3: 77–82.

Blake, Susan L. and James A. Miller 1984. "The Business of Writing: An Interview with David Bradley." *Callaloo* 21: 19–39.

Blight, David W. 1994. "W. E. B. Du Bois and the Struggle for American Historical Memory." In Geneviève Fabre and Robert O'Meally eds. 45–71.

Bouson, J. Brooks 2000. *Quiet As It's Kept: Shame, Trauma, and Race in the Novels of Toni Morrison*. Albany: State University of New York Press.

Bowers, Maggie Ann 2004. *Magic(al) Realism*. London and New York: Routledge.

Bradley, David 1990. *The Chaneysville Incident*. New York: Harper and Row.

Cao, Lan 1998. *Monkey Bridge*. New York: Penguin.

Carabi, Angels 1993. "Nobel Laureate Toni Morrison Speaks about Her Novel *Jazz*." In Carolyn C. Denard ed. 91–97.

Caruth, Cathy (ed.) 1995. *Trauma: Explorations in Memory*. Baltimore: The Johns Hopkins University Press.

Caruth, Cathy 1995a. "Recapturing the Past: Introduction." In Cathy Caruth ed. 151–157.

Caruth, Cathy 1995b. "Trauma and Experience: Introduction." In Cathy Caruth ed. 3–12.

Caruth, Cathy 1996. *Unclaimed Experience. Trauma, Narrative and History*. London: The Johns Hopkins University Press.

Caruth, Cathy 2011. "After the End: Psychoanalysis in the Ashes of History." Lecture given at the "Beyond Trauma: Narratives of (Im)possibility in Contemporary Literatures in English" Conference held at the University of Zaragoza, Spain, 31st March - 2nd April.

Clark, Kenneth B and Mamie P. Clark 1947. "Racial Identification and Preference in Negro Children." In T.M. Newcomb & E.L. Hartley (eds.) *Reading in social psychology*. New York: Holt, Rinehart & Winston. 169–178.

CNN 2010a. "AC 360° Black or White: Kids on Race." YouTube playlist (8 videos). 21 May 2018. <https://youtu.be/wYkUMqxr_o8?list=PLfmVNxXV6-8En6AgVD-yfKPw4wyV5a1eS>.

CNN 2010b. "CNN Pilot Demonstration." 28 Apr. 21 May 2018. <http://i2.cdn.turner.com/cnn/2010/images/05/13/expanded_results_methods_cnn.pdf>.

Conner, Marc C. (ed.) 2000. *The Aesthetics of Toni Morrison: Speaking the Unspeakable*. Jackson: University Press of Mississippi.

Conner, Marc C. 2000a. "From the Sublime to the Beautiful: The Aesthetic Progression of Toni Morrison." In Marc C. Conner ed. 49–76.

Conner, Marc C. 2000b. "Introduction: Aesthetics and the African American Novel." In Marc C. Conner ed. ix-xxviii.

Corey, Susan 2000. "Toward the Limits of Mystery: The Grotesque in Toni Morrison's *Beloved*." In Marc C. Conner ed. 31–48.

Cowan, Alison Leigh 2010. "When Special Delivery Meant Deliverance for a Fugitive Slave." New York Times 26 Feb. 11 Apr. 2012 <http://cityroom.blogs.nytimes.com/2010/02/26/when-special-delivery-meant-deliverance-for-a-fugitive-slave/>.

Craps, Stef 2010. "Learning to Live with Ghosts: Postcolonial Haunting and Mid-Mourning in David Dabydeen's 'Turner' and Fred D'Aguiar's *Feeding the Ghosts*." *Callaloo* 33.2: 467–475.

Craps, Stef and Gert Buelens 2008. "Introduction: Postcolonial Trauma Novels." *Studies in the Novel* 40.1/2: 1–12.

Dalsgárd, Katrine 2001. "The One All-Black Town Worth the Pain: (African) American Exceptionalism, Historical Narration, and the Critique of Nationhood in Toni Morrison's *Paradise*." *African American Review* 35.2: 233–248.

Darling, Marsha 1994. "In the Realm of Responsibility: A Conversation with Toni Morrison." In Danille Taylor-Guthrie ed. 246–254.

Davis, Christina 1994. "An Interview with Toni Morrison." In Danille Taylor-Guthrie ed. 223–233.

Davidson, Rob 2001. "Racial Stock and 8-Rocks: Communal Historiography in Toni Morrison's *Paradise*." *Twentieth-Century Literature* 47.3: 355–373.

Denard, Carolyn C. (ed.) 2008. *Toni Morrison: Conversations*. Mississippi: The University Press of Mississippi.

Dixon, Melvin 1994. "The Black Writer's Use of Memory." In Geneviève Fabre and Robert O'Meally eds. 18–27.

Donlon, Jocelyn Hazelwood 1995. "Hearing is Believing: Southern Racial Communities and Strategies of Story-Listening in Gloria Naylor and Lee Smith." *Twentieth Century Literature* 41: 16–35.

Drake, St. Clair and Horace R. Cayton 1993. *Black Metropolis: A Study of Negro Life in a Northern City*. Chicago: University of Chicago Press.

Duncan, Garrett A. 1996. "Space, Place and the Problematic of Race: Black Adolescent Discourse as Mediated Action." *Journal of Negro Education* 65.2: 133–150.

Eckard, Paula Gallant 1995. "The Prismatic Past in *Oral History* and *Mama Day*." *MELUS* 20.3: 121–135.

Edkins, Jenny 2003. *Trauma and the Memory of Politics*. Cambridge: Cambridge University Press.

Eiland, Howard and Michael W. Jennings (eds.) 2003. *Walter Benjamin: Selected Writings Vol. 4 1938-1940*. Cambridge: Harvard University Press.

Elliot, Emory et al. 2002. *Aesthetics in a Multicultural Age*. Oxford: Oxford University Press.

Ellison, Ralph 1967. "Flying Home." In Langston Hughes ed. 151–170.

Ellison, Ralph 1972. *Shadow and Act*. New York: Vintage.

Ellison, Ralph 1972a. "Richard Wright's Blues." In Ralph Ellison. 77–94.

Ellison, Ralph 1972b. "Twentieth-Century Fiction and the Black Mask of Humanity." In Ralph Ellison. 24–44.

Ensslen, Klaus 1988. "Fictionalizing History: David Bradley's *The Chaneysville Incident.*" *Callaloo* 35: 280–296.

Erdrich, Louise 2006. *Tracks*. London: Harper Perennial.

Erikson, Kai 1995. "Notes on Trauma and Community." In Cathy Caruth ed. 183–199.

Evans, Mari (ed.) 1984. *Black Women Writers (1950–1980): A Critical Evaluation*. New York: Anchor Press.

Eyal, Gil 2004. "Identity and Trauma: Two Forms of the Will to Memory." *History and Memory* 16.1: 5–36.

Eyerman, Ron 2001. *Cultural Trauma: Slavery and the Formation of African American Identity*. Cambridge: Cambridge University Press.

Eyerman, Ron 2004. "The Past in the Present: Culture and the Transmission of Memory." *Acta Sociologica* 47.2: 159–169.

Fabre, Geneviève and Robert O'Meally (eds.) 1994. *History & Memory in African-American Culture*. New York: Oxford University Press.

Fabre, Michel and Claude Julien (eds.) 1998. *Approches Critiques de la Fiction Afro-Américaine GRAAT* 18. Tours: Université François Rabelais.

Felman, Shoshana and Dori Laub 1992. *Testimony: Crises of Witnessing in Literature, Psychoanalysis, and History*. New York: Routledge.

Ferenczi, Sándor and Judith Dupont (ed.) 1995. *The Clinical Diary of Sándor Ferenczi*. Cambridge: Harvard University Press.

Flanagan, Joseph 2002. "The Seduction of History: Trauma, Re-Memory, and the Ethics of the Real." *Clio* 31.4: 387–403.

Flys Junquera, Carmen Lydia 1998. *Place & Spatial Metaphors in the Quest for Cultural and Artistic Epiphany: James Baldwin & Rudolpho Anaya*. Presented in Alcalá. (Unpublished Dissertation).

Ford, Andrew 1995. "*Katharsis*, the ancient Problem." In Andrew Parker and Eve Kosofsky Sedgwick eds. 109–132.

"forge." *Merriam-Webster Online Dictionary*. 2009. Merriam-Webster Online. 20 Aug. 2009 <http://www.merriam-webster.com/dictionary/forge>.

Freud, Sigmund 1922. *Beyond the Pleasure Principle*. London: The International Psycho-Analytical Press.

Friedman, Jonathan 1992. "The Past in the Future: History and the Politics of Identity." *American Anthropologist* 94.4: 837–859.

Friel, Brian 1981. *Translations*. London: Faber and Faber.

Furman, Jan 1996. *Toni Morrison's Fiction*. Columbia: University of South Carolina Press.

Gaines, Ernest 1983. *A Gathering of Old Men*. New York: Vintage.

Garbus, Lisa 1999. "The Unspeakable Stories of *Shoah* and *Beloved*." *College Literature* 26.1: 52–68.

Garland, Caroline 2002. *Understanding Trauma: A Psychoanalytical Approach*. New York: Routledge.

Gauthier, Marni 2005. "The Other Side of *Paradise*: Toni Morrison's (Un)Making of Mythic History." *African American Review* 39.3: 395-414.

Gilmore, Leigh 2001. *The Limits of Autobiography: Trauma and Testimony*. Ithaca: Cornell.

Hacking, Ian 1995. *Rewriting the Soul: Multiple Personality and the Sciences of Memory*. New Jersey: Princeton University Press.

Harding, Desmond 2006. "Bearing Witness: *Heartbreak House* and the Poetics of Trauma." *SHAW The Annual of Bernard Shaw Studies* 26: 6-26.

Harris, Leslie 1980. "Myth as Structure in Toni Morrison's *Song of Solomon*." *MELUS* 7.3: 69-76.

Harris, Norman 1981. "Locating the Self in Family and Racial History: *The Chaneysville Incident* by David Bradley." *Callaloo* 11/13: 203-205.

Hartman, Geoffrey 1996. *The Longest Shadow: In the Aftermath of the Holocaust*. Bloomington: Indiana University Press.

Hartman, Geoffrey 2004. "Trauma Within the Limits of Literature." *TRN-Newsletter* 2. 30 Aug. 2010 <www.traumaresearch.net/focus2/hartman.htm>.

Hefferman, Teresa 1998. "*Beloved* and the Problem of Mourning." *Studies in the Novel* 30.4: 558-573.

Heinze, Denise 1993. *The Dilemma of "Double Consciousness": Toni Morrison's Novels*. Athens: The University of Georgia Press.

Henry, Gordon D., Silvia Martínez Falquina and Juan Ignacio Oliva 2009. "'Walking Wounded': The Representation of Trauma in Postcolonial Fiction." In Marian Amengual, Maria Juan and Joana Salazar eds. 397-401.

Herman, Judith 2001. *Trauma and Recovery*. London: Pandora.

Hilberg, Raul 1996. *The Politics of Memory: The Journey of a Holocaust Historian*. Chicago: Ivan R. Dee.

Horvitz, Deborah 1989. "Nameless Ghosts: Possession and Dispossession in *Beloved*." *Studies in American Fiction* 17.2: 157-167.

House, Elisabeth B. 1990. "Toni Morrison's Ghost: The Beloved who is not Beloved." *Studies in American Fiction* 18.1: 17-26.

Hughes, Langston (ed.) 1967. *The Best Short Stories by Negro Writers*. Toronto: Little, Brown and Company.

Hutcheon, Linda 1988. *A Poetics of Postmodernism: History, Theory, Fiction*. Oxon: Routledge.

Ibarrola, Aitor 1995. *Fiction & Ethnicity in Northamerica: Problems of History, Genre and Assimilation*. Bilbao: Uncilla Press.

Jennings, Michael W., Howard Eiland and Gary Smith (eds.) 1999. *Walter Benjamin: Selected Writings Vol. 2 1927-1934*. Cambridge: Harvard University Press.

Jones, Bessie W. and Audrey Vinson 1994. "An Interview with Toni Morrison." In Danille Taylor-Guthrie ed. 171–187.

Jones, Gayl 1975. *Corregidora*. Boston: Beacon Press.

Kaplan, E. Ann 2005. *Trauma Culture: The Politics of Terror and Loss in Media and Literature*. New Jersey: Rutgers University Press.

Kearly, Peter R. 2000. "Toni Morrison's *Paradise* and the Politics of Community." *Journal of American and Comparative Cultures* 23.2: 9–16.

Kidd, Kenneth 2005. " 'A' is for Auschwitz: Psychoanalysis, Trauma Theory, and the 'Children's Literature of Atrocity'." *Children's Literature* 33: 120–149.

Kidron, Carol A. 2004. "Surviving a Distant Past: A Case Study of the Cultural Construction of Trauma Descendant Identity." *Ethos* 31.4: 513–544.

King, Nicola 2000. *Memory, Narrative, Identity: Remembering the Self*. Edinburgh: Edinburgh University Press.

Klein, Kerwin Lee 2000. "On the Emergence of *Memory* in Historical Discourse." *Representations* 69: 127–150.

Kogawa, Joy 1994. *Obasan*. New York: Anchor Books.

Kreyling, Michael 2007. " 'Slave life; freed life—everyday was a test and trial': Identity and Memory in *Beloved*." *Arizona Quarterly* 63.1: 109–136.

Kripke, Saul A. 1980. *Naming and Necessity*. Cambridge: Harvard University Press.

Krumholz, Linda 1993. "Dead Teachers: Rituals of Manhood and Rituals of Reading in *Song of Solomon*." *Modern Fiction Studies* 39.3&4: 551–574.

Kuo, Fei-hsuan 2009. *Spectre in the Dark: Trauma, Racism and Generational Haunting in Toni Morrison's Fiction*. Berlin: VDM Verlag Dr. Müller.

LaCapra, Dominick 1994. *Representing the Holocaust: History, Theory, Trauma*. Ithaca: Cornell University Press.

LaCapra, Dominick 1998. *History and Memory after Auschwitz*. Ithaca: Cornell University Press.

LaCapra, Dominick 2001. *Writing History, Writing Trauma*. London: The Johns Hopkins University Press.

LaCapra, Dominick 2004. *History in Transit: Experience, Identity, Critical Theory*. Ithaca: Cornell University Press.

Lamothe, Daphne 2005. "Gloria Naylor's *Mama Day*: Bridging Roots and Routes." *African America Review* 39.1-2: 155–169.

Langer, Lawrence 1975. *The Holocaust and the Literary Imagination*. New Haven: Yale University Press.

Langer, Lawrence 1991. *Holocaust Testimonies: The Ruins of Memory*. New Haven: Yale University Press.

Laub, Dori 1992a. "An Event Without a Witness: Truth, Testimony and Survival." In Shoshana Felman and Dori Laub. 75–92.

Laub, Dori 1995. "Truth and Testimony: The Process and the Struggle." In Cathy Caruth ed. 61–75.
Lawrence, David 1991. "Freshly Ghosts and Ghostly Flesh: The Word and the Body in *Beloved*." *Studies in American Fiction* 19.2: 189–201.
LeClair, Thomas 1994. "The Language Must not Sweat: A Conversation with Toni Morrison." In Danille Taylor-Guthrie ed. 119–128.
Lester, Julius 1969. *Black Folktales*. New York: Grove Press.
Lester, Julius 1969a. "Foreword." In Julius Lester vii-ix.
Lester, Julius 1969b. "People who Could Fly." In Julius Lester 147–152.
Levi, Primo 1959. *If This is a Man*. New York: The Onion Press.
Leys, Ruth 2000. *Trauma: A Genealogy*. Chicago: University of Chicago Press.
Linenthal, Edward T. 1995. *Preserving Memory: The Struggle to Create America's Holocaust Museum*. New York: Viking.
López Ropero, María Lourdes 2008. " 'Trust them to Figure it Out': Toni Morrison's Books for Children." *ATLANTIS* 30.2: 43–57.
Lowry, Lois 2008. *The Giver*. London: Harper Collins.
Luckhurst, Roger 2008. *The Trauma Question*. London: Routledge.
Marcus, James. "This side of Paradise." 21 May 2012 <http://www.amazon.com/exec/obidos/tg/feature/-/7651/002-5902217-4420056>.
Marshall, Paule 1969. *The Chosen Place, the Timeless People*. New York: Vintage.
Marshall, Paule 1983. *Reena and Other Stories*. New York: The Feminist Press.
Marshall, Paule 1983a. *Praisesong for the Widow*. New York: Plume.
Marshall, Paule 1983b. "Reena." In Paule Marshall. 69–91.
Martínez Falquina, Silvia 2009. "*Monkeys*: The Short Story Cycle Acting Out and Working Through Family Trauma." In Marian Amengual, Maria Juan and Joana Salazar eds. 513–517.
Matus, Jill 1998. *Toni Morrison*. Manchester: Manchester University Press.
McBride, Dwight A. 2001. *Impossible Witnesses: Truth, Abolitionism, and Slave Testimony*. New York and London: New York University Press.
McCarthy, Cormac 2009. *The Road*. New York: Picador.
McHugh, Kathleen 2002. "The Aesthetics of Wounding: Trauma, Self-Representation, and the Critical Voice." In Emory Elliot et al. 241–253.
McKay, Nelly 1994. "An Interview with Toni Morrison." In Danille Taylor-Guthrie ed. 138–155.
McKinney, Kelly 2007. " 'Breaking the Conspiracy of Silence': Testimony, Traumatic Memory, and Psychotherapy with Survivors of Political Violence." *ETHOS* 35.3: 265–299.
McNally, Richard 2003. *Remembering Trauma*. Cambridge: The Belknap Press of Harvard University Press.

Michaels, Walter Benn 1996. " 'You who never was there': Slavery and the New Historicism, Deconstruction and the Holocaust." *Narrative* 4.1: 1–16.
Middleton, Joyce Irene 1993. "Orality, Literacy, and Memory in Toni Morrison's *Song of Solomon*." *College English* 55.1: 64–75.
Miller, Nancy K. and Jason Tougaw (eds.) 2002. *Extremities: Trauma, Testimony, and Community*. Urbana: University of Illinois Press.
Morrison, Toni 1982. *Sula*. Westford: Plume Books.
Morrison, Toni 1984. "Rootedness: The Ancestor as Foundation." In Mari Evans ed. 339–345.
Morrison, Toni 1989. "Unspeakable Things Unspoken: The Afro-American Presence in American Literature." *Michigan Quarterly Review* 28.1: 1–34.
Morrison, Toni 1992. *Jazz*. New York: Alfred A. Knopf.
Morrison, Toni 1993. *Playing in the Dark: Whiteness and the Literary Imagination*. Cambridge: Harvard University Press.
Morrison, Toni 1999a. *Paradise*. London: Vintage.
Morrison, Toni 1999b. *The Bluest Eye*. London: Vintage.
Morrison, Toni 2005. *Beloved*. London: Vintage.
Morrison, Toni 2006. *Song of Solomon*. London: Vintage.
Morrison, Toni 2008. *A Mercy*. London: Chatto and Windus.
Morrison, Toni 2013. *Home*. London: Vintage.
Morrison, Toni 2015. *God Help the Child*. New York: Alfred A. Knopf.
Naylor, Gloria 1983. *The Women of Brewster Place: A Novel in Seven Stories*. New York: Penguin.
Naylor, Gloria 1985. *Linden Hills*. New York: Penguin.
Naylor, Gloria 1988. *Mama Day*. New York: Ticknor & Fields.
Nora, Pierre 1989. "Between Memory and History: Les Lieux de Mémoire." *Representations* 26: 7–24.
Offutt Mathieson, Barbara 1990. "Memory and Mother love in Morrison's *Beloved*." *American Imago* 47.1: 1–21.
Olick, Jeffrey K. 1999. "Collective Memory: The Two Cultures." *Sociological Theory* 17.3: 333–348.
Onega, Susana (ed.) 1995. *Telling Histories: Narrativizing History, Historicizing Literature*. Amsterdam and Atlanta: Rodopi.
Parker, Andrew and Eve Kosofsky Sedgwick (eds.) 1995. *Performativity and Performance*. New York: Routledge.
Peach, Linden 1995. *Toni Morrison*. Malaysia: Macmillan Press.
Pérez-Torres, Rafael 1993. "Knitting and Knotting the Narrative Thread—*Beloved* as Postmodern Novel." *Modern Fiction Studies* 39.3&4: 689–707.
Perry, Phyllis Alesia 1999. *Stigmata*. New York: Anchor Books.

Phelan, James 1993. "Toward a Rhetorical Reader-Response Criticism: The Difficult, the Stubborn, and the Ending of *Beloved*." *Modern Fiction Studies* 39.3/4: 709–728.

Phelan, James 1998. "Sethe's Choice: *Beloved* and the Ethics of Reading." *Style* 32.2: 318–333.

Ramadanovic, Petar 1998. "When '*To Die in Freedom*' is Written in English." *Diacritics* 28.4: 54–67.

Rand, Nicholas T. 1994a. "Introduction: Renewals of Psychoanalysis." In Nicholas Abraham and Maria Torok. 1–22.

Rand, Nicholas T. 1994b. "New Perspectives in Metapsychology: Criptic Mourning and Secret Love." In Nicholas Abraham and Maria Torok. 99–106.

Rand, Nicholas T. 1994c. "Secrets and Posterity: The Theory of the Transgenerational Phantom." In Nicholas Abraham and Maria Torok. 165–169.

Ricoeur, Paul 1990. *Time and Narrative*, Vol. III. Chicago: University of Chicago Press.

Ricoeur, Paul 2006. *Memory, History, Forgetting*. Chicago: University of Chicago Press.

Romero, Channette 2005. "Creating the Beloved Community: Religion, Race, and Nation in Toni Morrison's *Paradise*." *African American Review* 39.3: 415–430.

Rothberg, Michael 2003. "Dead Letter Office: Conspiracy, Trauma and *Song of Solomon*'s Posthumous Communication." *African American Review* 37.4: 501–516.

Rothberg, Michael 2009. *Multidirectional Memory: Remembering the Holocaust in the Age of Decolonization*. Stanford: Stanford University Press.

San José Rico, Patricia 2009. "Flying Away: Voluntary Diaspora and the Spaces of Trauma in the African-American Short Story." *Revista de Estudios Norteamericanos* 13: 63–75.

Schreiber, Evelyn Jaffe 2010. *Race, Trauma and Home in the Novels of Toni Morrison*. Louisiana: Louisiana State University Press.

Schwab, Gabriele 2009. "Replacement Children: The Transgenerational Transmission of Traumatic Loss." *American Imago* 66.3: 277–310.

Semprún, Jorge 1997. *Literature or Life*. New York: Viking.

Shackel, Paul A. 2003. "Archaeology, Memory, and Landscapes of Conflict." *Historical Archaeology* 37.3: 3–13.

Shange, Ntozake 2010. *Sassafrass, Cypress & Indigo*. New York: St. Martin's Griffin.

Singh, Amritjit, Joseph T. Skerrett and Robert E. Hogan. 1994. *Memory, Narrative, and Identity: New Essays in Ethnic American Literature*. Boston: Northeastern University Press.

Smitherman, Geneva 1977. *Talkin and Testifyin: The Language of Black America*. Michigan: Wayne State University Press.

Spivak, Gayatry Chakravorty 2008. *Other Asias*. Malden: Blackwell.

Stern, Katherine 2000. "Toni Morrison's Beauty Formula." In Marc C. Conner ed. 77–91.

Tal, Kalí 1996. *Worlds of Hurt: Reading the Literatures of Trauma*. Cambridge: Cambridge University Press.

Tal, Kalí 2003. "Chapter Three: Remembering Difference; Working Against Eurocentric Bias in Contemporary Scholarship on Trauma and Memory." In Kalí Tal, *Worlds of Hurt: Reading the Literatures of Trauma* (Revised online edition). 16 Apr. 2018. <http://worldsofhurt.com/chapter-three/>

Taylor-Guthrie, Danille (ed.) 1994. *Conversations with Toni Morrison*. Jackson: University Press of Mississippi.

Traditional 2009. "All God's Chillen Had Wings." 27 Feb. 2012. <http://site.bobshepherdonline.com/uploads/Africanamerican_folktale.pdf>.

Turner, Margaret E. 1992. "Power, Language and Gender: Writing 'History' in *Beloved* and *Obasan*." *Mosaic* 25.4: 81–97.

Vickroy, Laurie 2002. *Trauma and Survival in Contemporary Fiction*. Virginia: The University of Virginia Press.

Watkins, Mel 1994. "Talk with Toni Morrison." In Danille Taylor-Guthrie ed. 43–74.

Whitehead, Colson 2016. *The Underground Railroad*. London: Fleet.

Wilson, Judith 1994. "A Conversation with Toni Morrison." In Danille Taylor-Guthrie ed. 129–137.

Wilson, Matthew 1995. "The African American Historian: David Bradley's *The Chaneysville Incident*." *African American Review* 29.1: 97–107.

Wood, Michael 2000. "Sensations of Loss." In Marc C. Conner ed. 113–124.

Wright, Richard 1993. "Introduction." In St. Clair Drake and Horace R. Cayton. xvii-xxxiv.

Wyatt, Jean 2004. *Risking Difference: Identification, Race and Community in Contemporary Fiction and Feminism*. New York: State University of New York Press.

Yolen, Jane 2002. *Briar Rose*. New York: Tor.

Young, James E. 1988. *Writing and Rewriting the Holocaust: Narrative and the Consequences of Interpretation*. Bloomington: Indiana University Press.

Young, James E. 1993. *The Texture of Memory: Holocaust Memorials and Meaning*. Michigan: Yale University Press.

Yukins, Elizabeth 2002. "Bastard Daughters and the Possession of History in *Corregidora* and *Paradise*." *Journal of Women in Culture and Society* 28.1: 221–247.

Index

Abraham, Nicholas and Maria
    Torok   110n, 114
African American(s)   4, 26–27
    collective   23, 29
    community   3–4, 20, 26, 29, 29, 41–42, 47,
        61, 114, 147, 160–161, 190
    (contemporary) fiction   4n
    history of trauma/traumatic history   4,
        10, 45, 96, 140, 189
    literature   2–3, 15, 18, 30, 53, 80, 154–155,
        172–173, 189
    trauma   5–6, 11, 23–24, 26, 50, 74, 143, 148,
        161–162, 199, 201
Africans who could fly   5, 156–158, 200 *see*
    also Lester: "People Who Could Fly;"
    the Flying African, myth
Agency (political/social)   4–6, 23, 27, 43, 50,
    54–55, 112, 167–168, 190, 196, 199–201
Alexander, Jeffrey   20, 44
Amnesia   12, 110 *see also* forgetting
Ancestor(s)   27, 65, 66, 68, 88–89, 102,
    145–147, 153–156, 160–163, 178–180,
    181 *see also* forebear(s); forefather(s);
    predecessor(s)

Bachelard, Gaston   28
Baldwin, James   10, 37, 61, 171
Bear(ing) witness   22, 37–38, 45–46, 56,
    200–201 *see also* give voice
Beauty   78–81
Benjamin, Walter   9, 142, 144
Black Lives Matter   26
Black (Power) Movement   78 *see also*
    Malcolm X
Blackness   *see* Beauty
Blockage of memories   110, 110n, 116–117, 122
Bouson, J. Brooks   42, 70, 75, 77, 89, 112, 127,
    129, 150, 176
Bradley, David   195–196, 201
    The ChaneysvilleIncident   4–5, 8, 19, 51,
        54, 147, 178–197, 201
        C.K. Washington   187–188, 192–193
        Jack   180, 182–184, 186–187, 190
        John Washington   8, 19, 145, 148,
            178–187, 188, 190, 191–196

        Judith   19, 190–193, 196
        Moses Washington   180–182, 184–187,
            190, 192

Cao, Lan
    Monkey Bridge   13, 107
Caruth, Cathy   9, 12, 14, 24, 36, 56, 75,
    109, 145
Clark, Kenneth
    doll test(s)   79
Closure   54, 191–192, 193, 204–205 *see also*
    work(ing) through
Civil Rights   96
    Civil Rights Movement   *see* Malcolm X
Collective consciousness   20, 115
Colorism   *see* inverted racism
Concatenation of traumas   25–26, 66
    see also trauma: intergenerational/
    transgenerational
Craps, Stef   27, 50, 95

Denial   18, 111–113, 120–122, 125, 180 *see also*
    repression/suppression
Derrida, Jacques   27
Discrimination   6, 24, 26 *see also*
    oppression; racism
Dissociation   12, 17, 110n
Du Bois, W.E.B.,   47, 144
    double consciousness   165

Edkins, Jenny   35
Ellison, Ralph   40–41, 201
    "Flying Home,"   173
Empathy   6, 24, 28, 201–202
    empathic unsettlement   1
Erasure   56, 61, 200
Erdrich, Louise
    Tracks   132–133
Erikson, Kai   23, 68
Ethnicity   23
    ethnic identity   60
    ethnic literature   44–45
    ethnic minority   39–40, 74
Eyal, Gil   41
Eyerman, Ron   25, 45, 47

Felman, Shoshana and Dori Laub   2, 36, 43
Flashback(s)   12–14, 51, 53, 138, 144
Flying African, the, myth   172, 181 *see also* Africans who could fly; Lester: "People Who Could Fly"
Flys, Carmen   44–46
First World War   2
Forebear(s)   178 *see also* ancestor(s); forefather(s); predecessor(s)
Forefather(s)   27, 69–70, 85, 87, 98, 153, 161, 163, 180, 193–194 *see also* ancestor(s); forebear(s); predecessor(s)
Forgetting   5, 12, 28, 40, 47, 87, 118, 130–131, 191 *see also* repression/suppression
Founding event   5, 62, 69 *see also* trauma: founding/foundational
Fragmentation   35, 144
  of the self   18
  of narrative   51–53
Freud, Sigmund   10, 12, 14, 56, 75, 109, 110, 110n, 113, 145

Gaines, Ernest
  A Gathering of Old Men   32–33, 53
Ghost(s)   14–15, 54, 112, 122–123, 125, 130, 133, 156 *see also* haunting; specter(s)
Give voice   3–5, 8, 34, 37, 43, 48, 61, 74, 188, 189–190, 192, 205 *see also* bear(ing) witness

Halbwachs, Maurice   22, 59
Harding, Desmond   34, 45
Harlem Renaissance   78
Hartman, Geoffrey   10n, 50
Haunting   33, 124 *see also* ghost(s); specter(s)
Herman, Judith   2, 22, 40, 47, 109, 119, 201
Historiography   49, 57, 95
History   4, 7–9, 56–63, 86, 95, 99, 112, 142–144, 182, 195, 198, 200
  recreation of   3, 5–6
  recovery of   3–4, 6, 8, 106, 141, 143–144, 175, 179, 190, 197, 200, 201
  shared   4, 23
Holocaust   2, 10–17, 21, 25, 29, 35–37, 39, 46, 105, 124
Hutcheon, Linda   49
Hysteria   2

Identity
  formation   2–3, 7–8, 20n, 21–23, 27, 28, 57, 66, 87, 107–108, 114, 145–147
  politics   47, 60
  collective   2–3, 7–8, 20n, 21–24, 27, 44, 67, 73, 87, 90, 93–94, 105, 146
  cultural   44, 60
  individual   7, 22, 146
  group   45

Jim Crow   26
Jones, Gayl
  Corregidora   26–27, 60

Kaplan, Ann   2, 118, 146
King, Nicola   68, 124, 139, 147
Kogawa, Joy
  Obasan   39
Kuo, Fei-hsuan   60, 68, 124, 159, 200

LaCapra, Dominick   2–4, 10, 10n, 17, 22–23, 25, 46, 49, 57, 128n, 198–199, 204
Lacan, Jacques   10
Latency   2, 9, 111
Lester, Julius   159
  "People Who Could Fly"   158–159 *see also* Africans who could fly; the Flying African, myth
Levi, Primo   37
  If This is a Man   48
Leys, Ruth   2
Lowry, Louis
  The Giver   38–39
Luckhurst, Roger   2, 21, 24, 36, 43, 47, 54, 204

Magical realism   100, 129
Marshall, Paule
  Praisesong for the Widow   151, 154, 157, 181
  The Chosen Place, the Timeless People   30–32, 75, 86–87, 140
  "Reena"   80
Master narrative   42, 50, 63, 65, 67, 73, 74, 85, 115, 118, 147, 186, 189, 200
McNally, Richard   108–111, 191
Memoir   35, 39, 54
Memorialization   58, 147, 204 *see also* remembering/remembrance
Memory   21, 57–60, 107–108, 110
  collective   21, 32, 59–60, 91, 115, 146

INDEX

competitive   105
forgotten   189 *see also* repression/suppression
intrusive   12–14
of the past   21, 25, 50, 76–77, 126, 144
politics of   21n
recovered   50
recovery of   7, 189
recreation of   202
sites of   6, 8, 28 *see also* Nora, *lieux de mémoire*
transmission of   61
traumatic   38, 94, 108–110, 144
Miscegenation   67–68, 83
Morrison, Toni   4, 41–43, 45, 46, 61, 63, 80, 84, 128, 129, 155, 164, 201
   A Mercy   15–16, 18, 43, 51–52, 53
   Beloved   4, 6, 8, 15, 30, 43, 49, 53, 62, 112, 114–141, 200, 204
      Baby Suggs   117, 121–122, 136, 164
      Beloved   8, 15, 113, 115, 120–122, 130–131, 133–134, 138
      Denver   117, 122–123, 137–139
      Paul D   15, 119–120, 123, 130, 134–137
      Sethe   6, 30, 116–118, 126–127, 130–131, 133–136
   God Help the Child   80–82
   Home   13–14, 138–139
   Jazz   52, 62, 80, 121, 127
   national amnesia   43, 118, 124, 140
   Paradise   4, 7, 32, 58, 62–77, 83–89, 90, 93, 98, 99, 102, 106, 123, 177, 196
      Consolata   88
      Deacon "Deek" Morgan   69–72, 85, 87
      Misner   73, 84
      Patricia (Pat) Best   65, 71, 73–74, 77, 83
      The convent   76, 83, 87–88
      The Oven   70, 85
      Zechariah Morgan/Coffee   63–65, 71–72, 77
   Playing in the Dark   42, 63
   Song of Solomon   4, 5, 8, 54, 80, 145, 147, 148–156, 159–178, 181, 182, 197
      Guitar   149, 164–165, 167, 174, 176–177
      Jake Dead   149–150, 156, 167
      Macon Dead   149–151, 160, 163, 166–167, 168n
      Milkman   146, 147–149, 152–153, 155–156, 159–162, 170–174, 178–180, 183
      Pilate   149, 156, 159–160, 167, 172, 175, 177–178
      Shalimar   155–156, 160, 161, 163, 171, 174
   Rememory   124, 128–129, 162
   Sula   82–83, 170
   Tar Baby   15, 104
   The Bluest Eye   18, 42, 75, 80, 168
   Unspeakable, the   8, 112, 116, 117

Naming   163–172
Naylor, Gloria
   Linden Hills   43–44
   Mama Day   4, 5, 7, 51, 54, 58, 62, 80, 89–106, 129, 196
      Abigail   33, 99
      Cocoa   54, 80, 96, 97, 99–100, 101–104
      George   100–103, 104
      Miranda (Mama) Day   93, 97, 98, 100–101, 103–104
      Sapphira Wade   90–91, 93–94
      the other place   33, 97, 99
   The Women of Brewster Place   80, 126, 165
Nightmares   12, 126, 138
Nora, Pierre   57–58
   lieux de mémoire   7, 29–33, 55, 58, 128, 144 *see also* memory: sites of

Oppression   2, 3, 6, 20, 23, 26, 46, 50, 66, 75, 127, 173 *see also* discrimination; racism

Pass(ing) on   139–140
   of memory   25, 53, 69, 91
   of trauma   25, 57, 61
Past, the   *see* history
Peach, Linden   135, 153, 155, 167, 172n
Perpetuation   198
   of oppression/oppressive systems/systems of oppression   23, 24, 26, 27, 115, 124
Phelan, James   115n
Pilgrims, the   72, 75
Postmemory   25
Predecessor(s)   50 *see also* ancestor(s); forebear(s); forefather(s)
PTSD   12, 123

Race   23, 78–79
   racial discrimination   23, 24, 26–27
   racial oppression   6, 23

Racism   23, 26, 74 *see also* discrimination; oppression
   inverted racism   75–84
Remembering/remembrance   29, 39–40, 55, 59–60, 117, 124, 126–127, 139–141 *see also* memory
Repression/suppression   2, 4, 6, 8, 12, 42, 98, 107–114, 110n, 115–126, 135, 191–192 *see also* forgetting
   collective   42–43, 113–114
Return of the repressed   115, 120, 125–133
Reversal of stigmas   175–178
Ricoeur, Paul   3, 21n, 28, 43, 46, 57, 59, 69, 108, 112, 113, 144, 146, 163, 203, 204
Roots   101–102, 153–156
   rootlessness   104–105, 149, 154–155
Rothberg, Michael
   multidirectional memory   105, 108

Sankofa   142
Schuyler, George S.,
   Black No More   80
Second World War   2, 39, 66
Secondary victimhood   24
Secret   42–43, 71–72, 99, 113, 117
   secrecy   33, 40, 42, 99 *see also* silence
Segregation   26, 29, 96
Semprún, Jorge   35, 36–37
Shame   11, 42, 45, 66, 76, 89, 102, 112, 118, 124, 199
Shange, Ntozake
   Sassafras, Cypress & Indigo   163
Silence   4–5, 10, 15, 39–40, 43, 48, 54, 112, 114, 118–119, 124, 139–140, 199
   silencing processes   10–11, 39–43
Slavery   78, 118, 124, 136, 163–164, 187–188, 190
   slave narrative(s)   40, 41–42
Specter(s)   27, 132 *see also* ghost(s); haunting
Spivak, Gayatri
   strategic essentialism   3, 27
Stagnation   77, 87, 98, 198
Survivor   11 *see also* victim
   non-survivor   25, 28, 48–49, 59

Tal, Kalí   2, 10, 22, 38, 111
Talking cure, the   134
Testimony   21, 35–37, 45–46, 48
Trauma   1–4, 9–55
   clinical   7, 10

collective   5–6, 7, 20n, 21n, 9–23, 24, 27, 38, 49, 57, 154
cultural   19, 19n, 20n, 21–22, 205
founding/foundational   3, 5, 7, 22, 26–27, 50, 57, 87
historical   2, 7, 20n, 24, 44, 55, 205
intergenerational/transgenerational   25–27, 57, 149
literature/narrative/writing   34–55, 105, 204
postcolonial   3, 10, 105
recovery from   34, 88–89, 98, 137, 190, 200, 204
studies   2, 56, 109, 111
space(s) of   *see* memory: sites of; Nora: *lieux de mémoire*
unresolved   5, 132, 180
traumatic event(s)/experience(s)   1, 3, 9, 12–13, 17, 22–23, 37, 39–40, 108–109, 147
traumatic history   4, 7, 23, 25, 56, 66, 98
traumatic memories   7, 29, 50, 59–60, 94, 99, 110–112, 123
traumatic symptoms   12–19

Ugliness   *see* beauty
Unearthing   8, 46–47, 50, 143–144, 178–179, 182, 196, 197 *see also* recovery of memory

Vickroy, Laurie   35, 38, 46, 51, 54
Vicarious victimhood   *see* secondary victimhood
Victim   1, 1n, 17, 24, 43 *see also* survivor
Vietnam War   2, 11
Vonnegut, Kurt
   Slaughterhouse5   48

Whitehead, Colson
   The Underground Railroad   33
Whiteness   *see* beauty
Wiesel, Elie   36, 37
Work(ing) through   17, 18, 43, 47, 62, 86, 98, 103, 112, 121, 123, 134, 137–140, 196, 205
Wright, Richard   135–136
   Black Boy   165

X, Malcolm   164

Printed in the United States
By Bookmasters